P9-DUX-006

THE JEWISH RETURN INTO HISTORY

CAMERON'S BOOKS ELF
And Magazines

336 S.W. 3rd Ave.
Portland, OR 97204
503/228-2391

We Buy Books

2.50

91

THE JEWISH RETURN INTO HISTORY

Reflections in the Age of Auschwitz and a New Jerusalem

Emil L. Fackenheim

SCHOCKEN BOOKS · NEW YORK

First published by SCHOCKEN BOOKS 1978

10 9 8 7 6 5 4 3 2   80 81 82 83

Copyright © 1978 by Emil L. Fackenheim

Library of Congress Cataloging in Publication Data

Fackenheim, Emil L.
The Jewish return into history.

1. Holocaust (Jewish theology)—Addresses, essays, lectures.
2. Palestine in Judaism—Addresses, essays, lectures.   3. Israel
and the Diaspora—Addresses, essays, lectures.   I. Title.
BM645.H6F3   956.94′001   77-87861

Manufactured in the United States of America

To the Memory of
Lieutenant-Colonel Yonatan Netanyahu
Deliverer of the Entebbe Captives
And Student of Philosophy

Contents

PART THREE

The Centrality of Israel

Acknowledgments

ALMOST ALL THE essays in this volume have appeared previously. I wish to thank the original publishers for permission to reprint them.

In 1970 my wife and I were privileged to join members of the World Federation of Bergen-Belsen Associations, under the dynamic leadership of the late Josef Rosensaft, on a pilgrimage which took us first to Bergen-Belsen and then to Jerusalem. This unforgettable experience inspired far more in this volume than the essay written under its direct impact.

Summer Research Grants of the Canada Council enabled me to spend five consecutive summers in Jerusalem. I can no longer imagine how it is possible, for me or anyone else in the Diaspora, to write on most of the subjects of this book without such sojourns. The friends in Israel who have inspired and instructed me during these five summers are too numerous to name. But I must name my wife Rose, my daughter Suzy, and my son David who accompanied me. Without their presence I would have been a mere tourist or at best a visiting scholar. I would not have lived in Jerusalem.

Introduction

THE JEWISH essays contained in my *Quest for Past and Future* cover a period of no less than two decades and are, despite the turbulence of these decades themselves, marked by a relative tranquillity. The period covered by the present collection is less than a decade, and the essays are as marked by constant tension as has been the decade itself.

The earlier book climaxed with the one major change in my thinking and way of writing in more than thirty years of literary activity. Hence the essays contained in that book required a substantial introduction if they were still to speak. Here the briefest of introductions suffices. The tension I have referred to shows no sign of abating. One look at the newspapers is enough. These essays still speak for themselves.

Philosophical and religious thought widely take themselves to be immune and indeed indifferent to the "accidents" of "mere" history. The conscious repudiation of this view, first in abstracto and subsequently in relation to the events of our age, is the major change in my thinking to which I have referred. Thought, or at any rate Jewish thought, shows its strength precisely by making itself vulnerable. This is not to be confused with flirtations with the trivial shifts of fad and fashion, with happenings lent a spurious significance by manipulators, propagandists, ideologues. The vulnerability is to the stern challenge of epoch-making events. Thus it was at the beginning of Jewish history. Thus it remains—or has once again become—in our time.

There is a difference between an abstract, merely cerebral subscription to this view and a flesh-and-blood commitment to its consequences. Just how vast this difference is in our time may be gathered by comparing Part One of this book, composed of just one essay, already in some respects old-fashioned in tone and emphasis, with the other two parts. For the events to which Jewish thought is required to make itself vulnerable today are enormous, unprecedented, and ineluctable: the Holocaust and the rise of a Jewish state after two thousand years of Jewish statelessness.

So immense are these two events, and so close are we to them, that it is reasonable to doubt that thought in our time can grasp them. We may not, however, surrender totally to this doubt. For since one *need* not face that which one *cannot* face, such an absolutized doubt would lapse into the same evasion which is characteristic of its opposite—the certainty that, at least so far as theologians and philosophers are concerned, nothing radical has happened at either Auschwitz or Jerusalem, so that they can carry on their time-honored scholastic debates, safe in their dogmatic slumber.

How can we face that to which we are too close? Two duties are conferred on us. One is to confront the Holocaust honestly, without seeking refuge in a hundred available distortions. The other is to recognize the centrality of Israel in contemporary Jewish life, without seeking refuge in a hundred available equivocations.

The source of both duties is the same: the prohibition against blasphemy. Whoever dissolves the starkly unique tragedy of the Holocaust (whether in terms psychological, sociological, historical, moral, philosophical, or theological) sooner or later blasphemes against God, man, and in any case against the Truth. And whoever affirms that there are today two Jewish centers—or three, five, or none at all—averts his eyes from the fact that, had there been an Israel in the years 1933–

45, not one Jew able to flee from Hitler's gas chambers would have died in them.

But perhaps this is just one of two reasons why Israel is central today. This first reason is wholly compelling but starkly negative. Another, wholly positive but as yet ambiguous and obscure, is nevertheless felt by the soul and is beginning to reach the mind. Back in medieval times, the mystic Nahmanides wrote that while many nations had devastated the Land none had replanted it; that there had been many false messianic signs; and that the only true messianic sign would be the Land replanted. In the same age the poet Yehuda Halevi wrote that Jerusalem would not be rebuilt until Jews yearned for her very dust and stones. Today one travels through the replanted valleys of Galilee and is lost in wonder. And one walks through the Jewish Quarter of the Old City, ravaged by the Jordanians a generation ago, and is filled with a strange serenity. Much rubble remains. Yet in its midst are rising the rebuilt Jewish homes and synagogues, faithful to the past but surely exceeding its beauty—the palpable presence of the ancient yearning, intensified by despair in our time, and transfigured into determination.

> Written in Jerusalem in August 1977,
> the second half of the month of Av,
> the period of consolation over the
> destruction of the Temple.

Part One

OPENNESS TO SURPRISE, OR A BRIDGE TO SECULARITY

1. Man and His World in the Perspective of Judaism: Reflections on Expo '67

I

As a community of Jews and Christians, how should we welcome the more than seventy nations preparing to gather in Montreal for the great International Exhibition known as Expo '67? The theme under which they assemble—"Man and His World"—is a truly challenging one. Indeed, not many themes pose so great a challenge to this present generation of Jewish and Christian believers.

In a world full of strife, the gathering nations will meet in amity and concord. Yet although Judaism and Christianity preach amity and concord, it is not religion that makes this meeting possible: many of the assembling nations are non-Christian, and some avowedly atheist. And whereas to Jewish and Christian believers God is either all-important, or else of no importance, the theme of the gathering is the world of man, not that of God. Man "the Creator," "the Explorer," "the Pro-

Reprinted from *Judaism*, vol. 16, no. 2, Spring Issue 1967, pp. 166–75. The present paper was originally delivered at Temple Emanu-El, Westmount, Montreal in the series, "Man and His World," in observance of Canada's Centennial Year and Expo '67. The series was the 25th anniversary program of the founding of the Temple Emanu-El Institute on Judaism, under the leadership of Rabbi Harry J. Stern.

ducer," "the Provider," "Man and His Community"—these are all sub-themes of the overall theme which represent varieties of human, man-made culture; and if religion appears among them—for there will be religious pavilions—it is as but one of these varieties. It is secular culture, then, which has produced such unity among the nations as has made this meeting possible; and religion is allowed a place among them only because this culture is variegated enough to generate a spirit of pluralistic tolerance.

How then shall a believer in the biblical tradition respond to this gathering and to its guiding theme? This question may well seem to pose a fatal dilemma. On the one hand, we dare not accept on behalf of our God reduction to one or two pavilions among many others: can the all-important God of Israel or the Church be reduced to a mere religious "contribution" to human culture? On the other hand, to repudiate this gathering, on the grounds that it makes God marginal, would be both religiously perverse and historically reactionary. Religiously perverse because our God, the Father of all men and the Lord of Peace, is present wherever men meet in peace; historically reactionary, because it is on secular terms, and on secular terms alone, that in modern times those international bonds will be created without which the human race will not long survive. Ancient Roman internationalism could unite all pagan gods in a pantheon. Medieval internationalism could unite all European nations under the banner of Christianity. The worldwide internationalism which is so desperately needed in the modern age, and which we hope is coming into being, can only be secular. For Jews or Christians to turn against this internationalism, on the grounds of its inevitable secularity, would be religiously unthinkable; and it would also be utterly futile. How then shall we cope with this dilemma?

II

Implicit in the dilemma just stated is a question that has been with us for a long time—in the West, since the rise of the modern world. For it is the modern world that gave birth to the idea of radical secularity. Radical secularity means human autonomy; and the idea of human autonomy permeates all those modern activities that are distinctly modern. All science seeks rational knowledge; only modern science rests on the idea of rational self-sufficiency. All technology seeks rational control of nature; only modern technology—there is hardly a premodern technology worth mentioning—is fully rational. Every state is a system in which man governs man; only modern states eliminate kings ruling by divine right and wholly recognize that political power is human, and human only. In short, the modern-secular world is, as the Expo '67 theme so clearly indicates, a strictly human world. How shall the biblical believer— Jew and Christian—respond to it?

Four responses have been tried and found wanting in the past. The first is to ignore or simply to reject the modern-secular world. This response, most obvious in such forms as the nineteenth-century fundamentalist attacks on modern science, was all along foredoomed to failure. It might conceivably still win the odd victory, such as the demonstration that the theory of evolution is debatable. But victories of this kind are bound to be short-lived. The advance of modern science will not be stopped, even if some of its theories should turn out to be mistaken; for science will not conceivably repent of its basic idea of rational autonomy.

The second response—this, too, harking back to the nineteenth century—may be described as the fundamentalism of the intellectuals. These cannot deny or reject the claims of modern science. They are able, however, to shrink from the plebeian-democratic aspects of the modern world with an aesthetic-aristocratic horror. This occurs in religious romanticism, which longs for past medieval glories. But these glories, if glories they ever were, are gone beyond modern recovery; and they are presently alive, if at all, only in the minds and hearts of a self-styled aesthetic aristocracy. But no biblical believer, Jew or Christian, may flee from the real into an aesthetic world, afraid lest he dirty his hands—all the less if the aesthetic

world in question is fit for no one but reactionary aristo-
crats.

No more is another flight an authentic Jewish or Christian
possibility—from the modern-secular world into an unworldly
mysticism. To be sure, mysticism has always been an authentic
possibility within Christianity. Judaism, though less prone to
mysticism, has its Kabbalistic tradition; and of Hasidism, the
last great mystical movement within Judaism, Martin Buber
was able to say that it would be indispensable for any foresee-
able Jewish religious renewal. But mysticism-in-general is one
thing, a mystical flight from the world is another. This latter is
unacceptable for any Jew who believes that God has made the
world for man to live in, not to flee from. And today Christian
thinkers generally hold that such a flight is unacceptable for
Christians as well.

The above-mentioned three responses all fail because they
ignore, reject, or flee from the modern-secular world. This is not
true of the fourth response which must be noted—nineteenth-
century religious liberalism. This sought to come to terms with
the modern-secular world; and this was a merit to the extent
that it was motivated, not by the spirit of easy compromise, but
rather by the perception of the good in modern secularity. Enlightenment, liberty, progress—these are all ideals which, to
religious liberalism at its best, were not alien forces to which to
surrender, but rather friendly and indeed biblically-inspired
forces which deserved Jewish and Christian approval; and religious liberals were apt to accept them in a spirit of optimism
and hope, not in a spirit of defeat.

And yet, nineteenth-century liberalism *was* shot through
with the spirit of compromise, and this was its fatal weakness.
The great symptom of this weakness was that it approved the
modern-secular world indiscriminately, blind to those features
in it which are neither good nor, by any stretch of the imagination, compatible with biblical faith. (Thus in 1914, the year that
brought the nineteenth century to an end, liberal religion in
every European country surrendered to militant nationalism,

and the shock of this phenomenon, as much as anything else, provoked the neoorthodox protest against religious liberalism.) And the weakness itself was the spirit of "me-too-ism" with which religious liberalism approved the modern-secular world. There assuredly was nothing wrong with the approval, in the sphere of theory, of the search for scientific truth; and in the sphere of practice, of the search for greater human liberty and greater social justice. What was wrong, or at least a sign that there was something wrong, was the apologetic reaction to the fact that the secular forces could do nicely without religious approval. The reaction should have been that the modern earth, as much as any other, is, despite everything, the Lord's. Instead, there was retreat. The modern-secular world was handed over to secularism, and religion, once all-pervasive of life, became a mere segment of it. There was science, technology, secular morality, and politics, all of which were, or ought to be, devoted to the amelioration of the human lot. And then there was "religion," which made its own "contribution" to human betterment and had a sphere of its own.

Much effort was given to defining what this sphere was. But this was in the end of little moment: whether the religious sphere was the Unknowable which science could not know, or the Uncontrollable which technology could not control; whether it was at such limits of the human condition as death and guilt which, despite doctors and psychiatrists, will always be with us, or a "numinous" feeling present in religion alone and nowhere else. For the crucial fault was that "religion" was limited to one sphere among others, a fact that predetermined that the sphere reserved for it would diminish as the forces of secularism advanced. And as religious liberalism retreated under their impact its retreat revealed its basic weakness—a total loss of biblical radicalism. Ever since smashing the idols, the God of Israel has been the Radical who would tolerate no idols, and demanded total commitment in the center of life. Nineteenth-century religious liberalism, in contrast, reduced him to a mere contribution at the margins of modern secular-liberal culture. Under these circumstances, it was natural that doubt should arise as to whether this contribution was still necessary, and to what it was "relevant."

III

It is an impressive sign of religious vitality that religious radicalism should have reappeared in authentically twentieth-century Jewish and Christian thought. For it is dissatisfaction with liberal compromises, and a search for the roots, that characterize the great so-called neoorthodox thinkers of this century, such as Karl Barth and Reinhold Niebuhr among Christians, and Martin Buber and Franz Rosenzweig among Jews. Radicalism is characteristic, too, of those present thinkers, mostly Protestant, who seem temporarily to have eclipsed their immediate neoorthodox predecessors. Whatever one may ultimately think of these present thinkers, one must certainly listen to them. For in theological matters, unlike in many others, it is radicalism—including mistaken and indeed perverse radicalism—which is the road to truth.

These present thinkers may be called neoliberals. What distinguishes them from their nineteenth-century predecessors is precisely their radicalism. Thus from one quarter we hear that the biblical faith must be demythologized; and the demythologization demanded seems to include, not only ancient views of the world, but also the ancient God who is its Creator. From another quarter we hear the demand for so total an identification with the secular city and all its works as would involve the surrender of all attempts to speak in that city in a language different from its own. Going further, some thinkers assert that religious language has become meaningless; that, in the twentieth century, the word "God" is dead. The climax in radicalism is reached with the assertion that atheism is not a modern phenomenon which biblical faith must confront, but rather its own final consummation. "Christian atheism" is said to be not a contradiction in terms but, on the contrary, the result aimed at from the start by the Christian, if not the Jewish, faith. If it is radicalism that is wanted from theologians, we have, today, no cause for complaint.

As has been said, since in theological matters even wrong-headed radicalism is an instrument to truth, it is necessary for us, Jews and Christians, to listen to the radicals whose thought has just been sketched. And the service they perform is to confront us with a challenge that we have too long avoided. No longer can we behave as though the modern-secular world were no different from any other, i.e., ignore or soft-pedal the unprecedented challenge of its secularity. And no longer can we react by confining our faith to a mere department of life, hoping for safety in it. Not only is there no such safety; we also act unbiblically when we seek it. In biblical times, the God of our faith was in the midst of life, where the action was. If there is any one genuinely biblical motif in the neoliberal radicalism, it is the wish to be where the action is today—in the struggle against poverty and for racial justice, and in the concern with worldwide peace which overshadows, or ought to overshadow, all our other concerns. Today, the four above-criticized religious responses to the modern world are all dead.

The "radical" new theology teaches us two lessons. One is found in what it preaches, the other in the fate it suffers. It preachers that we, Jews and Christians, must be in the midst of the modern-secular world, radically self-exposed to its secularity. The fate it suffers is total dissipation into secularism. For, despite all protestations to the contrary, there can in the end be no real doubt that a theological radicalism of the present neoliberal sort must finally lead to wholesale surrender. This is still not quite certain when the radicalism is not itself quite radical, as when we are bidden to forsake the past voice of our God, and yet to hope that he who will speak with a wholly new voice will be the same God. All doubt is removed when it is asserted that the very word "God" is not meaningful to enlightened present believers, i.e., that its past use was a mere superstitious mistake. As for a "Christian atheism"—can it be taken seriously? At least to a Jew it must be clear that he who is the God of Israel and the Church appeared in history smashing all idols. And he must ask: Can those claim Christian warrant who now declare that this God himself is, and was all along, a mere idol? The question is seen in its full absurdity when it is remembered that the modern world in whose name the biblical God is rejected has brought forth, not only modern science, enlightenment, and democracy, but also Auschwitz and Buchenwald.

IV

We must then conclude that the present "radical" theologians have sharpened for us the dilemma with which we are concerned throughout the present discourse. Is the dilemma, then, unresolvable? Do we, Jews and Christians, have but the choice between surrender to secularism and half-hearted compromises doomed to increasing irrelevance? If so, we are in sore straits indeed; for both alternatives amount to a despair of the biblical God, who is sought, found, and obeyed in the very midst of the world.

When in such straits, a believer always does well to consult his classical sources, open to the possibility that they have the power to speak. On my part, I have been accustomed, for a quarter of a century, to consult Midrash; and I have time and again found unexpected light where I had previously thought there was none. Midrash, the work of the Talmudic rabbis, is the profoundest and most authentic theology ever produced within Judaism; and it is more rather than less profound and authentic for the fact that it is written, not in the form of system—final, airtight, and fully spelled out—but rather in the merely fragmentary and suggestive form of story and parable.

The Midrash which will be my text for the remainder of these reflections is the following:

When God created the world, He decreed: "The heavens are the heavens of the Lord; but the earth He has handed over to the children of man" (Ps. 115:16). Yet when He was about to give the Torah, He rescinded the first decree and said: "Those who are below shall ascend to those on high, and those who are on high shall descend to those that are below, and I will create a new beginning," as it is said: "And the Lord came down upon Mt. Sinai" (Exod. 19:20), and later "And unto Moses He said: 'Come up unto the Lord'" (Exod. 24:1). [*Exodus Rabba*, XII, 3]

V

All Midrash is symbolic. The first thing to be understood symbolically in the present Midrash is the idea of a temporal sequence in which the past has vanished from present reality. If creation, and the "decree" made at creation, were of the past only, they would be of no religious significance: creation is a religious reality, affirmed by faith, only because it is a present reality also, forever reaccepted and appropriated. Hence the subsequent "rescinding" of the decree made at creation is of a special sort. The second decree supersedes the first; yet it so wholly presupposes the continued reality of the first that it would lose its own meaning without it. The rabbis would never have thought of God as literally changing his mind; such a notion is at odds with their belief in the divine eternity and perfection. Yet so deeply were they impressed, at once with the reality of both decrees and the clash between them, that they dared to speak of God as though he changed his mind.

The first decree, then, is still a present reality, so much so that on its basis alone is the second possible. What does it establish? In the words of the 115th Psalm, "the heavens are the heavens of the Lord; but the earth He has handed over to the children of man." This tremendous passage, which incidentally figures prominently in Jewish literature and liturgy, with one stroke demythologizes the world. For mythological religion the world is "full of gods" (Thales). For biblical man—and hence for both Jew and Christian—the world is radically emptied of the gods because it is the work of God. Mythological man is subject to all sorts of demonic powers. Biblical man is radically liberated from these. Mythological man worships nature, or deified parts of nature. Biblical man worships the God who is wholly beyond nature because he is its Creator. As for nature, biblical man subdues it; for he is bidden to rule the earth which is handed over to him. It is God himself, then, who de-mythologizes the world, and his act of doing so is the primordial act of grace.

In the light of this truth, one must be extremely puzzled by the contemporary talk about the need to demythologize the Bible. One can readily admit that there is some important truth to this talk; for what scholar nowadays denies that the Bible borrows much of the imagery of contemporary culture? And who can affirm that this insight of biblical scholars is fully assimilated even by theologians, not to speak of the man in the street? Yet this truth must under no circumstances obscure the far more important truth that the biblical God himself stands in no need of contemporary demythologizing. He is demythologized from the start. It is the primordial event of his Presence which both destroys the idols and hands over the earth to the children of man.

It is, therefore, necessary to assert that an aspect of secularity is implicit in the biblical faith from the start. The philosopher A. N. Whitehead rightly connects the rise of modern science and technology with the modern Protestant return to the Bible. So long as man worships nature he will not "torture" it by means of scientific experiments; hence the Greeks, as well as medieval men still vitally affected by the Greeks, merely contemplated nature. Only a demythologization of nature—the maxim to subdue the earth rather than worship it—could have made the time ripe for modern science, for technology, and indeed for the modern secular world as a whole.

But what if *modern* secularity implied a radicalism which is in necessary conflict with the biblical faith? What if it made imperative the *conquest* of heaven as well as of earth? And what if to shrink from the former task were the result of mere medieval cowardice? It is true that there is no lack of heaven-stormers in the modern world; yet despite the infatuation of present theologians with Marx and Nietzsche, one wonders whether in the light of biblical faith these men must not ultimately be characterized as at best misguided and at worst idolaters.

For the view that there is a *necessary* conflict between modern secularity and the biblical faith is due to a tragic misunderstanding among secularists and believers alike. "The earth" handed over to man by no means includes our planet only; it includes the universe. The skies are not barred to our conquest, either in scientific understanding or technological control; for the skies are not heaven. The biblical God places no limitations upon the exercise of human reason; his gift of the earth to man is radical.

But what if the unlimited exercise of this human reason implied the *abolition* of heaven? What if it rendered superfluous the "hypothesis" of creation, and hence the Creator himself? In the biblical faith, creation is not and never has been a scientific or quasi-scientific hypothesis. It is, and always has been, the gift of existence—the world's and his own—to the man who in faith accepts it. And it is for this reason not an occurrence which took place once and for all in the past; creation is a gift which is renewed whenever there is human acceptance of it.

Such an acceptance is not at odds with secularity, modern secularity included; on the contrary, it makes inescapable the acceptance of its burden. We say "burden" even though it is a liberation also, and even though many present "radical" theologians are intoxicated in its celebration. Secularity *is* a burden. For to live a secular existence is to be responsible for the world. And indeed, so great is the burden of this responsibility in our own time that many among both the "religious" and the "irreligious" are in full flight from the world into a variety of fancies. The biblical believer—Jew or Christian—may not join their number. For his God bids him stay with, and assume responsibility for, the secular world. And if such an existence is, today, often solitary, it is the biblical God who makes this solitariness inescapable.

VI

But, according to our Midrash, God "rescinds" the first decree by means of a second. Like the first, this second decree is not a past event only but also a present reality, forever newly received. And since it forever rescinds the first decree, which yet remains forever real and presupposed, a "new beginning" occurs whenever such reception occurs; so new is the beginning as to produce radical surprise. The first decree has distinguished between the God who dwells in heaven and the man who has been given the earth. It is radically surprising that this God should, nevertheless, descend on earth; and that this man should, nevertheless, be commanded, and hence enabled, to ascend to heaven.

There is no parallel for this new beginning or this radical surprise in mythological, i.e. pagan, religion. Here the world is full of gods as a matter of course; and it is a matter of course, too, that man communes with them. Such communication, however, is not revelation. The biblical believer dwells, not in secure possession of the Divine, but in holy insecurity.

It is in this holy insecurity that the Jew experiences the joy of the Torah. For there is joy in a grace which in its heavenly power needs neither man nor the earth handed over to him, and which yet in its heavenly love chooses to need both; and which, having handed the earth over to man's profane possession, yet commands him, and hence enables him, to have a share in its sanctification. And as in this joy the Jew speaks and listens to the Christian, he discovers common ground. However they differ in their understanding of revelation, they share the knowledge of a "first decree" which has set apart heaven and earth; and of a "second decree" by virtue of which heaven descends to earth, and man may ascend to heaven.

For this reason, there exists the possibility of a joint Jewish and Christian testimony against ancient mythology. There exists, too, the possibility of a joint stand toward modern secularism. In the light of biblical faith, one may, indeed must, discriminate between different kinds of secularism, although doubtless these are less sharply distinguished in life than in thought. There is a modern secularism that presumes to destroy heaven; one that asserts that heaven is in principle inaccessible; and one that bears witness to being in fact cut off from heaven. The stance of biblical faith toward these three cannot be the same.

How can man on earth presume to destroy heaven? Only if, to begin with, he has failed to distinguish between them; that is, if he remains pagan. A secularism destructive of heaven remains bound to mythology even while it imagines itself to be its sworn enemy. It destroys the gods; yet in seeking to destroy God it deifies its own earthbound, and not wholly demythologized, powers. Today, we see on every side the ancient demons of the earth resurrected, however modern their guises. Such demons as blood, soil, race, and the capitalized Unconscious are not called gods; they are even given scientific or pseudo-scientific names: this serves but to augment their power. The biblical believer—Jew and Christian—must detect the ancient idols underneath their modern guises. And he must fight them with all his might.

In this fight he may well be joined by the second secularist. For in asserting heaven to be inaccessible to earth this secularist is free of the temptation to deify earth. His quarrel with the biblical believer is otherwise. The issue between them is whether or not, heaven and earth being divorced, revelation can take place.

How may the believer confront this second secularist? Open to all possibilities of the earth, this secularist is closed to the possibility that heaven may enter into it. Against such a dogmatism of earth, the biblical believer dare not pit a dogmatism of heaven, as if heaven could be his secure possession. He must, rather, testify against this secularist security with his own holy insecurity; against a control of earth immune to surprise with his own vulnerability to radical surprise. Could it be that this secularist's fear of error is, ultimately, a fear of truth?

What, finally, of the third secularist? He does not idolatrously presume to destroy heaven, nor does he dogmatically assert its inaccessibility. Like the believer, he has made himself open, insecure, and vulnerable. But what he has experienced is that heaven does not enter into his modern earth, and that all his modern attempts to ascend to heaven have come to grief. And in this experience he has discovered a fact of modern life.

For this reason, the believer may not bear witness against this third secularist one-sidedly. He must, rather, accept the discipline of mutual dialogue. And its mutuality, like all mutuality, involves risk; in this case, the risk is that, having listened to the testimony of this secularist, he, the believer, may himself be reduced to silence. He dare not shrink from this risk; for if indeed heaven still descends to earth this must be the modern earth. Yet he need not surrender to the fear that this risk is destructive of faith; for it but extends the range of its holy insecurity. And since revelation marks a new beginning whenever it occurs, he may stubbornly hope for the possibility of such a beginning, even today, even in the midst of our secular world.

How then shall we, Jews and Christians, welcome the international gathering in Montreal, and the secular theme under which it stands? We must welcome both wholeheartedly, unreservedly, and indeed do so with the knowledge that this secularity puts us to shame. Yet this knowledge must not mislead us into an indiscriminate admiration of secularism, let alone a surrender to it. For while the earth is handed over to man, he may not erect idols upon it. And while earth is set apart from heaven, it is yet incumbent upon us to bear witness to a grace which may descend upon this earth and command us to have a share in its sanctification.

Part Two

THE COMMANDING VOICE
OF AUSCHWITZ

2. The 614th Commandment

OUR TOPIC has two presuppositions which, I take it, we are not going to question but will simply take for granted. First, there is a unique and unprecedented crisis in this period of Jewish history which needs to be faced by all Jews, from the Orthodox at one extreme to the secularists at the other. (Thus we are not going to discuss the various forms of Judaism and Jewishness as though nothing had happened.) Second, whatever our response to the present crisis, it will be, in any case, a stubborn persistence in our Jewishness, not an attempt to abandon it or escape from it. (Thus we shall leave dialogues with Jews who do not want to be Jews for another day.)

How shall we understand the crisis of this period in Jewish history? We shall, I believe, be misled if we think in the style of the social sciences which try to grasp the particular in terms of the universal. We shall then, at best, understand the present Jewish crisis only in terms of the universal Western or human crisis, thus failing to grasp its uniqueness; at worst we shall

Reprinted from *Judaism*, vol. 16, no. 3, Summer Issue 1967, pp. 269–73. This essay was part of a symposium entitled "Jewish Values in the Post-Holocaust Future." The other participants were Richard H. Popkin, George Steiner, and Elie Wiesel, with Steven S. Schwarzschild acting as chairman. The symposium itself was held on March 26, 1967 (Purim day and coincidentally Easter Sunday), in New York City. The significance of these two dates was not lost on the participants.

abuse such an understanding as a means of escaping into the condition of contemporary-man-in-general. Instead of relying on the sociological mind, we must rely on the historical mind, which moves from the particular to the universal. But the historical mind. too, has its limitations. Thus no contemporary Jewish historian at the time of the destruction of the First or the Second Temple could have fully understood the world-historical significance of that event, if only because, in the midst of the crisis, he was not yet on the other side of it. We, too, are in the midst of the contemporary crisis, and hence unable fully to understand it. As for our attitude toward the future, this cannot be one of understanding or prediction, but only one of commitment and, possibly, faith.

How shall we achieve such fragmentary understanding of our present crisis as is possible while we are still in the midst of it? A crisis as yet unended can only be understood in terms of contradictions as yet unresolved. Jewish existence today is permeated by three main contradictions:

1. The American Jew of today is a "universalist," if only because he has come closer to the full achievement of equal status in society than any other Jew in the history of the Diaspora; yet this development coincides with the resurrection of Jewish "particularism" in the rebirth of a Jewish nation.

2. The Jew of today is committed to modern "secularism," as the source of his emancipation; yet his future survival as Jew depends on past religious resources. Hence even the most Orthodox Jew of today is a secularist insofar as, and to the extent that, he participates in the political and social processes of society. And even the most secularist Jew is religious insofar as, and to the extent that, he must fall back on the religious past in his struggle for a Jewish future.

3. Finally—and this is by far the most radical contradiction, and one which threatens to engulf the other two—the Jew in two of the three main present centers of Jewry, America and Israel, is at home in the modern world, for he has found a freedom and autonomy impossible in the premodern world. Yet he is but twenty-five years removed from a catastrophe unequaled

in all of Jewish history—a catastrophe that in its distinctive characterizations is modern in nature.

These are the three main contradictions. Merely to state them is to show how false it would be for us to see our present Jewish crisis as nothing more than an illustration of the general Western or human crisis. I will add to the general point nothing more than the mere listing of two specific examples. First, we may have a problem with "secularity," like our Christian neighbors. But our problem is not theirs, if only because for us—who have "celebrated" the secular city since the French Revolution—the time for such celebrating is past since the Holocaust. Second, while we have our problems with academically inspired atheism and agnosticism, they are central at best only for Jews who want to be men-in-general. For the authentic Jew who faces up to his singled-out Jewish condition—even for the authentic agnostic or atheistic Jew—a merely academically inspired doubt in God must seem sophomoric when he, after Auschwitz, must grapple with despair.

We must, then, take care lest we move perversely in responding to our present crisis. We must first face up and respond to our Jewish singled-out condition. Only thus and then can we hope to enter authentically into an understanding of and relation with other manifestations of a present crisis which is doubtless universal.

In groping for authentic responses to our present Jewish crisis, we do well to begin with responses which have already occurred. I believe that there are two such responses: first, a commitment to Jewish survival; and second, a commitment to Jewish unity.

I confess I used to be highly critical of Jewish philosophies which seemed to advocate no more than survival for survival's sake. I have changed my mind. I now believe that, in this present, unbelievable age, even a mere collective commitment to Jewish group-survival for its own sake is a momentous response, with the greatest implications. I am convinced that future historians will understand it, not, as our present detractors would have it, as the tribal response-mechanism of a fossil, but rather as a profound, albeit as yet fragmentary, act of faith, in an age of crisis to which the response might well have been either flight in total disarray or complete despair.

The second response we have already found is a commitment to Jewish unity. This, to be sure, is incomplete and must probably remain incomplete. Yet it is nonetheless real. Thus, the American Council for Judaism is an anachronism, as is, I venture to say, an Israeli nationalism which would cut off all ties with the Diaspora. No less anachronistic is a Jewish secularism so blind in its worship of the modern secular world as wholly to spurn the religious resources of the Jewish past; likewise, an Orthodoxy so untouched by the modern secular world as to have remained in a premodern ghetto.

Such, then, are the responses to the present crisis in Jewish history which we have already found in principle, however inadequately in practice. And their implications are even now altogether momentous. Whether aware of what we have decided or not, we have made the collective decision to endure the contradictions of present Jewish existence. We have collectively rejected the option, either of "checking out" of Jewish existence altogether or of so avoiding the present contradictions as to shatter Jewish existence into fragments.

But the question now is whether we can go beyond so fragmentary a commitment. In the present situation, this question becomes: can we confront the Holocaust, and yet not despair? Not accidentally has it taken twenty years for us to face this question, and it is not certain that we can face it yet. The contradiction is too staggering, and every authentic escape is barred. *For we are forbidden to turn present and future life into death, as the price of remembering death at Auschwitz. And we are equally forbidden to affirm present and future life, at the price of forgetting Auschwitz.*

We have lived in this contradiction for twenty years without being able to face it. Unless I am mistaken, we are now beginning to face it, however fragmentarily and inconclusively. And from this beginning confrontation there emerges what I will boldly term a 614th commandment: *the authentic Jew of today is forbidden to hand Hitler yet another, posthumous victory.*

(This formulation is terribly inadequate, yet I am forced to use it until one more adequate is found. First, although no anti-Orthodox implication is intended, as though the 613 commandments stood necessarily in need of change, we must face the fact that something radically new has happened. Second, although the commandment should be positive rather than negative, we must face the fact that Hitler did win at least one victory—the murder of six million Jews. Third, although the very name of Hitler should be erased rather than remembered, we cannot disguise the uniqueness of his evil under a comfortable generality, such as persecution-in-general, tyranny-in-general, or even the demonic-in-general.)

I think the authentic Jew of today is beginning to hear the 614th commandment. And he hears it whether, as agnostic, he hears no more, or whether, as believer, he hears the voice of the *metzaveh* (the commander) in the *mitzvah* (the commandment). Moreover, it may well be the case that the authentic Jewish agnostic and the authentic Jewish believer are closer today than at any previous time.

To be sure, the agnostic hears no more than the *mitzvah*. Yet if he is Jewishly authentic, he cannot but face the fragmentariness of his hearing. He cannot, like agnostics and atheists all around him, regard this *mitzvah* as the product of self-sufficient human reason, realizing itself in an ever-advancing history of autonomous human enlightenment. The 614th commandment must be, to him, an abrupt and absolute *given*, revealed in the midst of total catastrophe.

On the other hand, the believer, who bears the voice of the *metzaveh* in the *mitzvah*, can hardly hear anything more than the *mitzvah*. The reasons that made Martin Buber speak of an eclipse of God are still compelling. And if, nevertheless, a bond between Israel and the God of Israel can be experienced in the abyss, this can hardly be more than the *mitzvah* itself.

The implications of even so slender a bond are momentous. If the 614th commandment is binding upon the authentic Jew, then we are, first, commanded to survive as Jews, lest the Jewish people perish. We are commanded, second, to remember in our very guts and bones the martyrs of the

Holocaust, lest their memory perish. We are forbidden, thirdly, to deny or despair of God, however much we may have to contend with him or with belief in him, lest Judaism perish. We are forbidden, finally, to despair of the world as the place which is to become the kingdom of God, lest we help make it a meaningless place in which God is dead or irrelevant and everything is permitted. To abandon any of these imperatives, in response to Hitler's victory at Auschwitz, would be to hand him yet other, posthumous victories.

How can we possibly obey these imperatives? To do so requires the endurance of intolerable contradictions. Such endurance cannot but bespeak an as yet unutterable faith. If we are capable of this endurance, then the faith implicit in it may well be of historic consequence. At least twice before—at the time of the destruction of the First and of the Second Temples—Jewish endurance in the midst of catastrophe helped transform the world. We cannot know the future, if only because the present is without precedent. But this ignorance on our part can have no effect on our present action. The uncertainty of what will be may not shake our certainty of what we must do.

3. Jewish Faith and the Holocaust:
A Fragment

I

WITHIN THE PAST two centuries, three events have shaken and are still shaking Jewish religious existence—the Emancipation and its aftereffects, the Nazi Holocaust, and the rise of the first Jewish state in two thousand years—and of these, two have occurred in our own generation. From the point of view of Jewish religious existence, as from so many other points of view, the Holocaust is the most shattering. Doubtless the Emancipation and all its works have posed and continue to pose powerful challenges, with which Jewish thought has been wrestling all along—scientific agnosticism, secularism, assimilation, and the like. The Emancipation presents, however, a challenge *ab extra,* from without, and for all its well-demonstrated power to weaken and undermine Jewish religious existence, I have long been convinced that the challenge can be met, religiously and intellectually. The state of Israel, by contrast, is a challenge *ab intra,* from within—at least to much

Reprinted from *Commentary,* vol. 46, no. 2, August 1968, pp. 30–36. In somewhat different form this essay was also incorporated in chap. 1 of *Quest for Past and Future* (Bloomington: Indiana University Press, 1968; Boston: Beacon, 1970).

that Jewish existence has been throughout two millennia. But this challenge is positive—the fact that in one sense (if not in many others) a long exile has ended. That it represents a positive challenge was revealed during and immediately after the Six Day War, when biblical (i.e., preexilic) language suddenly came to life.

The Holocaust, too, challenges Jewish faith from within, but the negativity of its challenge is total, without light or relief. After the events associated with the name of Auschwitz, everything is shaken, nothing is safe.

To avoid Auschwitz, or to act as though it had never occurred, would be blasphemous. Yet how face it and be faithful to its victims? No precedent exists either within Jewish history or outside it. Even when a Jewish religious thinker barely begins to face Auschwitz, he perceives the possibility of a desperate choice between the faith of a millenial Jewish past, which has so far persisted through every trial, and faithfulness to the victims of the present. But at the edge of this abyss there must be a great pause, a lengthy silence, and an endurance.

II

Men shun the scandal of the particularity of Auschwitz. Germans link it with Dresden; American liberals, with Hiroshima. Christians deplore antisemitism-in-general, while Communists erect monuments to victims-of-Fascism-in-general, depriving the dead of Auschwitz of their Jewish identity even in death. Rather than face Auschwitz, men everywhere seek refuge in generalities, comfortable precisely because they are generalities. And such is the extent to which reality is shunned that no cries of protest are heard even when in the world community's own forum obscene comparisons are made between Israeli soldiers and Nazi murderers.

The Gentile world shuns Auschwitz because of the terror of Auschwitz—and because of real or imagined implication in the guilt for Auschwitz. But Jews shun Auschwitz as well. Only after many years did significant Jewish responses begin to appear. Little of real significance is being or can be said even now. Perhaps there should still be silence. It is certain, however, that the voices, now beginning to be heard, will grow ever louder and more numerous. For Jews now know that they must ever after remember Auschwitz, and be its witnesses to the world. Not to be a witness would be a betrayal. In the murder camps the victims often rebelled with no other hope than that one of them might escape to tell the tale. For Jews now to refrain from telling the tale would be unthinkable. Jewish faith still recalls the Exodus, Sinai, the two destructions of the Temple. A Judaism that survived at the price of ignoring Auschwitz would not deserve to survive.

It is because the world shrinks so fully from the truth that once a Jew begins to speak at all he must say the most obvious. Must he say that the death of a Jewish child at Auschwitz is no more lamentable than the death of a German child at Dresden? He must say it. And in saying it, he must also refuse to dissolve Auschwitz into suffering-in-general, even though he is almost sure to be considered a Jewish particularist who cares about Jews but not about mankind. Must he distinguish between the mass-killing at Hiroshima and that at Auschwitz? At the risk of being thought a sacrilegious quibbler, he must, with endless patience, forever repeat that Eichmann was moved by no such "rational" objective as victory when he diverted trains needed for military purposes in order to dispatch Jews to their death. He must add that there was no "irrational" objective either. Torquemada burned bodies in order to save souls. Eichmann sought to destroy both bodies and souls. Where else and at what other time have executioners ever separated those to be murdered now from those to be murdered later to the strain of Viennese waltzes? Where else has human skin ever been made into lampshades, and human body-fat into soap—not by isolated perverts but under the direction of ordinary bureaucrats? Auschwitz is a unique descent into hell. It is an unprecedented celebration of evil. It is evil for evil's sake.

A Jew must bear witness to this truth. Nor may he conceal the fact that Jews in their particularity were the singled-out victims. Of course, they were by no means the sole victims. And

a Jew would infinitely prefer to think that to the Nazis, Jews
were merely a species of the genus "inferior race." This indeed
was the theme of Allied wartime propaganda, and it is still
perpetuated by liberals, Communists, and guilt-ridden Christian theologians. Indeed, "liberal"-minded Jews themselves
perpetuate it. The superficial reason is that this view of Auschwitz unites victims of all races and creeds: it is "brotherly"
propaganda. Under the surface, however, there broods at least
in Jewish if not in some Gentile minds an idea horrible beyond
all description. Would even Nazis have singled out Jews for
such a terrible fate unless Jews had done *something* to bring it
upon themselves? Most of the blame attaches to the murderers:
must not at least some measure of blame attach to the victims as
well? Such are the wounds that Nazism has inflicted on some
Jewish minds. And such is the extent to which Nazism has
defiled the world that, while it should have destroyed every
vestige of antisemitism in every Gentile mind on earth, Auschwitz has, in some Gentile minds, actually increased it.[1]

These wounds and this defilement can be confronted only
with the truth. And the ineluctable truth is that Jews at Auschwitz were not a species of the genus "inferior race," but rather
the prototype by which "inferior race" was defined. Not until
the Nazi revolution had become an anti-Jewish revolution did it
begin to succeed as a movement; and when all its other works
came crashing down only one of its goals remained: the murder
of Jews.[2] This is the scandal that requires, of Germans, a ruthless examination of their whole history; of Christians, a pitiless
reckoning with the history of Christian antisemitism; of the
whole world, an inquiry into the grounds of its indifference for
twelve long years. Resort to theories of suffering-in-general or
persecution-in-general permits such investigations to be
evaded.

1. Witness the recent Polish propaganda campaign—tantamount to a rewriting of Holocaust history—in which it was suggested that the Jews had cooperated with the Nazis in their own destruction. Since I wrote these words, the
idea of a Nazi-Zionist axis has become standard Soviet propaganda.
2. See, e.g., George L. Mosse, *The Crisis of German Ideology* (New York:
Universal Library, 1964), especially chap. 17.

Yet even where the quest for explanations is genuine there is not, and never will be, an adequate explanation. Auschwitz is the scandal of evil for evil's sake, an eruption of demonism without analogy; and the singling-out of Jews, ultimately, is an unparalleled expression of what the rabbis call groundless hate. This is the rock on which throughout eternity all rational explanations will crash and break apart.

How can a Jew respond to thus having been singled out, and to being singled out even now whenever he tries to bear witness? Resisting rational explanations, Auschwitz will forever resist religious explanations as well. Attempts to find rational causes succeed, at least up to a point, and the search for the religious, ideological, social, and economic factors leading to Auschwitz must be relentlessly pressed. In contrast, the search for a purpose in Auschwitz is foredoomed to total failure. Not that good men in their despair have not made the attempt. Good Orthodox Jews have resorted to the ancient "for our sins we are punished," but this recourse, unacceptable already to Job, is in this case all the more impossible. A good Christian theologian sees the purpose of Auschwitz as a divine reminder of the sufferings of Christ, but this testifies to a moving sense of desperation—and to an incredible lapse of theological judgment. A good Jewish secularist will connect the Holocaust with the rise of the state of Israel, but while to see a causal connection here is possible and necessary, to see a purpose is intolerable. A total and uncompromising sweep must be made of these and other explanations, all designed to give purpose to Auschwitz. No purpose, religious or non-religious, will ever be found in Auschwitz. The very attempt to find one is blasphemous.

Yet it is of the utmost importance to recognize that seeking a purpose is one thing, but seeking a response quite another. The first is wholly out of the question. The second is inescapable. Even after two decades any sort of adequate response may as yet transcend the power of any Jew. But his faith, his destiny, his very survival will depend on whether, in the end, he will be able to respond.

How can a Jew begin to seek a response? Looking for prece-

dents, he finds none either in Jewish or in non-Jewish history.
Jewish (like Christian) martyrs have died for their faith, certain
that God needs martyrs. Job suffered despite his faith, able to
protest within the sphere of faith. Black Christians have died for
their race, unshaken in a faith which was not at issue. The one
million Jewish children murdered in the Nazi Holocaust died
neither because of their faith, nor in spite of their faith, nor for
reasons unrelated to faith. They were murdered because of the
faith of their great-grandparents. Had these great-grandparents
abandoned their Jewish faith, and failed to bring up Jewish
children, then their fourth-generation descendants might have
been among the Nazi executioners, but not among their Jewish
victims. Like Abraham of old, European Jews some time in the
mid-nineteenth century offered a human sacrifice, by the mere
minimal commitment to the Jewish faith of bringing up Jewish
children. But unlike Abraham they did not know what they
were doing, and there was no reprieve. This is the brute fact
which makes all comparisons odious or irrelevant. This is what
makes Jewish religious existence today unique, without support from analogies anywhere in the past. This is the scandal of
the particularity of Auschwitz which, once confronted by
Jewish faith, threatens total despair.

I confess that it took me twenty years until I was able to look
at this scandal, but when at length I did, I made what to me was,
and still is, a momentous discovery: that while religious thinkers were vainly struggling for a response to Auschwitz, Jews
throughout the world—rich and poor, learned and ignorant, religious and nonreligious—had to some degree been responding
all along. For twelve long years Jews had been exposed to a
murderous hate which was as groundless as it was implacable.
For twelve long years the world had been lukewarm or indifferent, unconcerned over the prospect of a world without Jews.
For twelve long years the whole world had conspired to make
Jews wish to cease to be Jews wherever, whenever, and in
whatever way they could. Yet to this unprecedented invitation
to group suicide, Jews responded with an unexpected will to
live—with, under the circumstances, an incredible commitment to Jewish group survival.

In ordinary times, a commitment of this kind may be a mere

mixture of nostalgia and vague loyalties not far removed from tribalism; and, unable to face Auschwitz, I had myself long viewed it as such, placing little value on a Jewish survival which was, or seemed to be, only survival for survival's sake. I was wrong, and even the shallowest Jewish survivalist philosophy of the postwar period was right by comparison. For in the age of Auschwitz a Jewish commitment to Jewish survival is in itself a monumental act of faithfulness, as well as a monumental, albeit as yet fragmentary, act of faith. Even to do no more than remain a Jew after Auschwitz is to confront the demons of Auschwitz in all their guises, and to bear witness against them. It is to believe that these demons cannot, will not, and must not prevail, and to stake on that belief one's own life and the lives of one's children, and of one's children's children. To be a Jew after Auschwitz is to have wrested hope—for the Jew and for the world—from the abyss of total despair. In the words of a speaker at a recent gathering of Bergen-Belsen survivors, the Jew after Auschwitz has a second *Shema Yisrael:* no second Auschwitz, no second Bergen-Belsen, no second Buchenwald—anywhere in the world, for anyone in the world!

What accounts for this commitment to Jewish existence when there might have been, and by every rule of human logic should have been, a terrified and demoralized flight from Jewish existence? Why, since Auschwitz, have all previous distinctions among Jews—between religious and secularist, Orthodox and liberal—diminished in importance, to be replaced by a new major distinction between Jews committed to Jewish survival, willing to be singled out and counted, and Jews in flight, who rationalize this flight as a rise to humanity-in-general? In my view, nothing less will do than to say that a commanding Voice speaks from Auschwitz, and that there are Jews who hear it and Jews who stop their ears.

The ultimate question is: where was God at Auschwitz? For years I sought refuge in Buber's image of an eclipse of God. This image, still meaningful in other respects, no longer seems to me applicable to Auschwitz. Most assuredly no *redeeming* Voice is heard from Auschwitz, or ever will be heard. However, a *commanding* Voice is being heard, and has, however faintly, been heard from the start. Religious Jews hear it, and they identify its source. Secularist Jews also hear it, even though perforce they leave it unidentified. At Auschwitz, Jews came face to face with absolute evil. They were and still are singled out by it, but in the midst of it they hear an absolute commandment: *Jews are forbidden to grant posthumous victories to Hitler*. They are commanded to survive as Jews, lest the Jewish people perish. They are commanded to remember the victims of Auschwitz, lest their memory perish. They are forbidden to despair of man and his world, and to escape into either cynicism or other-worldliness, less they cooperate in delivering the world over to the forces of Auschwitz. Finally, they are forbidden to despair of the God of Israel, lest Judaism perish. A secularist Jew cannot make himself believe by a mere act of will, nor can he be commanded to do so; yet he can perform the commandment of Auschwitz. And a religious Jew who has stayed with his God may be forced into new, possibly revolutionary, relationships with him. One possibility, however, is wholly unthinkable. A Jew may not respond to Hitler's attempt to destroy Judaism by himself cooperating in its destruction. In ancient times, the unthinkable Jewish sin was idolatry. Today, it is to respond to Hitler by doing his work.

In the Midrash, God is, even in time of unrelieved tragedy, only "seemingly" powerless, for the Messiah is still expected. In Elie Wiesel's *Night*, God hangs on the gallows, and for the hero of Wiesel's *The Gates of the Forest*, a Messiah who is able to come, and yet at Auschwitz failed to come, is not to be conceived. Yet this same hero asserts that precisely because it is too late we are commanded to hope. He also says the Kaddish, "that solemn affirmation, filled with grandeur and serenity, by which man returns to God His crown and His scepter." But how a Jew after Auschwitz can return these to God is not yet known. Nor is it yet known how God can receive them.

III

The Nazi Holocaust has brought Jews and Christians closer together—and set them further apart. The first truth is comforting and obvious. The second is painful, complex, and obscure, but perhaps in the end more necessary to confront. The gulf between Jews and Christians that Hitler succeeded in creating can be bridged only if it is recognized. But to bridge it is of incalculable importance for the future of both Judaism and Christianity.

Since an objective grasp of this issue is almost impossible, I had better state my views in terms of my own subjective development. Twenty years ago I believed that what once separated Jew and Christian was now dwarfed by what united them—namely their opposition to Nazism. I was of course not unaware of phenomena like the Nazi "German-Christian" church, or of the fact that respectable and indeed outstanding theologians were part of it. But so far as my native Germany was concerned, it was not the Christian Nazis who mattered to me; it was rather the Christian anti-Nazis, however small their number—not the "German-Christian" but rather the German confessional church. And what mattered theologically was thinkers like Barth and Tillich, able to recognize Nazi idolatry and to fight it courageously and unequivocally. To this day I still revere Kierkegaard, the first Christian thinker to perceive the nature and extent of modern idolatry, who would surely have been put into a concentration camp had he lived and written in Nazi Germany. To this day I am supported in my Judaism by the faithfulness of Christians to their Christianity. And when a new generation of Christian theologians arises to proclaim the death of God I feel, as a Jew, abandoned and betrayed.

The ancient rabbis recognized "righteous Gentiles" as being equal to the high priest in the sight of God; but they had no real acquaintance with Christianity and, of course, none with Islam. Medieval Jewish thinkers recognized Christianity and Mohammedanism as valid monotheistic religions, and considering the state of medieval Jewish-Christian and Jewish-Moslem relations, it is surprising that they did. But since the experience of Nazism and of Christian opposition to Nazism (which goes back to my adolescence), I have been convinced that there is now a need for Jewish recognition that the Christian (and the Mohammedan) not only affirms the One God but also stands in a living relation to him. Where to go from here I cannot say. I never could accept Rosenzweig's famous "double covenant" doctrine, according to which all except Jews (who are already "with the Father") need the Son in order to find him. How can a modern Jew pray for the conversion of the whole non-Jewish world to Christianity when even premodern Jews could pay homage to Moslem monotheism? Rosenzweig's doctrine seems altogether outmoded at a time when Christians themselves are beginning to replace missionary efforts with interreligious dialogue, and I wonder whether even for Rosenzweig this doctrine was more than a stage in his self-emancipation from modern paganism.

Thus, though I very much feel the need for a Jewish doctrine of Christianity, I am left without one and must for the time being rest content only with openness to Jewish-Christian dialogue. As regards the prospect of such dialogue, I confess that I have over the years become less optimistic in the hope that the long age of Christian triumphalism over Judaism is truly being superseded by an age of Jewish-Christian dialogue. In view of recent Christian developments, such as ecclesiastical declarations deploring antisemitism and absolving Jews of the charge of deicide, this may seem a strange, and even perverse, personal opinion. Yet I think that recent events have shown it to be realistic.

To most impartial observers it has always been a plain fact that, ever since the Age of Enlightenment, it was secularists who spearheaded the struggle for Jewish emancipation; organized Christian forces sometimes accepted emancipation, often opposed it, but rarely if ever led the fight. This fact, plain to so many, I myself failed to see (or refused to accept) until quite recently. I saw the distinction between the new Nazi and the old Christian antisemitism, but could not bear to admit a relation between them. In the grim years of Nazism and immediately thereafter, I found it humanly impossible to see enemies on every side. Twenty-five years later, however, it is necessary to confront yet another painful truth.

I will confine myself to two examples, both concerning German Christians opposed to Nazism. In 1933, many Jews then in Germany, myself included, made a veritable saint of Cardinal Faulhaber, crediting him with opposing both Nazism and Nazi antisemitism. This image remained with me for many years. I had read the Cardinal's relevant sermons, but had somehow not noticed what they said. Not until about three years ago, when I came upon Guenter Lewy's masterful *The Catholic Church and Nazi Germany,* did I realize that Faulhaber had confined his defense to the Jews of the Old Testament, and had gone out of his way to make clear that he was not defending his Jewish contemporaries. To quote Lewy:

> We must distinguish, he told the faithful, between the people of Israel before the death of Christ, who were vehicles of divine revelation, and the Jews after the death of Christ, who have become restless wanderers over the earth. But even the Jewish people of ancient times could not justly claim credit for the wisdom of the Old Testament. So unique were these laws that one was bound to say: "People of Israel, this did not grow in your own garden of your own planting. This condemnation of usurious land-grabbing, this war against the oppression of the farmer by debt, this prohibition of usury, is not the product of your spirit."[3]

Rarely has the Christian belief in the revealed character of the Hebrew Bible been put to so perverse a use.

My second example is even more painful, for it involves none other than the universally beloved Dietrich Bonhoeffer, brave anti-Nazi Christian witness and martyr to his cause. Even now I find it hard to believe that he should have confined his attack on Nazi Aryan legislation to its application to converted Jews; and I find it even harder to believe that these words were written by Bonhoeffer in Nazi Germany in response to Nazi antisemitism:

> Now the measures of the state toward Judaism in addition stand in quite special context for the church. The church of Christ has never lost sight of the thought that the "chosen people,' who nailed the redeemer of the world to the cross, must bear the curse for its action through a long history of suffering.[4]

3. Guenter Lewy, *The Catholic Church and Nazi Germany* (New York: McGraw-Hill, 1964), p. 276.
4. Dietrich Bonhoeffer, *No Rusty Swords* (London: Fontana, 1970), p. 222. See also below, pp. 74–75.

Rather than comment myself, I prefer to cite the comment of the American Christian theologian, J. Coert Rylaarsdam:

> We all think of Dietrich Bonhoeffer as a good Christian, even a martyr, perhaps. With great courage he insisted on "the crown rights of the Redeemer" within his own church. Moreover, he insisted that Jews who had converted to Christianity were entitled to the same rights in the church as other Christians, a position by no means unanimously held in the church of Hitler's Germany. Nevertheless, standing in the Christian tradition of the curse, Bonhoeffer did not hesitate to appeal to it to rationalize Hitler's program for Jews faithful to their own faith.[5]

To keep the record straight, one must add that the passages in question were written in 1933 (when, according to his friend Eberhard Bethge, Bonhoeffer still suffered from "lack of reality-relatedness"), that his opposition to Nazism became more complete as it came to assume secular-political expression, and, indeed, that he took personal risks to save Jewish lives. Even so, I know of no evidence yet (though I would dearly love to hear of any) to the effect that Bonhoeffer ever totally repudiated the Christian "tradition of the curse." From the very beginning he opposed the encroachment of racism upon the church and spoke up for Jews converted to Christianity. By 1940 he charged that the church "was silent when she should have cried out because the blood of the innocent was crying aloud to heaven . . . she is guilty of the deaths of the weakest and most defenseless brothers of Jesus Christ." But during the most grievous Jewish martyrdom in all of history, did he ever repudiate a millennial Christian tradition, and seek a bond (even if only in his own mind) with "Jews faithful to their own faith," because, and not in spite of, their faithfulness? How different would Bonhoeffer's struggle have been if he had repudiated the "Christian tradition of the curse" from the start! How different would Jewish fate have been in our time had his whole church repudiated it!

5. J. Coert Rylaarsdam, "The Disavowal of the Curse: A New Beginning?," *Dialogue*, Summer 1967, p. 192.

In America, to be sure, it has always been different, and the churches of the 1960s differ everywhere from those of the 1940s, there being historic changes in the making in Christian attitudes toward Jews. The question is, however, whether American differences are not mainly due to the effect of secular democracy, and also whether the changes in Christian attitudes toward Jews possess the radicalism which, after Auschwitz, is a categorical imperative. Here again, only ruthless truthfulness can save the future of Jewish-Christian dialogue. And the truth, as I am now forced to see it, is that the organized Christian forces will find it easiest to drop the ancient charge of deicide, harder to recognize roots of antisemitism in the New Testament, and hardest of all to face up to the fact that Jews and Judaism are both still alive. Confronted with the awkward fact of Jewish survival after the advent of Christianity, theologians have looked upon Judaism as a fossil, an anachronism, a shadow. It is not easy to reverse a doctrine which has persisted for two millennia (assuming not only religious, but also, as in Toynbee, secular, and, as in Marx, anti-religious forms), and to recognize that both Jews and Judaism have maintained an unbroken existence throughout the entire Christian era. But how can a Jew, however he may strain his ears, hear God speak to the Christian church, if even after Auschwitz this ancient calumny is not at length totally and categorically rejected? And how, he wonders, can a Christian enter into dialogue with a Jew unless he recognizes that the person across the table is no shadow but alive?

These questions became traumatically vivid for any Jew committed to Jewish-Christian dialogue during the momentous events of May and June 1967, when the state of Israel, the most incontestable proof that the Jewish people still lives, was threatened with destruction. The secular Western press understood well enough that Israel was fighting for her life. Yet only a handful of Christian spokesmen showed the same understanding. Why should Christian spokesmen have remained neutral as between Israel's claim to the right to live and Arab claims to the right to destroy her—if not because of old, unconscious, theologically-inspired doubts as to whether the "fossil" Israel did indeed have the right to live? Why has there always been much Christian concern for Arab refugees from Israel, but none whatever for Jewish refugees from Arab countries—if not because of old, no longer consciously remembered ecclesiastical doctrines to the effect that Jews (unlike Arabs) must be kept landless, and therefore rightless? Why were ecclesiastical authorities untroubled by two decades of Moslem control of the Christian holy places (and of Arab desecration of Jewish holy places), and yet now so deeply distressed by Jewish control?

But a still more ultimate question is raised by the events of 1967. For two long weeks in May the worldwide Jewish community perceived the specter of a second Jewish Holocaust in a single generation. For two weeks it listened to the same words emanating from Cairo and Damascus which had once emanated from Berlin, largely composed, one may be sure, by pupils of Joseph Goebbels. For two weeks it longed for Christian words of apprehension and concern. But whereas some such words came from secular sources, from the churches there was little but silence.[6] Once again, Jews were alone. This fact, transcending as it does all politics, is a trauma for Jews regardless of political persuasion—non-Zionists and even anti-Zionists as well as Zionists. Moreover, it stands between Jews and Christians even now, for when Jews ask why there was no moral Christian outcry against a second Auschwitz they are still widely misunderstood, as demanding of Christians that they side politically with Israel against the Arab states.

Any Jew pondering this ultimate question must surely reject the idea that the Christian churches abandoned Jews knowingly to a second Holocaust. What, then, was revealed by the Christian silence in the spring of 1967? Not, I believe, an old Christian antisemitism, but rather a new Jewish-Christian problem—the fearful truth that Hitler, against his will bringing Jews and Christians closer, also had his will in setting them further apart.

6. See A. Roy and Alice L. Eckardt, "Again, Silence in the Churches," *The Christian Century*, July 26 and August 2, 1967.

A Jew at Auschwitz was murdered because he was a Jew; a Christian was murdered only if he was a saint: but there are few saints among either Jews or Christians. Hitler gave a new and perverse reality to the ancient Jewish doctrine that anyone born a Jew is a Jew. He also gave a new and perverse reality to the ancient Christian doctrine that one becomes a Christian only through an act of voluntary commitment—and, with diabolical cunning as well as terror, he led Christians into temptation. Hitler tried to create an abyss between Jews and Christians; he succeeded; and—this is the horror—he continues to enjoy post-humous successes. The Jew after Auschwitz exists with the knowledge of abandonment; the Christian cannot bear to face his responsibility for this abandonment. He knows that, as a Christian, he should voluntarily have gone to Auschwitz, where his own Master would have been dragged, voluntarily or involuntarily, and he is wracked by a sense of guilt the deeper the less he has cause to feel it. Hence the Christian failure to face Auschwitz. Hence Christian recourse to innocuous generalities. Hence, too, Christian silence in May 1967. If in May 1967 the Christian community did not cry out against a second Auschwitz, it was not because of its indifference to the words emanating from Cairo and Damascus, but rather because it did not hear them. It failed to recognize the danger of a second Holocaust because it has yet to recognize the fact of the first.

To bridge the Jewish-Christian gulf which Hitler has succeeded in creating is a task of incalculable importance, and at a Jewish-Christian colloquium prior to the events of May 1967 I attempted a hesitant step in that direction. I said there that if every Christian in Hitler's Europe had followed the example of the King of Denmark and decided to put on the yellow star, there would today be neither confusion nor despair in the church, nor talk of the death of God. I said with every emphasis at my command that, as a Jew after Auschwitz, I did not and could not speak as a judge, but only as a witness. To remove every trace of ambiguity or doubt I stated not politely, but quite truthfully, that I had been sixteen years of age when Hitler came to power, and had not known then, any more than I knew now, whether I would have become a Nazi had I been born a

Gentile. Yet a leading Christian thinker, himself a lifelong anti-Nazi, mistook my statement for a case of Jewish triumphalism. So wide still is the gulf between Jews and Christians that Hitler opened decades ago. So close are we to handing him further, posthumous victories.

IV

On another public occasion, in March 1967, I asked the following question: Would we [like Job] be able to say that the question of Auschwitz will be answered in any sense whatever in case the eclipse of God were ended and He appeared to us? An impossible and intolerable question.[7] Less than three months later this purely hypothetical question had become actual, when at Jerusalem the threat of total annihilation gave way to sudden salvation, atheists spoke of miracles, and hardboiled Western reporters resorted to biblical images.

The question *is* impossible and intolerable. Even Job's question is not answered by God's presence, and to him children are restored. The children of Auschwitz will not be restored, and the question of Auschwitz will not be answered by a saving divine presence.

And yet, is a Jew after Auschwitz permitted to despair of salvation because of Auschwitz? Is it permitted him to cast out all hope and all joy? But on the other side, can there be any hope and any joy, purchased at the price of forgetting? Any one of these reponses would be further victories handed to Hitler, and are thus impossible.

It was into precisely this impossible and intolerable contradiction that believing Jews were placed by the events at Jerusalem in May and June 1967. Those events cast into clear relief the whole as yet unassimilated fact of an embattled, endangered, but nevertheless free Jewish state, emerging from

7. The discussion following the address reprinted in chap. 2 in this book; see *Judaism*, vol. 16, no. 3, Summer Issue 1967, p. 296.

ashes and catastrophe. Solely because of the connection of the events of May and June with Auschwitz did a military victory (rarely applauded in Judaism, and never for its own sake) acquire an inescapable religious dimension.

In this context, let me quote from a letter I recently received from Professor Harold Fisch of Bar-Ilan University in Israel:

> May I report to you a conversation I had last summer with a colleague, a psychologist, who had served during the war as an artillery officer in Sinai. I asked him how he accounted for the remarkable heroism of the quite ordinary soldier of the line, for, as you may know, exemplary heroism was the normal thing at that time; mere carrying out of duty was the exception. Where, I asked him, was the psychological spring? To my surprise, he answered that what deeply motivated each and every soldier was the memory of the Holocaust, and the feeling that *above all this must never happen again.* There had been an ominous similarity between the statements of Arab leaders, their radio, and newspapers, and the remembered threats of the Nazis: we had entered into a *Shoah* (holocaust) psychosis, all around us enemies threatening us with extermination and having both the means and the will to carry out their threat. As the ring closed in and help seemed far, one noticed one's neighbors who had been in Auschwitz and Bergen-Belsen going about whitefaced. It was all too obvious what was the source of their dread. The years in between had momentarily fallen away, and they were back in that veritable nightmare world. The dark night of the soul was upon us. *And it was the commandment which the Lord of history had, so to speak, pronounced at Auschwitz which saved us.* [Italics added.] I told my friend that I could not entirely accept his explanation because I knew that a majority of the soldiers had no personal or family recollections of the European Holocaust: they had come from North Africa or Yemen, or even the neighboring Arab countries where at that time such horrors were unknown. How could they feel the force of the analogy as could the survivors of Buchenwald? He told me that the intervening twenty years had brought it about that the Holocaust had become a collective experience pressing consciously and unconsciously on the minds of all, even the young, for whom Jewish history in the Diaspora had come to an end with the beginnings of Israeli independence.

It is solely because of this connection of the events of May and June with Auschwitz that a Jew must both tremble and rejoice. He must tremble lest he permit any light after Auschwitz to relieve the darkness of Auschwitz. He must rejoice, lest he add to the darkness of Auschwitz. Rejoicing after Auschwitz and because of Auschwitz, the Jew must be a Jew, *Am Yisrael Chai* ("the people Israel, alive"), a witness to the world, preparing a way for God.

4. *The People Israel Lives:*
How My Mind Has Changed

As I REREAD my theological writings of ten—or of fifteen or twenty—years ago I am filled with religious and theological guilt and repentance. In this report, however, I can deal only with the theological. More than thirty years ago, largely under the influence of Martin Buber and Franz Rosenzweig, I had responded to the demonic fact of Nazism by turning my back on my nineteenth-century liberal Jewish heritage and embracing what may broadly be called a neoorthodox faith and theology. I had rejected the dissipation of the distinction between the Word of God and the word of man, between the divine covenant with Israel and the random events of history—above all, an ideology that had confused the messianic days with the achievements and promises of the modern world.

To this day I remain largely within this neorthodox stance. I remain, too, in the bond with Christians made possible by that stance, a bond which first became fully actual for me when in a Nazi concentration camp before the war two of my closest fellow sufferers and witnesses were Christians. There was, how-

Reprinted from *The Christian Century*, May 6, 1970, pp. 563–68. This essay, appearing in the journal's "How My Mind Has Changed" series, was my first attempt in print to address Christians directly on the subject of the Holocaust. Hence, at the inevitable cost of some repetitions, I have made no changes, so as to be faithful to the original occasion.

ever, one omission in my position of that time, and that omission remained in my writings for more than two decades. Having recognized "the demonic" in principle, I abused that recognition to ignore the scandalous uniqueness of Auschwitz. Having taken hold of what, after Hitler, unites Jews with Christians, I overlooked the utter abandonment of the children of Treblinka by the world, Christians included. And even as my Jewish brethren in Europe suffered an agony without precedent inside or outside Jewish history, I was at work on a theology that sought to show that nothing unprecedented could call into question the Jewish faith—that it is essentially immune to all "secular" events between Sinai and the messianic days.

For the past half-dozen years or so I have recognized my guilt and sought to do repentance. And I can only plead that other Jews—religiously and nonreligiously minded—are likewise only now able to begin to face the Holocaust.

I

My mind and spirit are still numbed. I have, however, acquired one religious certainty as great as any in this religiously uncertain age. Søren Kierkegaard once perceived his "knight of faith" as forever obliged to retrace Abraham's road to Mount Moriah, the place where he was to sacrifice Isaac. The Jewish believer and theological thinker today—as well as a century or a millennium hence—is obliged to retrace, again and again, the *via dolorosa* that led one-third of his people to the human sacrifice in the Nazi gas chambers. He is forbidden the cheap and often sacrilegious evasions that tempt him on every side: the "progressive" ideology that asserts that memory is unnecessary, that Auschwitz was an accidental "relapse into tribalism" (an insult to any tribe ever in existence); the "psychiatric" ideology that holds that memory is masochism even as Auschwitz itself was sadism, thus safely belittling both; the "liberal-universalist" ideology that asserts that memory is actually immoral, that because Jews must care about Vietnam, the Black ghetto, and Arab refugees, they are obliged to forget the greatest catastrophe suffered by their own people.

That last-named ideology is especially insidious, for good Jews are tempted by it. When I first called Auschwitz unique my assertion was at once taken to mean that a dead Jewish child at Auschwitz is a greater tragedy than a dead German child at Dresden. That was a misunderstanding possible only because of an antisemitism (conscious or unconscious) that distinguishes "universalistic" Jews concerned with others to the point of consenting to group suicide, and "particularistic" Jews who deserve this nasty epithet if they show any concern whatever for the fate of their own people. This ideology, I say, tempts many: witness the countless Jews today who risk much in behalf of Vietnam or the Black ghetto but will not utter a word against Polish or Soviet antisemitism. Hatred of Jews on the part of others has always produced self-hating Jews—never more so than when disguised as a moral ideology.

I call Auschwitz unique because it *is* unique. As my wife, Rose, put it in a letter to a minister, Auschwitz was

overwhelming in its scope, shattering in its fury, inexplicable in its demonism. Unlike Hiroshima, it was no miscalculation of a government at war. It was minutely planned and executed over a twelve-year period, with the compliance of thousands of citizens, to the deafening silence of the world. Unlike slaughtered Russian villages, these were no chance victims of the fury of war. They were carefully chosen, named, listed, tabulated, and stamped. The Nazis went to incredible lengths to find even a single missing Jew. It did not help but hindered the war effort. For while antisemitism was in the beginning politically advantageous to the Nazis the actual crime of genocide had often to be carefully hidden from their own people. Troop trains were diverted from the Russian front in order to transport Jews to Auschwitz. Unique in all human history, the Holocaust was evil for evil's sake.

The woman who wrote those words is a Christian. I doubt whether I or any other Jew could have been so relentless as she was in her evaluation.

No wonder the mind seeks refuge in comparisons—some shallow, some obscene, all false—between Auschwitz and Hiroshima, or Vietnam, or the Black ghetto, or even the American campus. Indeed, the very words "Holocaust" and "six million" are evasive abstractions, empty universal substitutes for the countless particulars each of which is an inexhaustible mystery of sin and suffering. And when Jewish theologian Richard Rubenstein writes (in his essay in *The Religious Situation* [Beacon, 1968]) that "the facts are in" and that since "the theological options . . . will not magically increase with the passing of time" we may as well make our choice now, we must conclude that he does not know whereof he speaks.

Let me take just one of those particulars. In issuing "work permits" that were designed to separate "useless" Jews to be murdered at once from "useful" ones to be kept useful by diabolically contrived false hopes and murdered later, the Nazis customarily issued two such permits to an able-bodied Jewish man. One was untransferable, to be kept for himself; the other was to be given at his own discretion to his able-bodied mother, father, wife, or one child. The Nazis would not make the choice, even though to do so would have produced a more efficient labor force. Jewish sons, husbands, or fathers themselves were forced to decide who among their loved ones was—for the time being—to live, who to die at once.

I search the whole history of human depravity for comparisons. In vain. I would reject the comparisons cited above even if they compared the comparable: let each human evil be understood in its own terms. What makes the comparisons utterly odious is that in effect if not intention they abuse Auschwitz, deny that it ever happened, rob its victims even of memory. There is a qualitative distinction between evils—even gigantic ones—perpetuated for such "rational" ends as gain, victory, real or imagined self-interest, and evils perpetrated for evil's sake.

Moreover, there can be a difference even among evils for evil's sake. Theologians call these "the demonic," and I myself once found escape in this theological abstraction. I find it no more. In the history of demonic evil (which, incidentally, in this age of uncritical theological celebrations, someone should write) conceivably there are examples comparable to the Nazi custom of issuing the two work permits. But until such examples are found my religious life and theological thought must lack the comfort of comparisons as I retrace the *via dolorosa* that leads to Auschwitz, trying at the desperate utmost to match the solitude, the despair, the utter abandonment of every one of my brethren who walked that road. And I shall always fail.

II

If the crime of Auschwitz is unique, so is the threat to the faith of its victims. I search the history of religious suffering for comparisons. Once again, in vain. Other believers (Jewish and Christian) have been tortured and murdered for their faith, secure in the belief that God needs martyrs. Black Christians have been tortured and murdered for their race, finding strength in a faith not at issue. The children of Auschwitz were tortured and murdered, not because of their faith nor despite their faith nor for reasons unrelated to the Jewish faith. The Nazis, though racists, did not murder Jews for their "race" but for the Jewish faith of their great-grandparents. Had those great-grandparents failed to show the minimum commitment to the ancient covenant on the raising of Jewish children, their twentieth-century offspring might have been among the Nazi murderers; they would not have been among the Jewish victims. At some time in the mid-nineteenth century, European Jews, like Abraham of old, brought a child sacrifice; but unlike Abraham they did not know what they were doing—and there was no reprieve. It is as if Satan himself had plotted for four thousand years to destroy the covenant between God and Israel, and had at last found the way.[1]

For the desperate question for us after Auschwitz is this: nineteenth-century European Jews did not know—what if they

---

1. See above p. 30 and below p. 136. I find myself compelled to keep returning to this fundamental point (and indeed to quote myself verbatim) since it would seem to be *the* shibboleth of post-Holocaust Jewish self-understanding, whether religious or secular.

had known? And what of us who *do* know? Dare we *morally* raise Jewish children, exposing our offspring to a possible second Auschwitz decades or centuries hence? And dare we *religiously not* raise Jewish children, completing Satan's work on his behalf?[2]

My soul is aghast at this impossible choice, unprecedented in the annals of faith anywhere. And I am filled with shame of mind as well as of soul when I consider that my earlier theology had ruled it out on neat a priori grounds, when it implied that nothing radically new could happen in Jewish religious history between Sinai and the messianic days. My intentions, I still think, were good, for I had sought to make the Jewish faith immune to "merely empirical" and "secular" history, irrefutable as well as unprovable. The result, however, was a betrayal, however unwitting, of the victims of Auschwitz—a betrayal committed even as they were suffering their unique martyrdom.

Moreover, I now think that my earlier theological aim lacked Jewish authenticity. To be sure, when the Romans destroyed the second Temple the talmudic rabbis refused to despair of God's covenant with Israel, but at the same time they let the catastrophe call it into question. Whether picturing God as in exile with Israel or as lamenting his own decision or even as engaged in bitter self-recrimination, they showed the courage to make their faith vulnerable to actual—i.e., empirical and "secular"—history. How shall we live with God after Auschwitz? How without him? Contend with God we must, as did Abraham, Jacob, Job. And we cannot let him go.

Rather than venturing to enter in this brief essay into this still-unknown territory, I quote here two texts, both of which have been used in prayers in Jewish services:

---

2. This contradiction, unlike Kierkegaard's teleological suspension of the ethical, does not involve morality on one side only. Among the worst of the Spanish inquisitors were descendants of converted Jews, and Reinhard Heydrich is said to have had a Jewish ancestor. By choosing for our children not to be victims, may we be exposing them to the possibility, or the likelihood, that they will be murderers?

The Resurrection

One day they will assemble in the valley of bones—
Ashes sifted out of furnaces, vapors from Luneburg,
Parchments from some fiend's books, cakes of soap,
Half-formed embryos, screams still heard in nightmares.
God will breathe upon them. He will say: Be men.

> *But they will defy Him: We do not hear you. Did
> you hear us?*
> *There is no resurrection for us. In life it was a won-
> drous thing*
> *For each of us to be himself, to guide his limbs to
> do his will.*
> *But the many are now one. Our blood has flowed
> together,*
> *Our ashes are inseparable, our marrow commingled,*
> *Our voices poured together like water of the sea.*
> *We shall not surrender this greater self.*
> *We the Abrahams, Isaacs, Jacobs, Sarahs, Leahs,
> Rachels*
> *And now forever Israel.*

Almighty God, raise up a man who will go peddling
    through the world.
Let him gather us up and go through the world selling
    us as trinkets.
Let the peddler sell us cheaply. Let him hawk his wares
    and say:
Who will buy my souvenirs? Little children done in soap,
A rare Germanic parchment of the greatest Jew in Lodz.
Men will buy us and display us and point to us with
    pride:
A thousand Jews went into this and here is a rare piece
That came all the way from Crakow in a box car.
A great statesman will place a candle at his bedside.
It will burn but never be consumed.
The tallow will drop with the tears we shed
And it will glow with the souls of our children.
They will put us in the bathrooms of the United Nations
Where diplomats will wash and wash their hands

With Polish Jews and German Jews and Russian Jews.
Let the peddler sell the box of soap that once was buried
With Kaddish and Psalms by our brothers.

> *Some night the statesman will blow upon the candle*
> *And it will not go out.*
> *The souls of little children will flicker and flicker*
> *But not expire.*
> *Some day the diplomats will wash their hands and*
>   *find them stained with blood.*
> *Some day the citizens of the German town*
> *Will awake to find their houses reeking*
> *With all the vapors from all the concentration camps,*
> *From Hell itself, and the stench will come from the*
> *Soap box.*

Then they will all rise up, statesmen, diplomats, citizens
And go hunting for the peddler: You who disturb our
    rest
And our ablutions, you who haunt us with your souvenirs,
You who prick our conscience, death upon you!

> *But the peddlers shall never cease from the earth*
> *Until the candles die out and the soap melts away.*[3]

Yossel Rakover's Appeal to God

. . . I believe in You, God of Israel, even though You have done
everything to stop me from believing in You. I believe in Your laws
even if I cannot excuse Your actions. My relationship to You is not
the relationship of a slave to his master but rather that of a pupil to
his teacher. I bow my head before your greatness, but will not kiss
the lash with which You strike me.

You say, I know, that we have sinned, O Lord. It must surely be
true! And therefore we are punished? I can understand that too! But
I should like You to tell me whether *there is any sin in the world
deserving such a punishment as the punishment we have received!*

You assert that you will repay our enemies? I am convinced of it!
Repay them without mercy? I have no doubt of that either! I should

3. David Polish, "The Resurrection." From *High Holy Day Book*, published by the Jewish Reconstructionist Foundation. Used by permission.

like You to tell me, however—*is there any punishment in the world compensating for the crimes that have been committed against us?*

You say, I know, that it is no longer a question of sin and punishment, but rather a situation in which Your countenance is veiled, in which humanity is abandoned to its evil instincts. But I should like to ask You, O Lord—and this question burns in me like a consuming fire—*what more, O what more, must transpire before You unveil Your countenance again to the world?*

I want to say to You that now, more than in any previous period of our eternal path of agony, we, we the tortured, the humiliated, the buried alive and burned alive, we the insulted, the mocked, the lonely, the forsaken by God and man—we have the right to know *what are the limits of your forbearance?*

I should like to say something more: Do not put the rope under too much strain lest, alas, it snap! The test to which You have put us is so severe, so unbearably severe, that You should—You must—forgive those members of Your people who, in their misery, have turned from You.

. . . I tell You this because I do believe in You, because I believe in You more strongly than ever, because now I know that You are My Lord, because after all You are not, You cannot possibly be after all the God of those whose deeds are the most horrible expression of ungodliness!

. . . I die peacefully, but not complacently; persecuted but not enslaved; embittered but not cynical; a believer but not a suppli-cant; a lover of God but no blind amen-sayer of His.

I have followed Him even when He rejected me. I have fol-lowed His commandments even when He has castigated me for it; I have loved Him and I love Him even when He hurls me to the earth, tortures me to death, makes me the object of shame and ridicule.

. . . God of Israel, . . . You have done everything to make me stop believing in You. Now lest it seem to You that You will succeed by these tribulations to drive me from the right path, I notify You, my God and God of my father, *that it will not avail You in the least!* You may insult me, You may castigate me, You may take from me all that I cherish and hold dear in the world, You may torture me to death—I shall believe in *You*, I shall love You no matter what You do to test me!

And these are my last words to You, my wrathful God: nothing will avail You in the least. You have done everything to make me renounce You, to make me lose faith in You, but I die exactly as I have lived, a believer!

Eternally praised be the God of the dead, the God of vengeance, of truth and of law, Who will soon show His face to the world again and shake its foundations with his almighty voice.

Hear, O Israel, the Lord our God, the Lord is One.

Into your hands, O Lord, I consign my soul.[4]

Authentic Jewish theology cannot possess the immunity I once gave it, *for its price is an essential indifference to all history between Sinai and the messianic days.* The distinction between "sacred" and "secular" history is in any case Christian in origin, and whether Christianity (for which the decisive divine incursion into history has already occurred) can pay the price of indifference to "secular" history I must let Christian theologians decide. Jewish theology, at any rate, cannot pay that price, for *its* God of history (whose work is as yet incomplete) must be capable of continued presence *in* history, not merely at its messianic end.[5]

III

I must strain my mind and heart to enter into the soul of the father or son or husband subjected to the Nazi "two work permits" custom. As my thought enters into this terrible solitude it is itself solitary, for it finds no help from any source. Camus's reflections on suicide and Sartre's philosophy of the absurd seem childish games in comparison. Moreover (if Orthodox Jews will forgive me), I find no help in pious rabbis slaughtered by the crusaders; nor (if refugees from the iron curtain will forgive me) in the victims of Stalin's massacres; nor (if Chris-

4. From "Yossel Rakover's Appeal to God," by Zvi Kolitz. The prayer appears in *Out of the Whirlwind,* ed. Albert H. Friedlander (New York: Doubleday, 1968; New York: Schocken, 1976), pp. 390–99. Quoted by permission of the author. (There actually was a Yossel Rakover who died in the flames. The "appeal" which Kolitz has him making to God is faithful to the Hasidic tradition to which he belonged.)

5. I have sought to deal with this subject in my *God's Presence in History* (New York: New York University Press, 1970; New York: Harper Torchbook, 1973).

tians will forgive me) in the solitary self-sacrifice of the Christ. Indeed, I am attempting the impossible. The father and son and husband I speak of must be multiplied many times. And the soul of each is a many-sided mystery which can never be fathomed, but only revered.

Yet my impossible attempt is necessary. Moreover, it has uncovered for me a revelation that, as I again and again behold it, fills me with an ever-new radiating light and power. I ask: Why did not each and every father, husband, and son subjected to the Nazi two work permits go mad? Or not going mad and surviving, why did he not commit suicide? Or choosing life rather than death, why did he stay a Jew, remarry and raise Jewish children? Why did even a single Jew who stayed sane and chose life and remained a Jew and raised Jewish children remain faithful to his ancient God?

Elie Wiesel has dared to compare Auschwitz with Sinai in its revelatory significance—and he has added that we are not listening. As, still shrinking from such a listening, I attempt to listen at least to those who survived, I hear in the very existence of each and every one a totally astonishing, albeit totally frag-mentary, faithfulness and testimony: in him who stayed sane, to the sacredness of sanity; in him who chose life, to the sacred-ness of life; in him who raised Jewish children, to the sacred-ness of the survival of the Jewish people; in him who stayed with his God, to a sacred bond between God and Israel which even Satan himself did not break.

I cannot resort to a glib theologizing which holds fast to but one of these testimonies, implicitly presuming to judge among them. (Where was I at the time of Auschwitz? Who would I be today if I were a survivor?) If, nevertheless, I focus attention on the last two testimonies, it is because, taken together, they re-veal a fact revolutionary for Jewish theology.

Once there was a sharp, perhaps ultimate, dichotomy be-tween "religious" and "secular" Jews. It exists no longer. After Auschwitz the religious Jew still witnesses to God in history, albeit in ways that may be revolutionary. And the "secular" Jew has become a witness as well—against Satan if not to God. His mere commitment to Jewish survival without further grounds is a testimony; indeed, Jewish survival after Auschwitz is neither "mere" nor without grounds. At Auschwitz *every* Jew represented all humanity when for reasons of birth alone he was denied life; after Auschwitz every Jew represents all humanity when he commits himself to Jewish survival. For this commitment is *ipso facto* testimony that there can be, must be, shall be, no second Auschwitz anywhere; on this testimony and this faith the secular no less than the religious Jew stakes his own life, the lives of his children, and the lives of his children's children. A secular holiness, side by side with religious, is becoming manifest in contemporary Jewish existence.

Nowhere is this more obvious than in the state of Israel. When I set out on my first visit to Israel two years ago I expected religious Jews to be religious and secular Jews to be secularists. Brought up in an anti-Zionist tradition, I had been taught a neat distinction between Jewish "religion" and Jewish "nationalism." And though I had long rejected these inapplicable pseudo-Protestant distinctions (and along with them, anti-Zionism) I was still altogether unprepared for one totally astonishing discovery: *the religious quality of the "secularist" Israeli Jew.* Perhaps I would not have seen it had I still been in headlong flight from the Holocaust. Of the truth of what I saw, however, I have no doubt. Jerusalem, while no "answer" to the Holocaust, is a response; and every Israeli lives that response. Israel is collectively what every survivor is individually: a No to the demons of Auschwitz, a Yes to Jewish survival and security—and thus a testimony to life against death *on behalf of all mankind.* The juxtaposition of Auschwitz and Jerusalem recalls nothing so vividly as Ezekiel's vision of the dead bones and the resurrection of the household of Israel. Every Israeli—man, woman, or child—stakes his life on the truth of that vision.

IV

This vision came alive for all with eyes to see when, in June 1967, Jews at Jerusalem had no choice but to fight for life, whereas twenty-five years earlier Jews at Auschwitz had had no choice but death. Why did this vision come less alive for the Christian press, which might have remembered Ezekiel, than for the secular press, which presumably did not remember him?[6]

This brings me to a most painful aspect of my recent religious and theological development. Thirty years ago I had become convinced that what had once divided Jews and Christians was now dwarfed by the demonic forces threatening both. In the years that followed I became involved in Jewish-Christian dialogues on that basis and formed lasting personal and theological friendships. Today I am confronted by another, less comforting aspect of Jewish-Christian relations. In regard to it I find myself misunderstood or even abandoned by most, though not all, Christian theologians. *Nazi antisemitism, while anti-Christian, would have been impossible without centuries of Christian antisemitism.* Why drag up this dead past? Because, alas, I can view it as past no longer, and because I owe the victims of Auschwitz (and, as I shall endeavor to show, Christianity itself) a relentless truthfulness.

Once I held the mild view that Christian antisemitism was vanishing in the wake of Jewish-Christian dialogues that confined attention to what the two faiths have in common. I have now been forced into a more radical view: antisemitism exists wherever it is held (or implied) that "the Jewish people" is an anachronism that may survive, if at all, only on sufferance. Antisemitism of this kind survives in such post-Christian phenomena as a liberalism that maintains that of all peoples Jews alone are obliged to be men-in-general, and in a communism that affirms that of all nationalisms Jewish nationalism alone is "petty-bourgeois." Its ultimate root, however, lies in the Christian view—perpetuated through the centuries, lingering on even where Christianity itself is undermined by atheism or agnosticism—that the birth of the new Israel entails the death of the old. Deliberately using hyperbole in order to shock Christian conscience, the Christian theologian J. Coert Rylaarsdam has said that Christians have generally thought that the only good Jew is a dead Jew or a Christian.

Such a formulation is enough to show that after Auschwitz

6. See A. Roy Eckardt's "Again, Silence in the Churches," *The Christian Century,* July 26 and August 2, 1967.

any kind of antisemitism is intolerable. Yet antisemitism survives in Christian attitudes—in none so obviously as those vis-à-vis the state of Israel. Why did the Christian press remain undisturbed by nineteen years of Jordanian control of the Christian holy places (and desecration of Jewish cemeteries and synagogues), but become greatly agitated by Israeli control?[7] Why does it fill its pages with accounts of the plight of Arab refugees but rarely even mention the nearly as numerous Jewish refugees from Arab countries? Why are there moral equations between Israel's claims to the right to exist and Arab claims to the right to destroy her? I have no answer to these questions except a theology of a new Israel to which, consciously or unconsciously, the resurrected old Israel remains an affront.

Few Jews are indifferent to the plight of the Arab refugees. For my part, I cannot deny the Palestinian Arabs the right to a state of their own which I claim for my own people. What fills me with a frustration bordering on despair—and indeed with doubt whether, after all, such a thing as Jewish-Christian dialogue is possible—is any Christian view that the survival of the Jewish state is a "merely political" matter to which I must be "religiously" indifferent if I am to be a worthy partner in Jewish-Christian dialogue.[8] Do Christians think that Judaism could survive a second Holocaust—or that Israel could survive without her army? Are they to have dialogue with dead Jews?

7. The press reports that in an address the Rev. A. C. Forrest, editor of *The United Church Observer*, "publicly retracted [his statement that] Arab peoples should recognize Israel," compared Arab terrorists to "the freedom fighters of France," and added that Christian churchmen are "concerned with the loss [sic!] of the Holy Places" (*Don Mills, Ontario Mirror*, December 10, 1969).

8. In a widely publicized letter to a Canadian Arab organization, the Rev. E. E. Long, general secretary of the United Church of Canada, wrote that his church "deplored the fact that Jewish people everywhere seemed to identify the preservation of the state of Israel with the preservation of the Jewish religion." At about the same time the Rev. R. H. Bennett, associate secretary of the Canadian Council of Churches, wrote that the "new Palestine Liberation Force [whose actions include the indiscriminate murder of women and children—Jewish, Christian and Arab—anywhere in the world]—terrible as it may sound—has brought a new sense of dignity and national identity to the Palestinian, whether in or out of Israel" (*The United Church Observer*, December 1, 1969). The juxtaposition of these two clerical statements reveals a grisly dialectic between Arabs who may do anything, "terrible as it may sound," for the sake of "dignity" and Jews who may exist only if they stay on the cross.

I speak bluntly for the sake of Christianity as well as for the sake of Judaism. Dostoevsky once wrote a legend about the Grand Inquisitor and the returning Christ. No Christian has yet been able to write the infinitely more traumatic legend of the Christ returning to Nazi-occupied Europe. Hitler gave a perverse reality to the ancient fact that one is born into the Jewish covenant but that one chooses the Christian covenant. He murdered Jews if they had one Jewish grandparent, Christians only if they chose to be saints. And, alas, there are few saints among Jews or Christians. (Had I been born a Gentile, would I have been a saint? Or a bystander? Or a Nazi murderer?)

Christians cannot yet face the fact that the returning Christ would have gone to Auschwitz voluntarily, for few of them did so. Still less can they face the fact that he would have gone involuntarily if not voluntarily. For not only is the view that his people are dead in spirit—a view without which physical death at Auschwitz would have been impossible—an evil, centuries-old heritage within Christendom itself; it survives, consciously or unconsciously, in the Christian mind to this day.

Like all evil, centuries-old heritages, that view will continue to survive until Christians themselves turn consciously and uncompromisingly against it. To do so will be an act of spiritual self-liberation. I have no doubt that if masses of Christians in Hitler's Europe had voluntarily put on the yellow star there would today be no doubt or confusion in the Christian churches, no talk of the death of God. I also have an uncanny feeling that Christians might find the renewal they presently seek if they were to close the tragic, centuries-old gulf between themselves and the "old" Israel; if their souls were to enter into the despair and the hope-despite-despair of Auschwitz.

May one hope that a Christian will one day be able—nay, compelled—to write the legend of the Christ returning to Nazi-occupied Europe? White Christians even now are turning against one great sin of their past, sharing in the chant of their erstwhile black slaves: "Freedom now!" Will the time come when all Christians will turn against their other, far older sin—when, dancing in Jerusalem with the people of their Lord, they will chant in astonishment, gratitude and joy: *"Am Yisrael Chai*—The people Israel lives"?

5. Sachsenhausen 1938: Groundwork for Auschwitz

IN THIS ESSAY I shall argue three separate, but in this case interrelated, theses: (1) that, following the events of *Krystallnacht* in 1938, Sachsenhausen was a groundwork for the Holocaust; that is, whether the Nazis at that time already planned murder camps for Jews or made that terrible decision only later on, the 1938 concentration camp possessed certain features without which the murder camps of the war years would not have been possible;[1] (2) that a built-in feature of the system of 1938 was deception of the victims; for them to *recognize* the features I will outline was extraordinarily difficult if not totally impossible; (3) that for the reason just offered, certain hermeneutical rules normally accepted in historical research become questionable in the extreme case under discussion. It is normally assumed that, with all due allowance for bias of perception and memory, the eyewitness is the most reliable source of "what actually happened." When the eyewitness is caught in a scheme of things systematically calculated to deceive him, subsequent reflection is necessary if truth is to be given to his testimony.

The occasion of this paper was the study of a document

Reprinted from *Midstream*, April 1975, pp. 27–31.
1. The notorious Wannsee Conference did not take place until January 20, 1942.

entitled *Konzentrationslager Sachsenhausen* (1938), by Dr. K. J.
Ball Kaduri, which is found in the Yad Vashem Archives. My
method on this occasion is critical reflection upon what I, then a
youth of twenty-two, remembered of the camp of which I myself had been an inmate, in the light of what I read about it more
than thirty years later, in an account given by a man much older
than myself, much more trained to observe and analyze—an
account, moreover, that the author himself apparently did not
compose until 1946. In order to *understand* what I myself had
experienced, I had to *see* it, so to speak, *objectified on paper*, in
a report written by someone more articulate than I was, or could
have been, at the time. Hence I feel that my personal idiosyncrasies, while entering into the following account, play no important role in my three theses. Everybody has *some* idiosyncrasies; and it was a built-in feature of the Nazi system to
exploit them all.

I. Torture through Senseless System

As a rule those of us considered fit to work were sent every
day to work in a tile factory several miles outside the camp. I
begin with Ball's description of the customary march to and
from that factory.

> The marching columns are formed in the camp in rows of four, and
> then the march begins through the gate to the *Klinkerwerke*. How
> refreshing such a march could be after the stay in the camp in the
> morning, or even after a day's hard labor at night! But what hap-
> pens? The march is made into a hellish torture, through a diabolical
> system which produces perpetual chaos. Normally such a large col-
> umn would be divided into groups, with a distance between them.
> Here, however, the unit is as large as 1000 men. . . . Suddenly the
> front is being slowed down, but no command is issued to this effect.
> Consequently, those behind are unaware of it and run into those in
> front of them. Whereupon those in front are ordered to run, to run as
> fast as possible, with the result that front and back fall apart again,
> and those behind are ordered to run even faster, until they barge
> into those before them once more.

In this spurious march *the fiction is maintained* that each row must keep in step, that no one must fall behind. The moment disorder occurs, either when those in the back fall behind, or those in front are too far ahead, the stormtroopers hit the offenders with their rifle butts, and someone is an offender even if his heavy breathing shows that he finds it difficult to keep up. (Italics added)

The moment I read this passage I understood it. Then why, so far as I recall, had I *never once* understood the spuriousness of this "march" during the three months when, many times, I participated in it? True, I was twenty-two and athletic, while Dr. Kaduri was more than twenty years older, so that running never bothered me, and my friends were in the same position. However, none of us young ones were heartless or insensitive, and I recall many an occasion when two of us would take an older man between us and support him on his "march." Was I, then, too young and naive to understand *any part* of the "diabolical system"? Yet some of it we understood well enough. Our work at the *Klinkerwerke* was partly ordinary labor directed to a purpose. Partly, however, it was also so obviously senseless that the fact could escape no one. Thus, many a day we spent carrying sand—always on the double!—from place A to place B, only in order to be ordered the next day to carry it back from place B to place A. The senselessness of this labor was so obvious that everyone understood it. Moreover—this is the crux—understanding it, we formed inner defenses against it. With regard to the meaningful labor we too had our inner defenses. Like the British officer in *The Bridge on the River Kwai,* we were many times tempted by the meaningfulness of the labor to find meaning in it and perform it well, forgetting that it was labor for the enemy, but then we would recognize this and resort to small acts of sabotage. We never fooled ourselves into thinking that we did or could do any noticeable harm to the Nazis. Still, even small acts of sabotage maintained our morale.

In the case of the back-and-forth sandcarrying race (whose senselessness was obvious) we kept our morale through humor. We *knew* that this system had no purpose. Hence we also knew that its only purpose could be torture for torture's sake—to break us down. *And, aware of this purpose, we resisted it.* I recall an incident early in our imprisonment (when we were still quite naive) when a well-known Berlin rabbi and I lined up outside the medical barrack for treatment for a sore or infected leg (I forget which). After a while the Nazi medical officer came out, kicked us with his jackboots and shouted "Run, Jews!" As we were running, the rabbi turned to me and asked: "Are you still sick?"

In contrast with these two cases of obviously meaningful and obviously meaningless labor, the *Klinker*-march, as described by Dr. Kaduri, was *meaningless labor systematically endowed with a fictitious meaning*. This fooled me and, I am sure, almost everyone else. Moreover, it was clearly *designed* to fool us, so as to rob us of the means of inner defense. With the wisdom of hindsight—and with the truth objectified for me in Dr. Kaduri's perceptive account—I am certain that as early as 1938 the concentration camp had *one* purpose, i.e., slave labor, but also a *higher* purpose superseding slave labor and its benefits to the Nazi system, i.e., to rob its victims of their humanity if not yet of their lives. I am also certain that, as early as then, the Nazis recognized that in order to achieve the higher purpose (or at any rate in order to achieve it most effectively) it was not enough to have two labor systems of which one was obviously meaningful and the other obviously meaningless. They had to produce (and did produce) a Kafkaesque system in which there *appeared* to be meaning, *was* none, and in which this truth was either systematically *kept from* the victims, or in any case *the fiction was still maintained even when the secret was out*. Thus a clear line of development leads from the *Klinker*-march at Sachsenhausen in 1938 to the incredible and unprecedented legend on the gate to Auschwitz—*Arbeit macht frei*.

II. *System of Supermen and Subhumans*

I give my second quotation from Ball Kaduri's account:

The first and most severe rule of the camp was that the slaves were absolutely forbidden to initiate a conversation with any member of the SS. Such an "address" was simply unthinkable. On the other

hand, they were naturally required to answer any question addressed to them. Most of these questions were simple cases of
chicanery, containing no order, and having the sole purpose of reacting to the prisoner's answers with insults or blows. Most of
these questions concerned one's profession, and the only thing that
mattered was a prompt answer. *Whether the answer was true or
false did not matter in the slightest and was never investigated.*
(Italics added)

Let me comment on the last part of this passage first. On our
first day in Sachsenhausen, following a whole night of alternatively having to stand at attention and march about, there took
place an "investigation" lasting several hours. An S.S. officer
would stroll along, leisurely look at this or that person, and at
length pick someone and ask him for his profession. And no
matter what answer the person would give—"doctor,"
"lawyer," "businessman," etc.—it was an occasion for insults
and blows. "You have defiled German women!" "You have
perverted German law!" "You have cheated your German cus-
tomers!" and so forth. The remarkable thing that first day was
not the Nazi behavior but rather that of us Jews. As if by a silent
compact we all felt that this day could be our last, and that we
would not lower ourselves to the level of the Nazis by telling
lies. One man was ordered to say that he had betrayed Germany, and although they beat him for a long time, he refused to
say it. (I need hardly add that any form of physical resistance
was out of the question. The S.S. man with the machine gun
stood in readiness right behind the investigating officer.)

On the second day we changed our minds. It was, we began
to feel, a rather foolish bit of heroics to tell the truth to these
Nazis, particularly since it became clear that no one checked
our answers, and that one could spare oneself insults and blows
by telling believable but inoffensive lies. Thus, for example, we
rabbinical students decided that "public school teacher" was
a prudent answer, and experience proved we were right.

All this was clear. What was not clear to me until I read
Ball's account was that *in resisting the Nazis as we did we fell
into their trap.* In retrospect and in the light of hindsight
knowledge, it is quite absurd to assume that their system of

asking-all-questions-and-checking-no-answers was accidental. We *were meant* to tell our innocent lies, for in so doing, to be sure, we protected ourselves, but at the same time we also lost some of our dignity. *To them* Jews were subhumans whose answers did not matter, and *we*, considering ourselves pretty smart, fell into the trap. Of course, the trap was rather harmless at the time. It did not, however, remain so, for one begins compromising one's dignity on behalf of safety a little, then a little more, until finally a sliding scale is reached where it becomes more and more difficult to escape from the system.

This was one side of the trap. The other, as Ball puts it quite brilliantly, was that it was "unthinkable" for us to initiate a conversation with a stormtrooper. We didn't do so, of course. In fact, we wouldn't have dreamed of either wanting to speak to them or drawing attention to ourselves. What I did not realize until I read this account is that *this too was part of the system*. If the inmates were not only *considered* subhuman but lured into *accepting themselves as such*, the masters, unknown to us and not understood by us, were placed in a position of being superhuman. You not only *didn't* address them, but it was *unthinkable* that you should do so, not because of who they were but because of the black uniforms that they wore. Here in essence is the system that not only caught us but, for long years, the whole world. How well those of us old enough remember the surprise that filled us when we saw those pictures of the Nuremberg trials where the big Nazi leaders were finally shown as the little, contemptible men they were! Yet while the system lasted it was almost invincible. *And among the first to break it were the Jewish fighters of the Warsaw Ghetto.*

Note this remarkable statement by Itzhak Cukierman, óne of the leaders of the Warsaw Ghetto uprising:

> On the second day our fortified division achieved new victories without having even one casualty. We were able, with great determination, to overcome the Germans. By following guerrilla warfare theory, we saved lives, added to our supply of arms and—most important—*proved to ourselves that the German was but flesh and blood, as any man.*

*And prior to this we had not been aware of this amazing truth!
If one lone German appeared in the Ghetto, the Jews would flee en
masse, as would Poles on the Aryan side.* Now it became clear that
the armed Jew had the advantage over the German . . . something
for which to fight. And now the German—once cocky and bent on
murder and plunder—felt insecure, knowing that he might not
emerge alive from a Jewish house or cellar; and he ceased harrass-
ing Jews. (Italics added)[2]

In the situation in which it was acquired, with a desperate
heroism that passes belief and understanding, this insight must
be considered as nothing short of revelation. Yet with how little
effort the evil Nazi system might have been wiped out a few
years earlier—assuredly not by its inmates and victims, but by
the outside world which chose either to look on or, more fre-
quently, to look away! Except for good fortune—the Nazi loss of
the war—the "Holocaust Kingdom," which had come close to
running itself, might today run the world.

III. The Use of Christian Antisemitism
by Nazi Antisemitism

The two above phenomena were general. My last example
concerns what may well be confined to the special idiosyncrasies of a small minority. However, as I have said, this appears to me of no significance, since everyone has *some*
idiosyncrasies, *and the Nazi system sought to exploit them all.*
Quoting once again from Ball's document, I cite a "poem"
which on one occasion he was forced to bellow again and again:

> Dear old Moses, come again,
> Lead our Jewish fellowmen
> Once more to their promised land.

2. Meyer Barkai, tr. and ed., *The Fighting Ghettos* (New York: Tower,
1962), pp. 26–27.

> Split once more for them the sea,
> Two huge columns let it be
> Fixed as firmly as two walls.
> When the Jews are all inside
> On their pathway, long and wide,
> Shut the trap, Lord, do your best!
> Give the world its lasting rest!

I confess that, no matter how hard I have tried since I first read this utterly obscene "poem" more than a year ago, I cannot recall ever having heard it before, to this day. Yet I *must* have heard it for, as Ball reports, it was not the product of Nazi antisemitism, but rather a heritage from Stoecker's Christian antisemitism of the 1880s. In other words, my failure to remember is a textbook case of repression. The particular repression may be mine, but repression *as such* was inevitably a general phenomenon during the entire Nazi period—and the Nazis counted on it. It was simply humanly impossible, first for German Jews, then for European Jews, to recognize that the enemies were so many and so vicious. Hence, on the Jewish side, wishful thinking, and on the Nazi side, its systematic exploitation. Believe it or not, in the early period of the Nazi régime, Jews sometimes felt that maybe Göring wasn't so bad after all—after Goebbels had just made a particularly blood-curdling speech. In Sachsenhausen itself it sometimes seemed that one *Sturmführer* was quite human—because another dwarfed him in viciousness. I no longer doubt that the "human" *Sturmführer* was deliberately planted. The abnormal situation shook all our normal standards—*and to shake them was part of the machine.*[3]

3. Dr. Ball Kaduri has seen the present article and agrees with the rest of it but disagrees with this particular point. He is of the opinion that the togetherness of relatively "human" with more vicious stormtroopers was not part of a plot but rather chance. This disagreement between us reflects a current disagreement in scholarship in which a "monolithic" view of Nazism as a thoroughgoing totalitarian system is attacked by another which stresses "the limits of Hitler's power," if indeed it does not go so far as to view Nazism as a "totalitarian anarchy." This is not the place to take sides in this debate, except

In my own case, why did I block the above "poem," i.e., the fact that Christian antisemitism was used by and built into Nazi antisemitism? Why did I live for months and years afterward by the comforting illusion that Nazism was equally opposed to Jews and Christians? Generally, because it was hard to recognize enemies on so many sides; specifically because I happened to know, and be friends with, a handful of stoutly anti-Nazi Christians, exactly *three* (sic!) of them (one a "non-Aryan") fellow inmates in Sachsenhausen itself. I then did not and could not face the fact that the vast majority of German Christians were Nazis, Nazi sympathizers, or at any rate passive accomplices. Far more true to the situation of the time than the testimony of the few anti-Nazi Christians was a telegram addressed to Hitler by a certain *Landesbischof* Wiedemann of the city of Bremen.[4] (If I had seen that telegram at the time, I would not have believed it.) Its text was as follows:

To: The *Führer* and *Reichskanzler* Adolf Hitler:
The three churches of gratitude in Bremen have been inaugurated. They bear your name, *mein Führer*, in gratitude to God for the miraculous redemption of our nation at your hands from the abyss of Jewish-materialistic bolshevism. I thank you for having enabled us to express in these new churches what is a deep confession for us who are fully conscious Christian National Socialists.

Heil, mein Führer!

This telegram is dated November 28, 1938—less than two weeks after the synagogues burned all over Germany, Jewish homes and stores were looted in the broad light of day, and

---

to stress that the second school would become mendacious and apologetic if it failed to give full attention to the fact that, however "twisted" may have been the road that led the various Nazi fiefdoms to Auschwitz, it *did* lead there without *radical* opposition from *any* of them.

4. I am indebted to Professor Uriel Tal of Tel Aviv University for acquainting me with this document.

Jews themselves disappeared one knew not where. It was this time that *Landesbischof* Wiedemann, and countless other Christians with him, chose to hand their churches over to Satan, without ever being able to say: "Lord, forgive us, for we knew not what we did."

6. The Nazi Holocaust as a Persisting Trauma for the Non-Jewish Mind

> Hitler envisaged the camps as places where his prisoners expiated their crimes; instead, the camps created saints and martyrs on an unprecedented scale.
>
> ROBERT PAYNE,
> *The Life and Death of Adolph Hitler*

IN 1973 *Der Spiegel* published a series of articles about Hitler. The May 28 installment makes the following asseverations. Until 1938, or perhaps 1939, Hitler confined himself to such worthy conservative objectives as "correcting" the unfavorable results "for Germany of the first world war." Then his "friends and supporters" were "horrified" by Hitler's "new course." Göring bellowed that the great pogrom of November 1938 was "the last infamy" for which he would cover up (the same Göring who three months later decreed the confiscation of all Jewish gold and jewelry!). The march into Prague was "illegitimate imperialism" for Gestapo Chief Werner Best (the subsequent Nazi ruler of Denmark!). A war criminal at Nuremberg, Seyss-Inquart was a "moderate" Nazi, and so was Hitler himself—until that "radical change" of 1938 (or perhaps 1939) which is

Reprinted from *Journal of the History of Ideas*, vol. XXXVI, no. 2, April-May 1975, pp. 369–76.

nothing less than a "mystery to this day." On this note the installment ends, in true serial fashion.

The next installment devotes exactly one page to the Holocaust (giving the statistics accurately enough), then disposes of the countless murderers with the casual explanation that, after all, Himmler and his men were "faithful" to the *Führer*, and is at length climaxed with a long, detailed revelation of the great mystery: the poor, prematurely aged Hitler was sick. In this way, after a whole generation has heard again and again that only one was responsible, that all the others were "only following orders," we are now told that this one was not responsible either, for he was ill. It is the ultimate whitewash.

Der Spiegel is no neo-Nazi rag. Of the two coauthors, Werner Maser is the respected scholarly writer of, among other works, *Hitler: Legend, Myth, and Reality*, while the other, Heinz Höhne, is the respected journalist and author of *The Order of the Death's Head*.[1] Their works belong to the hitherto insufficiently identified genre of literature for which the Holocaust is a trauma. That this unique catastrophe should, after a generation, still traumatize the non-Jewish as well as the Jewish mind is natural. However, one may evade the trauma or confront it.

Since a philosopher should not quarrel with historians about facts, I begin with one fact of which I have eyewitness knowledge—the *Krystallnacht* of November 1938 in which synagogues all over Germany were burned, Jewish stores were smashed and looted, and tens of thousands of Jews were carried off to concentration camps. (I was one of them.) There is a current thesis that Nazism was neither monolithic nor efficient but consisted of conflicting fiefdoms or was even a "totalitarian anarchy." This thesis (well argued, for example, in E. N. Peterson, *The Limits of Hitler's Power*[2]), is put to some strange uses.

1. Werner Maser, *Hitler: Legend, Myth, and Reality* (New York: Harper & Row, 1971); Heinz Höhne, *The Order of the Death's Head* (London: Pan, 1972).

2. E. N. Peterson, *The Limits of Hitler's Power* (Princeton, N.J.: Princeton University Press, 1969).

Who instigated *Krystallnacht?* Not S.S. leaders Himmler and Heydrich but Goebbels, replies Höhne, who writes about the S.S.![3] Not Hitler but Goebbels and the S.A., hazards Peterson, who writes about the limits of Hitler's power![4] Goebbels acted only because Hitler forced him to, guesses V. Reimann—in his biography of Goebbels![5] And we already know that, if Hitler *did* instigate it, *his* biographer Maser considers him sick—and thus not responsible. *What goes on here?* And how shall we fare with Auschwitz when this shirking of responsibility happens with the *Krystallnacht* which was merely a tame prelude? (The buck-passing game is all the more strange because it is based on the false assumption that *Krystallnacht* was an on-the-spot decision following the assassination of von Rath in Paris: on our arrival in Sachsenhausen the old inmates told us that they had been awaiting us for months, ever since they had built the new barracks.)

This question finds some answers in Höhne and Maser. Thus Höhne distinguishes (fairly enough) between "anti-Jewish fanatics" and "SD intellectuals" who had a "horror" of such men as Streicher, who "wanted to be regarded as decent," and had "as their sole object . . . to solve the so-called Jewish problem in a cold rational manner."[6] However, he does not ask whether the "decency" was perhaps more deadly than the "fanaticism," which is why he offers only moralistic platitudes when finally confronting the "cold rational manner" in which the "problem" was "solved" at Auschwitz.[7] It appears that no *radical* probing is necessary or possible—a whole generation after.

That Maser's *Führer* was "sick" at the time of Auschwitz we already know. What, then, about the "healthy" *Führer* before 1938? Maser gives a lengthy account, footnotes and all, about

3. Höhne, p. 313.
4. Peterson, pp. 20, 46, 144.
5. Viktor Reimann, *Dr. Joseph Goebbels* (Vienna: Molden, 1971); had Hitler permitted it, Goebbels "in all likelihood would have left the Jews alone."
6. Höhne, pp. 301 ff.
7. Ibid., pp. 536 ff. On this point, see further below, chap. 14, sec. 3.

The Nazi Holocaust as a Persisting Trauma 71

Hitler's "intellectual background," ludicrous in its Teutonic
scholarly solemnity, absurd when the "background" includes
Plato, Stoicism, and Hegel, and scandalous when it descends to
the assertion that Hitler had a "remarkable knowledge" of the
Talmud.[8] (Hitler "knew" about the Talmud only from antisemitic trash.) Yet of an early (1919) Hitler letter on antisemitism Maser merely cites the relevant portions, *without a word
of comment*.[9] In this letter Hitler distinguishes between a
"merely emotional" antisemitism which can lead to nothing
more effective than "pogroms," and one "based on reason"
which alone can have as "its final goal . . . the removal of the
Jews as a whole." Maser either does not wish to consider the
explosive significance of this distinction, or else (more likely) it
is lost on him.

What is lost on the Teutonic scholar is not lost on a current
bestselling British popular author who writes:

> What is really disturbing about the letter is that it is all so intricate
> and passionless. . . . Hitler had not read or was totally indifferent to
> the *Protocols of the Elders of Zion*. . . . Hitler's letter is just as
> terrifying as the *Protocols*, but the terror is of a different order. It is
> wholly German: as methodical as a German soldier's jackboots as he
> stamps out everything in his path.[10]

The authors cited hitherto all abuse legitimate inquiries into
details to mitigate, or avoid altogether, what is fully grasped in
Payne's popular masterpiece: *the horror of the whole*.

There is no necessary conflict between inquiring into the
parts and confronting the whole; nor are the above criticisms
intended to contrast German with non-German writers. Both
points are superbly illustrated in K. D. Bracher's *The German
Dictatorship*.[11] Bracher sees Nazi Germany as a dual system.
One system—the inner core—revealed itself ultimately as the

8. Maser, p. 123.
9. Ibid., p. 116.
10. Robert Payne, *The Life and Death of Adolf Hitler* (Toronto: Popular
Library, 1973), p. 132.
11. K. D. Bracher, *The German Dictatorship* (New York: Praeger, 1971).

S.S. state. The other was the traditional system, composed of the civil service, the army, and the educational and religious establishments. This latter was, on the one hand, permitted separate existence and, on the other, increasingly penetrated, manipulated, and perverted by the former. It remained distinguished from the S.S. system to the end. It even sporadically opposed it. But since the opposition was only sporadic and never radical, and since it otherwise cooperated passively and even actively with the S.S. system, *it enabled that system to do what it could never have accomplished by itself.*

With so precise an insight into the modes of the German implication in Nazism, Bracher is able to confront the trauma of the Holocaust authentically, that is, to relate it honestly without pretending to explain it. Who could explain a system correctly described as follows:

> The cost of the S.S. in terms of men, material, buildings and railroad tracks especially constructed for the extermination camps ran into hundreds of millions of marks. With rare exceptions the S.S. only killed people who presented no threat to the regime. The killing served no purpose. The soap made of human fat, the hair used for stuffing mattresses, the gold fillings that were melted down to add to the gold reserves of the Central Bank were only marginally more useful than the lamp-shades made of human skin by Ilse Koch, the wife of the commandant of Buchenwald.[12]

Bracher adds: "The reality and unreality of National Socialism were given their most terrible expression in the extermination of the Jews."[13]

Once one grasps and accepts Bracher's "dual system" theory, one will expect that the writings traumatized by the Holocaust include those dealing with any of the implicated institutions—the German army, the civil service, the professors, and the churches. One will also not be surprised to find that the objective implication of the institutions is often belittled or even denied by diversion of attention to the few individuals or

12. Payne, p. 468
13. Bracher, p. 431

groups within them that resisted. Among these few were the plotters of July 20, 1944, and the confessional church. Of the first group Payne writes:

> The colonels and generals who so ineffectively attempted to assassinate [Hitler] . . . on July 20, 1944, were already corrupted because they had fought in his wars and were accessories to his crimes . . . when they spoke of "saving Germany's honor" they were speaking of something that was beyond saving. The Germans who fought cleanly against Hitler were so few that they can be counted on the fingers of two hands, and most of them were to be found among the young students of Munich University who formed a conspiratorial society called "The White Rose."[14]

Payne may be too sweeping. (One would wish to exempt such as Stauffenberg from his judgment.) However, the record of the pitifully few students and professors calling themselves "The White Rose" *does* put nearly everyone, and not Germans alone either, to shame. Why did these few organize, mimeograph, and distribute anti-Nazi pamphlets, almost certain that they would fail, be caught, and murdered? (Almost no one escaped.) In *Students against Tyranny* we read:

> "We will have to let the truth ring out as clearly and audibly as possible in the German night," said Professor Huber. . . . "Perhaps we will succeed in the eleventh hour in shaking off the tyrannical oppressor and using that great moment for building, in concert with the other nations of Europe, a new and more humane world." "And what if we don't succeed?" someone asked. "I doubt very much that we'll be able to storm these iron walls of fear and terror, which strangle every move toward rebellion at its inception." "Then we must risk it anyway," answered Christl with strong emotion. "Then it is our duty by our behaviour and by our dedication to demonstrate that man's freedom still exists. Sooner or later the cause of humanity must be upheld, and then one day it will again prevail."[15]

14. Payne, p. 571.
15. Inge Scholl, ed., *Students against Tyranny* (Middletown, Conn.: Wesleyan University Press, 1970), pp. 36 ff.

Simple? Impossible? Simple but impossible! Impossible but simple! This is a moving book, describing what may well be the purest "student rebellion" of all time, against the most evil "establishment" ever. And it did succeed in one aim—it saved what was left of German honor.

Among Payne's handful is certainly Dietrich Bonhoeffer, whose biography by his friend and fellow anti-Nazi Christian Eberhard Bethge is not likely to be surpassed.[16] That even so sound a work on so noble a subject by so worthy an author is not without serious flaws reflects the trauma of Nazism—and of the Holocaust. Thus, first, Bonhoeffer's long and painful transformation from confessional witness to political plotter (and martyr) is not *really* made intelligible by Bethge who, indeed, does not seem to understand it himself. (In 1936 confessional churchmen addressed a *private* written protest to Hitler, naively expecting a reply. The true heroes were the two who leaked the document to the foreign press, *thus transforming a futile gesture into a political act.* How did the subsequent incarceration of the two affect the thinking of the others? Bethge does not say.)

Politically stodgy (Bonhoeffer's prayer for the defeat of Nazi Germany needs explanation in Bethge's eyes to this day!), Bethge is, secondly, theologically stodgy as well: Bonhoeffer's identification of Hitler with the Anti-Christ has inspired Christians and non-Christians alike, yet Bethge wonders whether Bonhoeffer could ever have considered it sound doctrine.

The most serious flaw involves Bonhoeffer himself as well as his biographer. Bethge and others tell us that Bonhoeffer led the fight against the "Aryan paragraph." Only indirectly does it emerge that, while Bonhoeffer *the man* helped save Jewish lives, Bonhoeffer *the theologian* confined his fight to converted Christians. As for Bonhoeffer's own theological antisemitism—expressed at least in 1933—Bethge cannot bring himself to mention it at all.[17] With this crucial aspect suppressed,

16. Eberhard Bethge, *Dietrich Bonhoeffer* (New York: Harper & Row, 1970).

we do not learn whether the later Bonhoeffer who changed so radically in other respects ever overcame his theological antisemitism, or whether, by the traumatic but necessary standard of Auschwitz, Bonhoeffer acted not because but in spite of his theology. A non-German, J. S. Conway, is better able without seeming self-exculpation to stress the fact that the German churches were themselves persecuted by the Nazi regime and yet also to recognize the special weaknesses of the German churches that enabled Hitler to manipulate and use them. (His is, on the whole, a thorough and well-balanced book.[18]) Yet his concluding summary of these weaknesses—among them, unworldly pietism, obedience to state authority, and distrust of democracy—has a strange omission. There is no mention of Christian antisemitism.[19]

This is no accident. Conway reports faithfully the antisemitism of the pro-Nazi Christians. He is embarrassed by the meagerness of pro-Jewish statements and actions by the anti-Nazi Christians. And he hardly notices that even these meager responses were hardly ever made for Jews *as Jews* but only as human beings or proto-Christians. This clash between scholarly objectivity and Christian embarrassment reaches a climax when the book promises to report Christian resistance in behalf of church property, Christian morality, and Jewish lives, and yet, a mere seven pages later, the chapter dealing with the third topic is forced to contradict the promise in its very title, "The Failure of Brotherly Love toward the Jews."[20]

The trauma of the Holocaust for Christianity, then, extends beyond the German churches. In response to the catastrophe

17. Dietrich Bonhoeffer, *No Rusty Swords* (London: Fontana, 1970), pp. 222 ff: "The church of Christ has never lost sight of the thought that the 'chosen people,' who nailed the redeemer of the world to the cross, must bear the curse of its action through a long history of suffering. . . . The conversion of the Jews, that is to be the end of the people's period of suffering." See also above, pp. 35–36.

18. J. S. Conway, *The Nazi Persecution of the Churches 1933–1945* (New York: Basic Books, 1968).

19. Ibid., pp. 334 ff.

20. Ibid., pp. 254 ff., 261.

the churches have turned against antisemitism, most dramatically so in the events set in train by Vatican II. Yet they rarely confront the trauma directly. Indeed, the fact that Nazism was manifestly anti-Christian (together with the heroism of the anti-Nazi Christian witnesses whose *own* stand toward antisemitism is not scrutinized) is often used to avoid a Christian encounter with Auschwitz. But what if Nazi antisemitism was not *simply* anti-Christian but rather the nemesis of a bimillennial disease within Christianity *itself*, transmuted when Nazism turned against the Christian substance? In that case, Auschwitz would be *the* central theological event of this century not only for the Jewish but also for the Christian faith.

Few Christian thinkers have stated this view as forcefully as Franklin H. Littell; none has tried as energetically to confront his fellow Christians with it. His efforts have produced a series of Jewish-Christian conferences, and now, *The German Church Struggle and the Holocaust*,[21] an attempt to articulate the relation and lack of relation between these two events. The project is bold, but both dangerous and promising. To be sure, *any* resistance to Nazism must be praised, and those who plead against all the critics, "You do not know what it was like!" are quite right. Yet such pleas easily become self-exculpating and, deadlier still, interfere with the search for truth even in hindsight. And without that search there is no hope.

Littell's volume reflects all these elements. Thus the revered Wilhelm Niemoeller does not recognize, even now, the vast difference between Mussolini and Hitler.[22] On her part, Beate Ruhm von Oppen admits the "deadly reality" of "Christian" antisemitism in Nazi Germany, but weakens this admission not only by the above use of quotation marks but also by turning at once to the deadlier realities of Nazi antisemitism.[23]

---

21. F. H. Littell and H. G. Locke, eds., *The German Church Struggle and the Holocaust* (Detroit: Wayne State University Press, 1974).
22. Ibid., p. 54.
23. Ibid., p. 67.

On the one hand, Peter Hoffmann's piece—the most self-exculpating—asserts that Germany too was "in a real sense" an "occupied country."[24] On the other, the essays of W. J. Allen and F. Bonkovsky analyze the limits, German and Christian, of the resistance.

Most striking of all is that in a collection on "Church Struggle" *and* "Holocaust" few essays dealing with the former subject touch on antisemitism, and that not one focuses on the crucial distinction between "non-Aryan" Christians and Jews. The two themes fall apart, for there was no "church struggle" on behalf of Jews but at most only on behalf of "non-Aryan" members of the church itself. This is the book's inherent anguish, most eloquently expressed by T. A. Gill who, having listened to the papers on *both* themes, writes:

> I simply cannot get gooseflesh over . . . Barmen's discovery that the attacks on the Jews must be resisted because they were in reality attacks on Jesus Christ. That is not high theology. That is blasphemy . . . unwitting blasphemy, I hope. . . . It was played out to the end, too. In the letter sent around preparing for the Stuttgart confession after the war, was there much about the guilt against the Jews? Was there anything?[25] We have little to learn from any church or any prophet who cannot recognize murder until it is murder in the cathedral. . . . Since the Holocaust, what word can we hear but Bonhoeffer's who, on the little he could have known, said that thereafter the Germans could not speak again evangelically to the Jews? I enlarge it from Germans to Gentiles.[26]

These sentiments, if taken seriously, impose two tasks upon Christian thinkers—the exposure and elimination of the basic (i.e., theological) foundations of Christian antisemitism, and the restructuring of the Christian faith itself so as to enable it, at last, to confront the Jew as an authentic witness to religious

24. Ibid., p. 112.
25. The final Stuttgart confession in fact spoke only of "the sins of our people toward Poles, Danes, Frenchmen, etc."
26. Littell and Locke, pp. 286, 288.

truth on his own Jewish terms. Rosemary Ruether's *Faith and Fratricide*[27] not only takes these two tasks upon itself but treats them as systematically intertwined. A specialist in Patristics and its *anti-Judaeos* literature (suspiciously neglected by most scholars in the field), well acquainted with Jewish as well as Christian thought, she spurns evasions and is a "radical" theologian, one of the few among the many who devotes serious attention to the oldest of Christian sins. Ruether does not hesitate to see the New Testament itself as anti-Jewish, and, far more significantly, as not accidentally or sporadically so but rather by dint of a fatal inner logic. The Jewish Bible and the midrashic literature generated by it exhibit the dialectical tensions *between* law and grace, letter and spirit, the particular and the universal, sin and repentance, error and truth, abandonment and redemption. The New Testament replaces these structures *with a series of antitheses,* in which the "new" Israel can find itself (undialectically) affirmed only by means of an (undialectical) negation of the "old." On Ruether's definitive showing, formidable in the case of Patristic anti-Jewish stereotypes and shatttering in the resemblance of these to the modern ones, this fatal dualism has haunted Christianity—not merely "Christendom"—ever since, and did not end when liberal theology replaced the old orthodoxies. (Indeed, smug in its "universalism," liberal Christian theology has its own hostility to Jewish "particularism."[28]) Such, in the simplest terms, is the long and complex disease. Its cure, in Reuther's view, can only be a Christian theological repentance of its original sin, that is, a total repudiation of antithetical theology and the "realized eschatology" which is its source. "Is it possible to say, 'Jesus is Messiah' without, implicitly or explicitly, saying at the same time 'and the Jews be damned'?"[29] Ruether replies: only if the Christian affirmation is "relativized" into a "theology of hope"

27. Rosemary Ruether, *Faith and Fratricide* (New York: Seabury Press, 1974).

28. E.g., H. Fishman, *American Protestantism and a Jewish State* (Detroit: Wayne State University Press, 1973).

29. Ruether, p. 246.

which will free it of anti-Jewish and indeed all religious imperialism.

Whether the link between the classical Christian affirmation and Christian antisemitism is essential or, despite their bimillennial coexistence, after all only contingent is a question for Christian thought. (After Auschwitz, is it not its central question?) Not confined to Christian thought is the insight that *any* answer is suspect of "false consciousness" (Gregory Baum) which shows no signs of agony. Six million Jewish crucifixions in our time, redeemed by no resurrection, have left all except an agonized Christianity without credibility; and the agony, too, especially when made into a *theologoumenon*, can be an evasion. No Christian thinker has faced this truth more bravely than A. Roy Eckardt. It is a measure of this unique theologian that his books have become ever less theologically self-enclosed, thus more vulnerable. His latest book[30] is authentically theo-political precisely by virtue of his theological courage. But it is a sign of the times that his most recent, important article,[31] deals not with God but with the devil.

If Auschwitz is a trauma for Christianity, the state of Israel, being the Jewish declaration of independence from Christian charity, is a trauma for Christian antisemitism. The devil, however, disguises this fact, and Eckardt's article examines some of his works. God afflicts the comfortable and comforts the afflicted; "the devil . . . afflicts the afflicted and comforts the comfortable." He therefore *times* his actions carefully. Why did Father Daniel Berrigan "condemn Israel in the very hour of her aloneness and peril," i.e., immediately after the Yom Kippur War? Why did Professor Robert Cushman wait for that same "devil's *kairos*" to assert that "decent respect to the opinion of mankind" dictates that the price of Israel's existence is too

30. A. Roy Eckardt, *Your People, My People* (New York: Quadrangle, 1974) works toward an "authentic Jewish-Christian relationship," virtually unique as a testimony at once firmly rejecting all Christian theologizing about the Jewish people.

31. A. Roy Eckardt, "The Devil and Yom Kippur," *Midstream*, August–September 1974.

high? While obeying the above maxim, the devil at the same time denies doing so; hence he brands the victims of attack as the true aggressors. He disguises himself still more effectively when he resorts to the "higher method" of "even-handedness." The World Council of Churches' even-handed "plea for peace" was implicitly an "approval of Arab holy wars." And when in the uneven conflict between Israel's claim to the right to exist, and Arab claims to the right to destroy her, Christian spokesmen refuse to make an "absolute commitment" to the first claim they are either unable or unwilling to recognize that "there is no such thing as a partial right to exist."[32] To this fundamental truth the devil's lying reply ("the Arab states, too, are threatened with destruction") Professor Eckardt has doubtless anticipated. For he understands that, indefinitely transmutable and disguisable, antisemitism, like theology itself, is a system incapable of refutation and curable only by conversion. Doubtless these characteristics attach to other kinds of deep-seated prejudice as much as antisemitism. But this admission and insistence becomes itself the devil's ploy if it obscures the fact that antisemitism is "totally unique," that there are "no parallels" to it.

But can the devil be converted? This raises for the Christian mind the most traumatic question of all; yet there is no evading it. In this grim century, *has Christian theology even in its most saintly and profound characters played into the devil's hands?* In 1942 Karl Barth wrote: "There is no doubt that Israel hears; *now less than ever* can it shelter behind the pretext of ignorance and inability to understand. But Israel hears—and does not believe."[33] The translation of these words was authorized in 1957 when all was known. At the time they were written a certain Rabbi Israel Shapiro of Grodzisk was telling his flock about to die at Treblinka that their ashes would purify Israel and help redeem the world.[34]

32. Ibid., p. 74.
33. *Church Dogmatics*, II, 2 (Edinburgh: T. & T. Clark, 1957), p. 235; italics added.
34. Cited by M. M, Kasher, ed., *Haggadat Pessach Arzi-Yisraelit* (New York: American Biblical Encyclopedia Society, 1950), p. 137.

7. The Human Condition after Auschwitz: A Jewish Testimony One Generation After

I

A MIDRASH IN Genesis Rabba disturbs and haunts the mind ever more deeply. It begins as follows:

> Rabbi Shim'on said: "In the hour when God was about to create Adam, the angels of service were divided. . . . Some said, 'Let him not be created,' others, 'Let him be created.' . . . Love said, 'Let him be created, for he will do loving deeds.' But Truth said, 'Let him not be created, for he will be all falsity.' Righteousness said, 'Let him be created, for he will do righteous deeds.' Peace said, 'Let him not be created, for he will be full of strife.' What then did God do? He seized hold of Truth, and cast her to the earth, as it is said, 'Thou didst cast Truth to the ground.'" [Dan. 8: 12][1]

No Midrash wants to be taken literally. Every Midrash wants to be taken seriously. Midrash is serious because its stories and parables address the reader; they are not confined to the past. It is religious because, while it may contain beauty and poetry, its essential concern is Truth. And when, as in the pres-

The B. G. Rudolf Lecture in Judaic Studies, published as a pamphlet by Syracuse University Press, 1971.
1. *Midrash Genesis Rabba*, VIII: 5.

ent case, a Midrash tells a story of human origins, the religious truth it seeks to convey is universal. Its theme is nothing less than the human condition as a whole.

Why does this Midrash disturb and haunt us? Not simply because it is realistic rather than romantically "optimistic" about man. Midrash is always realistic. We are haunted because Truth is cast to the ground. This climactic part of the story (as thus far told) does not say that all is well, that the good Lord has the power, so to speak, of indiscriminately silencing all opposition. Were this its message, then Peace as well as Truth should be cast to the ground. That Truth alone is singled out for this treatment suggests the ominous possibility that *all* that might be said in favor of the creation of man is nothing but pious illusion; that Truth is so horrendous as to destroy *everything* for us unless we shun it, avoid it, evade it; that *only* after having cast Truth to the ground can God create man at all.

But then we ask: whom does God deceive? Surely one thing even God cannot do is, as it were, fool himself. Are we the ones, then, who are fooled? Are we *radically* deceived in our belief that at least *some* of that which we undergo, do, are, is *ultimately* worthwhile—a belief without which we cannot endure?

But such a divine deception (if a deception it is) does not succeed. We can see through it. The midrashic author *knows* that Truth is cast to the ground. So do all the devout Jews who have read his story throughout the generations. But what is the effect of this knowledge? Can it be other than despair?

The Midrash itself deals with this question when it repudiates despair. It ends as follows:

> Then the angels of service said to God, "Lord of the universe, how canst Thou despise Thy seal?[2] Let Truth arise from the earth, as it is said, 'Truth springs from the earth.'" [Ps.85:12]

Somehow it is possible for man to face Truth and yet to be. But do we know how?

2. Truth is the seal of God.

II

Without doubt to say yea or nay to existence is the ultimate question in all religion and all philosophy. Judaism is firmly committed to being when it sees God himself as the Creator of the world, and the Creation as good. Yet many a deep religious and philosophical spirit has chosen nonbeing, and has considered the tragic ultimate. And the most vocal of these in the West, Arthur Schopenhauer, blames all the "vulgar" Western "optimism" on Judaism and its creation story. Is Jewish "optimism" vulgar? Is it blind to the tragic? Must we follow Schopenhauer when he suggests that Jewish and indeed all optimism reflects but a self-congratulatory human "egoism" which is blind to all except our all-too-frail human goals and aspirations?[3] Our Midrash suggests a very different view. Not until Truth is cast to the ground is God able to create man. And not even God himself can despise his own "seal" of Truth. "Jewish optimism" affirms existence while at the same time confronting a Truth that is tragic. Yet, in our Midrash at least, the grounds for this togetherness remain inscrutable. "Jewish optimism" is not a "vulgar" optimism. It is an enigmatic optimism.

III

When Judaism came to North America the enigma became obscured. Faith in God often became faith in ever-evolving Reason, with idolatry becoming superstition gradually vanishing in an age of enlightenment. Halakha—the discipline of divine commandments that recognizes both the greatness and the misery of man—moved toward "customs and ceremonies" that had no discipline and no authority, and that stood in no need of them since man himself stood in no need of them. Radical evil,

3. Arthur Schopenhauer, *Works*, trans. R. B. Haldane and J. Kemp (London: Kegan Paul; Trench: Trübner & Co., 1909), vol. III, pp. 305 ff., 446 ff.

if recognized at all, was considered to have been left behind in Europe. Wars and colonialism were European affairs; poverty was an evil progressively conquered by American conscience, initiative, and know-how; antisemitism shrivelled into a "medieval prejudice."

In retrospect, this American Jewish optimism simply is a version of American optimism. Who but an American political leader could ever have seriously and sincerely waged a war to end all wars, when all experience shows that even "just wars" serve at best but limited ends? Who except Americans could still hope, in this century, that the complex Arab-Israeli conflict would vanish if only American know-how came on the scene and irrigated the Jordan waters?

That this and indeed all American optimism was always shot through with illusion is obvious today. Indeed, to scorn it as superficial has become the fashion. Yet the paramount task of the hour is not a rehearsal of the obvious, but rather a discriminating search for such truth as may remain behind all the superficialities and illusions. For a robust, ebullient affirmation of life is of the American essence. And if "American optimism" were ever *wholly* lost, America itself would be lost.

That such discrimination is hard to come by is evident on every side. If traditional American optimism was sweeping and indiscriminate, it has now found a nemesis that shows these same qualities. No political, religious or philosophical quarter has remained exempt. Only in a single camp does the old American optimism seem to survive wholly intact, and this, ironically, is the camp that would destroy America. Where except in America has a group of revolutionaries arisen which does not ask what social forces might be available to build the new world on the ruins of the old—which speaks and acts as though, with the act of destruction accomplished and "the system" destroyed, paradise will come of itself? Perhaps alone of all the present groupings, the American New Left has not abandoned the American Dream. It has merely transformed and postponed it.

IV

No professional historical expertise is required for the discovery of the causes of our present crisis. Hiroshima made known that America had lost her political innocence; and while the Vietnamese war was a daily, tragic reminder that indiscriminate international involvement is neither politically nor morally tenable, retreat to the idyllic isolationist view that the problems of power politics are confined to Europe has become, in a shrinking world, quite impossible. At home, all America now recognizes that in her collective affirmation that all men are created equal the Black man was somehow forgotten; and the nemesis of this past forgetfulness is a racial conflict that seems insoluble. For all their traumas, these two experiences are overshadowed by yet a third, for this assails at its roots the very mainspring of the traditional self-confidence of America. No nation has matched America in the modern certainty that, whatever nature and history have set wrong, human ingenuity and initiative can set right. No nation has staked greater faith in modern technology or has shown greater ability to develop it. Indeed, to this day the word "know-how" has American connotations. Yet this know-how, in no way diminished in energy and ability, has now produced a nemesis of which we read daily in our newspapers. Nature, subdued for human use, is becoming increasingly unusable. The city, built for human habitation, is becoming increasingly uninhabitable. Man himself, the sovereign creator of all the machinery, is himself being turned into part of it: as his power over nature and society increases, so diminishes his ability to be human. And we somehow seem unable to stop the process or to alter its course.

The search into causes is the task of the historian. The search for remedies is the task of the leaders of society. The philosopher's task is the critical examination of our collective human self-image. *A virtually all-pervasive human self-deprecation is today abroad in the land. It is as indiscriminate, or even enthusiastic, as was the former human self-elevation.*

*And just as the one once called for philosophical discrimina-
tion and criticism, so, now, does the other.*

Two illustrations must suffice. Once the characteristically
American movie was the cowboy picture. With clear villains
and clear heroes, it was a morality play whose happy end was
foreordained. (In Europe it used to be a bit of a joke that all
American movies, cowboy or not, had to end happily.) Today,
only the midnight cowboy remains. And foreordained are
gloom, disaster, and every kind of degradation and depravity.
The odd movie may still dare to portray heroism. It then still
remains foreordained that, regardless of the merits of the movie,
the critics will pan it. Are there no heroes left?

From the down-to-earth sphere of popular culture we turn to
the rarefied sphere of theology—nearly always a sound indi-
cator of the general consciousness even when it is bad. That
Harvey Cox's celebration of the secular city[4] should have been
a theological bestseller is hard to believe slightly more than ten
years later, when this very city is obviously so near to the core
of our technological despairs. The phenomenon clearly reflects
a religious consciousness that runs hither and thither in search
of hope and light but seems unable to find it. Hence, in quick
succession, the God-is-dead theology, itself already dead except for one lone, dark voice which moves us but cannot guide
us;[5] the theology of hope which, arousing hope if only because
its place of origin was post-Nazi Germany, could find no
grounds for hope because the grounds of our despair were not
confronted;[6] and, finally, a political theology which, deriving as
it does most of its strength from the well-warranted militancy of
Black Americans, seems at best either a confession of guilt on
the part of the ex-Constantinian white Christian, or else a mere
theological endorsement of a Black American militancy that is

4. Harvey Cox, *The Secular City: A Celebration of Its Liberties and an
Invitation to Its Discipline* (New York: Macmillan Co., 1965).

5. See T. J. J. Altizer, *The Gospel of Christian Atheism* (Philadelphia:
Westminster, 1966); *The Descent into Hell* (Philadelphia: Lippincott: 1970).

6. See e.g., J. Moltmann, *The Theology of Hope* (New York: Harper & Row,
1967).

able to dispense with all theological endorsements. In short, current American theology (its core, of course, is Protestant, but Catholic and Jewish representatives are not lacking) may seek to transcend our present crisis; in fact, however, it seems merely to reflect that crisis.

V

The above observations should be taken as a description of our present state of affairs, and not without further ado as a criticism arrived at from some superior standpoint—as if such a standpoint were readily available.

For many centuries this availability was taken for granted. Theologians would resort at once to the Word of God, with or without the help of ecclesiastical authority. Philosophers would affirm a human "nature" immune to the vicissitudes of history—an immunity which in turn guaranteed a timeless access to the True, the Good, and the Beautiful. And a long alliance between these two disciplines produced a firm stand in behalf of "eternal verities" against perpetually shifting "arbitrary opinion."

These centuries are past. Theologians (Jewish and Christian) should always have known that the Word of their God is manifest *in* history if it is manifest at all: because of the historical self-consciousness of contemporary man, this knowledge can now no longer be evaded. If nevertheless seeking refuge in the eternal verities of philosophy, they find that these, too, have vanished. For modern philosophy has found itself forced to abandon the notion of a permanent human nature—and along with this all timelessly accessible visions of the True, the Good, and the Beautiful.

This fact is most profoundly if not uniquely manifest in the philosophies arising from the work of Immanuel Kant. These philosophies do not deny aspects of the human condition that remain more or less permanent throughout human history. Such aspects, however, are now confined to man's natural constitution. What makes man *human* (we are told) is neither given nor permanent, but rather the product of his own individual or collective activity. *Man qua man is a self-maker.* This formula sums up the deepest of all the many revolutions in modern philosophy. We may wish to quarrel with its central thesis. We may wish to qualify it. We may even wish to reject it outright. One thing, at any rate, seems for better or worse impossible— the return to the premodern philosophical wisdom.

Not so long ago theologians of liberal stamp greeted this revolution in philosophy with rejoicing. Who has not heard sermons (and in particular American sermons) about the "infinite perfectibility of man?" The notion of man as a self-maker seemed (and in some respects surely is) far more grandiose than the notion of a human nature given by another—even if this Other was not (rather vaguely) "Nature" or "the Universe," but the Lord of Creation himself. Add to this what was said above about the American tradition of optimism, and it is not surprising that for a considerable period of time all talk about "the nature of man" and "*the* True, *the* Good, and *the* Beautiful" seemed in many circles to be timidly conservative, if not downright reactionary.

But now the crisis of American optimism has disclosed for us that the concept of man as a self-maker gives us grounds for apprehension and dread as well as for hope. The lack of a permanent nature may hold the promise that unforeseeable ways of human self-perfection are possible; since this lack is an unlimited malleability, however, it implies the possibility of unforeseeable negative as well as positive developments. And thus the specter comes into view that man, *qua* unlimited maker, may reach the point of making his whole world into a machine, while at the same time, *qua* infinitely malleable, himself being reduced to a mere part of the machine, that is, to a self-made thing. Nor is this possibility today a mere unsubstantial fancy confined to philosophers. For some of our futurologists have begun to conjure up a future in which man, the proud self-maker, will have lost control over the world he has made, and the reduction to self-made thinghood will be complete. Indeed, even popular consciousness is haunted by the prospect that the whole bold and exciting story of the one being in the universe capable of making his own nature—the story of the only truly *free* being—will come to an end, the pathos of which is matched only by its irony.

With prospects so terrifying, it is no wonder that some simply opt out of history; that others hanker after a simpler, more innocent past; and that, as if anticipating catastrophe, we are all tempted even now to deprecate indiscriminately all things human.

The philosopher may not yield to the temptations of escapism or indiscriminate despair. Nor may he simply throw in his lot with the futurologists, for (as we shall show at least in part) their entire approach calls for considerable philosophical suspicion. At this point, we shall be well advised to suspend the future and confine ourselves to the present. Is a genuinely *human* existence possible *even now?* Or, in order to make it possible, must we cast Truth to the ground? Must we suppress all knowledge of a future that is sure to come and force Truth to *stay* cast to the ground?

VI

We have thus far made no reference to Jewish experience in this century. We do so at this point because the direst predictions any futurologist might make have already been fulfilled and surpassed at Auschwitz, Mauthausen, Bergen-Belsen and Buchenwald. One shrinks from speaking of these unspeakable places of unique horror in any context that might invite false generalizations and comparisons. Yet one simple statement may safely be made. In the Nazi murder camps no effort was spared to make persons into living *things* before making them into dead things. And that the dead had been human when alive was a truth systematically rejected when their bodies were made into fertilizer and soap. Moreover, the criminals *themselves* had become living things, and the system, run by operators "only following orders," was well on the way toward running itself. The thoughtful reader of such a work as *The Holocaust King-*

dom[7] reaches the shocking conclusion that here was indeed a "kingdom," that is, a society organized to a purpose; that, its organization near-perfect, it might in due course have dispensed with the need for a "king"; and that such was its inner dynamic and power for self-expansion that, given a Nazi victory, it might today rule the world. This "society," however, was an antisociety, indeed, *the* modern antisociety *par excellence:* modern because unsurpassably technological, and antisociety because, while even the worst society is geared to life, the Holocaust Kingdom was geared to death. It would be quite false to say that it was a mere means, however depraved, to ends somehow bound up with life. As an enterprise subserving the Nazi war effort the murder camps were total failures, for the human and material "investment" far exceeded the "produce" of fertilizer, gold teeth, and soap. The Holocaust Kingdom was an end in itself, having only one ultimate "produce," and that was death.

It is not without *prima facie* plausibility that Richard Rubenstein, Jewish theologian long preoccupied with the Holocaust, should in his more recent spoken utterances have characterized the Nazi murder camp as simply the extreme technological nightmare. Taking his cue from Lewis Mumford[8]

---

7. Alexander Donat, *The Holocaust Kingdom* (New York: Holt, Rinehart & Winston, 1963; New York: Holocaust Library, 1978).

8. Mumford writes: "Well before the first atom bomb was tested, the American Air Force had adopted the hitherto "unthinkable" practice of the wholesale, indiscriminate bombing of concentrated civilian populations: this paralleled, except for the distance of the victims, the practice employed by Hitler's sub-men in extermination camps like Buchenwald and Auschwitz." (*The Myth of the Machine* [New York: Harcourt, Brace & World, 1970], p. 256.)

In the following it will emerge that, despite admittedly terrifying similarities, this "parallel" is totally false. Mumford's (unexplained) use of the word "sub-men" in the above passage already suggests that, rather than *argue* for a parallel, he simply begs the question. Elsewhere he even lapses into self-contradiction. His case for Nazism as *nothing but* a megamachine requires that (following Hannah Arendt) he must view Eichmann as a "banal" bureaucrat (p. 279), while at the same time murder-camps serving no end except murder itself require an (unexplained) "pathological hatred" in the Nazi leaders (p. 250). If even Eichmann was a mere banal bureaucrat who were the "pathological" leaders? How many? In the end, perhaps just one? And what made all those "merely following orders" follow orders *such as these*—with a "faith" not and others, he in these utterances understands Auschwitz as but the extreme of a technological dehumanization which, to varying degrees, may in the end become the fate of us all. Nazism was simply the machine radically dehumanized, and its millions of victims, its "waste products."[9]

In this view Richard Rubenstein, the Jewish theologian overwhelmed by the Holocaust, is at one with Martin Heidegger, the German philosopher who, so far as is known to us, never mentions the Holocaust in any of his writings. Heidegger omits this subject. He makes much, however, of "world wars" and their "totality," of the human "raw material" of technology, and of *Führers.* Of all these he writes:

> "World wars" and their "totality" are mere consequences of a loss of Being. It is only as consequences of this loss that they drive toward securing a stable form of dissipation-through-use. Man himself is drawn into this process, and his condition of being the most important raw material of all is no longer concealed. . . . The moral indignation of those who do not yet recognize what is the case often concentrates on the arbitrariness and claim-to-power made by *Führers.* This, however, is the most fatal way of lending them dignity. . . . In truth, the *Führers* are merely the necessary consequences of the fact that what-is [cut loose from Being] has gone astray, has spread itself out into the emptiness that has come to pass, and demands a single order and a making-secure of what-is.[10]

In linking Rubenstein with Heidegger we pay Rubenstein a tribute, for of all the philosophical thinking that has thus far been done about the involvement of modern man's very being with modern technology Heidegger's is doubtless the deepest. Heidegger goes beyond the mere external manifestations of

---

shrinking from total self-sacrifice? Nazism was a demonic compact between *Volk* and *Führer* in which each exalted the other in an orgy of death and destruction—with the consequence that the view of Nazism as *simply* the extreme megamachine lies in shambles.

9. Ibid., p. 279.

10. Martin Heidegger, "Überwindung der Metaphysik," *Vorträge und Aufsätze* (Pfullingen: Neske, 1967), pp. 84–85. (The translation is mine.) I deal more fully with these and related Heideggerian views in chap. 5 of my *Encounters between Judaism and Modern Philosophy* (New York: Basic Books, 1973).

technology. He goes to man, the autonomous self-maker, who stands behind these manifestations. Moreover, he goes beyond this self-maker's purported "autonomy" to a modern loss of an original presence of Being, to a *Seinsvergessenheit* and a *Seinsverlassenheit* of which that autonomy, for better or worse, is but a derivative result. And the reward for this search in depth is that, unlike all the far more superficial futurologists, Heidegger offers us at least a glimmer of justified hope.

Yet we are forced, equally by the very depth of Heidegger's philosophy and by the very agony of Rubenstein's preoccupation with the Holocaust, to ask of both thinkers essentially the same question. Can either Nazism or its murder camps be understood as but one particular case, however, extreme, of the general technological dehumanization? Or (to use language which theologians are equipped to understand) does not a scandal of particularity attach to Nazism and its murder camps which is shied away from, suppressed or simply forgotten when the scandal is technologically universalized? To be sure, there have been "world wars"—but none like that which Hitler unleashed on the world. There have been (and are) "total" political systems—but none like Nazism, a truth suppressed when "fascism" is used as a generic term in which Nazism is included. And while there have been (and are) "cults of personality," there have been no *Führers* but only one *Führer.*

Nor is it possible to distinguish between the goals of Nazism-in-general, as one system, and those of the murder-camp-in-particular, as a second system subserving the first. In essence, Nazism *was* the murder-camp. That a nihilistic, demonic celebration of death and destruction was its animating principle was evident to thinkers such as Karl Barth from the start; it became universally revealed in the end, when in the Berlin bunker Hitler and Goebbels, the only true Nazis left, expressed ghoulish satisfaction at the prospect that their downfall might carry in train the doom, not only (or even at all) of their enemies, but rather of the "master race." The mind shrinks from systematic murder that serves no purpose beyond murder itself, for it is ultimately unintelligible. Yet in Nazism as a whole (not only in the murder camps) this unintelligibility was real. And except for good fortune this diabolical celebration might today rule the world.

Even this does not exhaust the scandalous particularity of Nazism. The term "Aryan" had no clear connotation other than "non-Jew,"[11] and the Nazis were not antisemites because they were racists, but rather racists because they were antisemites.[12] The exaltation of the "Aryan" had no positive significance. It had only the negative significance of degrading and murdering the "non-Aryan." Thus Adolf Eichmann passed beyond the limits of a merely "banal" evil when, with nothing left of the Third Reich, he declared with obvious sincerity that he would jump laughing into his grave in the knowledge of having dispatched six million Jews to their death. We must conclude, then, that the dead Jews of the murder camps (and all the other innocent victims, as it were, as quasi-Jews, or by dint of innocent-guilt-by-association) were not the "waste product" of the Nazi system. They were *the* product.

VII

Despite all necessary attempts to comprehend it, the Nazi system in the end exceeds all comprehension. One cannot comprehend but only confront and oppose. We can here at-

---

11. Except only for "non-Gypsy." The fate of the Gypsies in Nazi Germany is in at least one respect more tragic than that of the Jews—no one seems to bother remembering it.

12. "Antisemitism" itself is nothing but a synonym for "Jew-hatred," concocted in the nineteenth century when hatred of Jews was fanned without explicit recourse to its ancient theological rationalizations. A secret Nazi order, dated May 17, 1943, reads as follows: "When the Grand Mufti visited *Reichsleiter* Rosenberg, the *Reichsleiter* promised to instruct the press that the word "antisemitism" was henceforth to be abandoned. This term seemed to include the Arab world which, according to the Grand Mufti, was overwhelmingly pro-German. The Allies utilize our use of that term in order to argue falsely that it is the nationalist socialist intention to view Jews and Arabs in the same light." Poliakov-Wulf, *Das Dritte Reich und die Juden* (Berlin: Arami, 1955), p. 369. (The translation is mine.)

This secret Nazi order might be pondered by those who believe (or pretend to believe) that "anti-Zionism" by definition cannot be antisemitic, on the grounds that Arabs as well as Jews are "Semites."

tempt to confront only one miniscule manifestation.[13] When issuing "work permits" designed to separate "useless" Jews to be murdered at once from "useful" ones to be kept useful by diabolically contrived false hopes and murdered later, the Nazis on occasion issued two such permits to able-bodied Jewish men. One was untransferable and to be kept for himself; the other was to be given *at his own discretion* to his able-bodied father, mother, wife, or one child. On those occasions the Nazis would not make this choice, although to do so would have resulted in a more efficient labor force. Jewish sons, husbands and fathers themselves were forced to decide who among their loved ones was—for the time being—to live and who to die at once.

The mind seeks escape in every direction. Yet we must confront relentlessly the Nazi custom of the two work permits, recognizing in this custom not the work of some isolated sadists, but rather the essence of the Nazi system. Hence we ask: where here was Heidegger's "dissipation-through-use?" Where was Rubenstein's technological dehumanization with its human "waste products?" Had utility been the principle of Nazism it would not have left the choice between "useful" and "useless" Jews to its victims. Not utility (however dehumanized), but rather torture and degradation was the principle. Indeed, there is no greater contrast between the technological exaltation of utility (even when out of control) and a celebration of torture *contrary* to all utility when it is not incidental but rather *for torture's sake*.

Why is this scandalous particularity overlooked, denied, or repressed by Rubenstein and Heidegger, not to speak of all the other writers who lack the agony of Rubenstein and the profundity of Heidegger? The theologian (Jewish or Christian) may

13. See above p. 46. I have resisted the temptation to change the example to avoid repetition. The two-work-permit custom illustrates unsurpassably not only the demonic (as in the above context), but also (as in the present context) my contention that the Nazi murder camp was so far from being a utilitarian system as to be, on the contrary, fundamentally at odds with the principle of utility.

hazard a guess if he falls back on his own authentic resources. For he is himself acquainted with scandalous particularity, for better (in the presence of God) and for worse (in the presence of the demonic). Moreover, he is acquainted with our all-too-human desire to evade or deny each and every scandalous particularity, and he knows this tendency to be pagan. And if he modernizes what he already knows he will understand that in a scientific age the characteristic form of evading or denying scandalous particularity is to explain it away. Hence it may be no coincidence that Heidegger's later thought is pagan,[14] that Rubenstein advocates a Jewish return to paganism; and that the dire predictions of the futurologists have a strong resemblance to ancient pagan fatalism.

We cannot be sure how the ancient rabbis, were they alive, would respond to the death camps. We *can* be sure that they would not explain them away. In their own time, they knew of idolatry, and considered groundless hate to be its equivalent. They knew, too, that it could not be explained but only opposed. Alive today, they would reject all fatalistic futurological predictions as so many self-fulfilling prophecies which leave us helpless. Instead, they would somehow seek to meet the absolute evil of the death camps in the only way absolute evil can be met—by an absolute opposition on which one stakes one's life.[15]

The authentic Jew after Auschwitz has no privileged access to explanations of the past. He has no privileged access to predictions of the future, or to ways of solving the problems of the present. He is, however, a witness to the world. He is a witness against the idolatry of the Nazi murder camps. This negative testimony is *ipso facto* also the positive testimony that man shall *be*, and shall be *human*—even if Truth should be so horrendous that there is no choice but to cast it to the ground.

14. See Hans Jonas, "Heidegger and Theology," *The Phenomenon of Life* (New York: Harper & Row, 1966), pp. 235–61.
15. For an attempt to bring rabbinic wisdom concerning idolatry to bear on Nazism, see chap. 4 of the work cited in n. 10.

VIII

The Jew in whom this testimony is unsurpassably manifest is the survivor of the two-work-permit custom. When the torture occurred he had no choice but compliance. Armed resistance was impossible. So was suicide. So was the transfer of his own work permit to another member of his family. Any of these attempts would have doomed the one member of his family who was to live. To save this one member, he was forced to become implicated in the diabolical system that robbed him of his soul and made him forever after innocently guilty of the murder of all his family except one member.

We ask: having survived (if survive he did), why did this Jew not seek blessed release in suicide? Choosing to live, why did he not seek refuge in insanity? Choosing to stay sane, why did he not do all he could to escape from his singled-out Jewish condition but rather affirmed his Jewishness and indeed raised new Jewish children? How could even one stay with his God?

These are unprecedented questions. They required unprecedented responses. Why not suicide? *Because after the Nazi celebration of death life has acquired a new dimension of sanctity.* Why not flight into madness? *Because insanity had ruled the kingdom of darkness, hence sanity, once a gift, has now become a holy commandment.* Why hold fast to mere Jewishness? *Because Jewish survival after Auschwitz is not "mere," but rather in itself and without any further reasons or theological justifications a sacred testimony* to all mankind *that life and love, not death and hate, shall prevail.* Why hold fast to the God of the covenant? Former believers lost him in the Holocaust Kingdom. Former agnostics found him. No judgment is possible. All theological arguments vanish. Nothing remains but the fact that the bond between him and his people reached the breaking point but was not for all wholly broken. Thus the survivor is a witness against darkness in an age of darkness. He is a witness whose like the world has not seen.

We do not yet recognize this witness, for we do not yet dare to enter the darkness against which he testifies. Yet to enter that darkness is to be rewarded with an altogether astonishing discovery. *This may be an age without heroes. It is, however, the heroic age* par excellence *in all of Jewish history.* If this is true of the Jewish people collectively (not only of the survivor individually), it is because *the survivor is gradually becoming the paradigm for the entire Jewish people.*

Nowhere is this truth as unmistakable as in the state of Israel. The state of Israel is collectively what the survivor is individually—testimony on behalf of all mankind to life against death, to sanity against madness, to Jewish self-affirmation against every form of flight from it, and (though this is visible only to those who break through narrow theological categories) to the God of the ancient covenant against all lapses into paganism.

We ask: having survived, why did the survivor not seek both safety and forgetfulness among such good people as the Danes, but rather seek danger and memory in the nascent and embattled state of Israel? Indeed, why do not even now Israeli Jews in general, survivors or not, flee by the thousands from their isolated and endangered country, in order that they might elsewhere find peace and safety—not to speak of the world's approval? Why do they hold fast to their "law of return"—the commitment to receive sick Jews, poor Jews, oppressed Jews, rejected by the immigration laws of every other state? A world that wants no part of Auschwitz fails to understand. Indeed, perpetuating antisemitism, despite Auschwitz or even because of it, it often does not hesitate to resort to slander. Yet the truth is obvious: the state of Israel is a collective testimony against the groundless hate which has erupted in this century in the heart of Europe. Its watchword is *Am Yisrael Chai*—"the people Israel *lives.*" Without this watchword the state of Israel could not have survived for a generation. It is a watchword of defiance, hope, and faith. It is a testimony to all men everywhere that man shall *be,* and be *human*—even if it should be necessary to cast Truth to the ground.

And now, astonishingly, this watchword has come alive among the Jews of the Soviet Union. What makes these Jews affirm their Jewishness against the overwhelming odds of a ruthless system, when they could gain peace and comfort by disavowing their Jewishness? Though we can only marvel at their heroism and not understand it, its mainspring is obvious enough. No American Jew has experienced the Holocaust as every Russian Jew has experienced it. Hence every Russian Jew must have felt all along that to be denied the right to his Jewishness is not, after what has happened, a tolerable form of discrimination or prejudice but rather an intolerable affront; it is, as it were, a secular sacrilege. And if now these Jews increasingly dare to convert secret feeling into public action, it is because of the inspiration incarnate in the state of Israel.

Is heroism in evidence among ourselves, the comfortable, mostly middle-class Jews of North America? In order to perceive any trace of it, we must break through the false-but-all-pervasive categories of a world that does not know of Auschwitz and does not wish to know of it.

In America this is a time of identity crises. Among these there is a specific Jewish identity crisis which springs from the view that a Jew must somehow achieve a "universal" transcendence of his "particular" Jewishness if he is to justify his Jewish identity. Thus it has come to seem that a Jew shows genuine courage when he rejects his Jewish identity, or when he at least seeks a "universal" justification of that identity by espousing all noble causes except the Jewish. And the North American Jewish hero may seem to be he who actually turns against his own people, less because he seeks the creation of a Palestinian Arab state than because he seeks the destruction of the Jewish state.

Such may be the appearances. The truth is otherwise. Just as the Black seeking to pass for white has internalized racism, so the Jew joining al-Fatah has internalized antisemitism, and this is true also (albeit to a lesser degree) of the Jew espousing all except Jewish causes. Where is the universalism in this exceptionalism—a "universalism" that applies to everyone with one exception—Jews? There is only sickness. To the extent to which the world still wants the Jew either to disappear or at least to become a man-in-general, it still has the power to produce Jews bent on disappearing, or at least on "demonstrating" their exceptionalist "universalism."

These may seem harsh judgments. They are necessary because Jewish identity crises such as the above have become a surrender to Auschwitz. For a Jew after the Holocaust to act as though his Jewishness required justification is to allow the possibility that none might be found, and this in turn is to allow the possibility, after Hitler murdered one-third of the Jewish people, that the rest should quietly pass on. But merely to allow these possibilities is *already* a posthumous victory for Hitler. It is *already* an act of betrayal. And the betrayal is as much of the world as of the Jewish people.

Is there any trace of Jewish heroism among ourselves? The question transcends all conventional distinctions, such as between old and young, "right" and "left," and even "religious" and "secular." The North American Jewish hero is he who has confronted the demons of Auschwitz and defied them. It is the Jew who has said "No!" to every form, however mild or disguised, of antisemitism without and self-rejection within. It is the Jew at home in his Jewish skin and at peace with his Jewish destiny. It is the Jew who is whole.

IX

But if this is the age of heroism in the history of the Jewish people, it is, after all, also an age of unprecedented darkness in world history, and Jewish heroism itself is possible only at the price of perpetually verging on despair. The question therefore arises what meaning the Jewish *Am Yisrael Chai* might have for contemporary man.

One shrinks from so large a question for two opposite reasons. At one extreme, the singled-out Jewish testimony may all-too-easily dissipate itself into a vacuous and thus cheap and escapist universalism. At the other extreme, it may express its universal significance at the false price of deafness to quite different, and yet not unrelated testimonies, such as might come from Vietnam, Czechoslovakia and Bangladesh. Perhaps one avoids both dangers best by concretizing the question. Earlier we dwelt on the American tradition of optimism, which is now in a state of crisis, and stressed that, while much in this optimism was always false, America itself would be lost if American optimism were wholly lost. What may the Jewish *Am Yisrael Chai* reveal about American optimism? What was always false about the American Dream? What—if anything—remains true?

Always false was precisely the "Dream." The innocence that produced that dream is lost. If the saving of America were dependent upon the recapturing of the innocence and the Dream there would be no hope. However, the Midrash that has furnished the text for the present discourse is not the product of a dream. Truth may be cast to the ground. The midrashic author *knows* that it is cast to the ground. He knows, too, that in the end Truth must rise again from the earth.

When dreams are shattered, men are wont to seek refuge in wishful thinking. Our age is no exception. In a half-hearted version, collective make-believe is manifest in our current, self-enclosed, middle-class apotheosis of psychoanalysis. (Within its sober bounds, that discipline gives limited help to disturbed individuals, and quite possibly we are all disturbed. Expanded into systematic wishful thinking, it turns into a panacea for all the ills of our world.) In a radical version, collective make-believe is manifest in a self-enclosed ideologizing which would refashion all reality in its own image, while being itself out of touch with reality.

Being self-enclosed, collective make-believe can survive for a long period of time. Yet its nemesis is sure to come, and by dint of its greater honesty it is the radical version which is bound first to experience it. To be sure, ideology seeks to refashion reality. Being divorced from reality, however, it in fact refashions only ideology, and the conflict between ideality and reality in the end becomes so total as to result—when Truth springs from the earth—in despair.

Is despair, then, the only *truthful* outcome? Richard Rubenstein does not lack the courage of radically opposing the entire Jewish tradition with his affirmation that the only messiah is death. Long before him Arthur Schopenhauer wrote as follows:

> Death is the great reprimand which the will to life, or more espe-
> cially the egoism which is essential to it, receives through the
> course of nature; and it may be considered as a punishment for our
> existence. Death says: thou are the product of an act which should
> not have been; therefore to expiate it thou must die.[16]

Once the sentiment expressed in this passage was attractive
only to idle drawing room speculation. Today one can detect on
every side a veritable fascination with every kind of negation
and death itself. Once the denial of the will to live could seem
to be a noble rejection of "egoism." Today it stands revealed as
the foe, nothing short of obscene, of a will to live which, far
from "egoistic," is a heroic act of defiance. And the revelation is
nowhere as manifest as in the survivor of the Nazi custom of the
two work permits. He is not blind to the shadows of death but
has walked through its valley. He does not cling to life but
rather affirms it by an act of faith which defies comprehension.
He relives, in a form without precedent anywhere, that great
"nevertheless" which has always been the secret of the enigmatic optimism of Judaism. His testimony is a warning to men
everywhere not to yield to death when Truth springs from the
earth. It is an admonition to endure Truth and to choose life. It
is a plea, anguished and joyous, to share in a defiant endurance
which alone reveals that Truth, despite all, remains the seal of
God.

16. Schopenhauer, *Works*, vol. III, p. 306.

8. *Transcendence in Contemporary Culture: Philosophical Reflections and a Jewish Testimony*

I

APPEARANCES SUGGEST that the modern world has lost Transcendence beyond all possible recovery. No avenue seems left.

The Greeks contemplated nature and sought first causes. The modern scientist seeks mere uniformities, and his purpose with nature is not the contemplation of it but rather control over it. But who will find—or even seek—Transcendence in what he controls? Some may still find Transcendence in nature where it is uncontrollable and certainly as yet uncontrolled. Yet such is even now the effect of technology on contemporary culture that henceforth any such recourse to nature is destined to be judged not as an access to Transcendence, but rather as a flight from immanence. And the flight is in vain.

The picture is no different for consciousness within than for nature without. Mystics of all times and all places have found Transcendence within the soul, when in a moment of ecstasy it "stands outside itself," touched by an Infinity beyond it. In the modern world, however, mystical experiences are a rarity, and, more importantly, distrusted even when they occur. The pale

Reprinted from H. W. Richardson and D. R. Cutler, eds., *Transcendence* (Boston: Beacon Press, 1969), pp. 143–52.

cast of psychological and sociological thought has reduced what was once "Reality"to a mere feeling projected on reality, thus destroying the feeling itself. And whatever the present limitations of psychological and sociological reflection, such is its hold on contemporary culture even now as to make every purported mystical access to the infinite self seem in truth to be a mere flight from the finite self. And the flight is as vain when it is into a long lost mythical past as when it occurs in a chemically induced present.

What of the avenue to Transcendence most characteristically associated with the Western world? This is neither nature-contemplation, which has had no real home in the West since ancient times, nor mysticism, whose home is more in the Eastern than in the Western world. Since biblical times, the Western, Judeo-Christian world has found Transcendence in history. This has happened for better: in the midst of the human-historical world was found a Transcendence other-than-human and higher-than-human which gave meaning, if not to all of history, so at any rate to crucial, epoch-making events within it. Perhaps it has happened also for worse, for at least to non-Western minds it must often seem that the West lays a greater burden on history than it can bear.

Transcendence in history, too, seems to have vanished. Biblical man heard a commanding and promising divine Voice, and he perceived divine salvation with his own eyes. Modern man has reduced all divine to human voices, for whether inspired by Kant or Dewey, Nietzsche or Marx, he has "transvalued" divine commandments into manmade "values," and transformed promises to be redeemed by God into hopes to be realized by man. As for saving acts of divine Presence, perceived in moments of radical surprise when the unexpected and unexpectable become actual,[1] modern man has lost radical surprise, and treats unexpected and unexpectable events either as subject to explanation after all, or else as the product of chance.

Such is the consensus concerning Transcendence in our modern, technological, secular civilization. It is shallow at least

1. For the notion of radical surprise referred to here see above, chap. 1.

when it is certain of itself and takes itself to be conclusive, and it is more rather than less shallow when it derives this certainty concerning present and future from scientific evidence. The voice of God is rarely heard in scientific generalizations, and is apt to confound scientific predictions. The cautious social scientist is well advised to confine himself to the short-range future. As for the wise historian, he never plays prophet anyhow.

The philosopher, too, is well advised to exercise caution. Part of his native equipment, philosophical caution is never more apposite than on the accessibility of Transcendence, and never more so than when the temptation is to make a priori assertions concerning it. Throughout history men have found access to Transcendence in the most varied ways. Is it likely that they were, one and all, simply deluded—and that with very little effort a priori rational or linguistic analysis can now disclose what has all along been the truth? What if any truth thus arrived at were at best only a twentieth-century truth? What if the human condition presupposed, described, or postulated by logical positivism, linguistic empiricism, and atheistic existentialism were merely a modern secularist condition and the philosophies describing it nothing more than a reflection of that condition? Long ago Hegel said that philosophy cannot transcend its time.[2] In the crisis of the present age, might not a philosopher match the historian's caution and refuse to play prophet?

Hegel himself compared the modern crisis to that of late Roman antiquity. Were he alive today (when the crisis already evident at his time has advanced much further) he might have perceived both much closer analogies and a much greater need to refrain from predictions, prophecies, and even any except the most cautious sociological generalizations. In the Roman pantheon the gods were all assembled and, because they had been made subservient to human use, they were demythologized and destroyed. Sociologists might have predicted

2. For the understanding of Hegel reflected in this essay see my *The Religious Dimension of Hegel's Thought* (Bloomington: Indiana University Press, 1968; Boston: Beacon, 1970).

that there could be no new gods, while theologians might have prophesied that all the gods had died. All this might have happened. Yet Christianity was just about to conquer the Western world.

The above, Hegelian-style reflections are themselves in the biblical tradition in that they suggest the possibility that Transcendence, rather than accessible either always or not at all, may differ in its accessibility according to historical circumstances. Such a view raises at all times the immediate question as to how, in any given historical here-and-now, Transcendence may be authenticated. In an age such as the present one (when access to Transcendence seems lost), it raises the additional question of how there can be any authentication of its very possibility. The second question can be answered at once. There can be no authentication if access to Transcendence is either a mere memory or a mere hope. A past which can no longer be reenacted and a future which cannot yet be anticipated are mere flights from present reality. An age that is one of "eclipse of God" (Buber), or that is "too late for the gods and too early for being" (Heidegger), can be recognized for what it is only if there is divine revelation in the divine self-concealment itself.

What of the first question? Authentication is possible only by a witness who *exists in* his particular situation, not by scientific observers, philosophers, or theologians who fancy themselves as transcending every all-too-particular situation. Public-opinion polls, conducted in the waning days of the Roman Empire, would have corroborated the pagan despair of the gods and dismissed Jews and Christians as oddballs and cranks. Similar polls, conducted in the Middle Ages, would have confirmed Christianity, but in so doing subscribed to the assumptions of Constantinian imperialism. One can be witness to a Transcendence which transcends the historical situation only *within* one's historical situation; nor can others who could appraise or respond to this testimony do so except from within *their* historical situation. There is no impartial, independent vantage point. But as for the objective uncertainty and the historical existential limitations bound up with this state of affairs, these are, so far as men's relation to Transcendence is concerned, boundaries that they cannot escape. In a unique situation, a witness or group of witnesses can never be quite certain that Transcendence speaks to them, and they must always be open to the possibility that it speaks differently to others.

Yet there are at least negative criteria by which claims to authenticity may and must be appraised. Neither Jewish nor Christian witnesses could have survived the collapse of the Roman Empire had they failed to satisfy two conditions. The God of Israel and the church, who had already proved to be unassimilable to the Roman pantheon while its gods were still alive, had to be capable of surviving their death, thus being a God of the present and the future as well as of the past. And he had to be a God commanding not idle curiosity or passing fancy, but faithfulness unto death. An anachronistic god could not have been kept alive even by the blood of martyrs; and even the most up-to-date god is not a living God unless he can raise up witnesses, however few in number, who are faithful unto death.

The question that arises in the present age is therefore as follows: *Can there be, in the present age, ways of testimony to Transcendence which, on the one hand, are totally present, contemporary and nonanachronistic and which, on the other hand, are not idle fancies or abstract conceits, but are forced on men or groups of men in their contemporary condition and by that condition so as to command absolute loyalty?*

With this question, a Jewish philosopher's reflection *about* the present general situation must necessarily turn into a Jewish testimony from within his present particular Jewish situation. This would be true in any age. It is truer in this age than in almost all others. For Jews of this generation have been singled out by the Nazi Holocaust as Jews have not been singled out since the events at Mount Sinai.

II

The Nazi Holocaust is totally present, contemporary, and nonanachronistic. The passage of time has brought it closer rather than moving it farther away, disclosing that the world has thus far shied away from it but must at length confront it with an unyielding realism and, if necessary, despair.

A secular liberalism which celebrates the loss of Transcendence in the modern world would dismiss the Holocaust as a mere lapse into atavistic tribalism. This is but one of many ways in which attempts have been made to avoid the stark contemporaneity of its horror. Others making such attempts include Christian theologians ignoring the implications of the fact that the Holocaust occurred in Christian (or post-Christian) Europe, Germans who disconnect it with the remainder of German history, and Communists who cover it with the blanket term "fascism," and who bury fascism itself in the Marxist dialectic. Historians too disregard the Holocaust—or, if they do not ignore it, they find it hard to return from it to their normal business.

Secularist-liberal ideology is not wholly blind to the fact that the blessings of the secular city are ambiguous. The anonymity produced by the fragmentation of communal ties alienates as well as liberates. The Promethean power provided by modern technology has destructive as well as constructive potentialities. The freedom from a premodern religious oppressiveness permits the permissible—and suggests that all things are permitted. Secularist-liberal ideology can face these ambiguities so long as it can ignore their demonic possibilities, pretending that the demonic is a mere species of "prejudice and superstition," safely destroyed by modern enlightenment.[3]

The Nazi Holocaust destroys this pretense. Nazi antisemitism was not "prejudice," but a groundless, infinite, and implacable hate. Nazi racism was not "superstition," but mass murder infused with infinite passion and elevated to pseudoreligious absoluteness, not a finite means to the winning of a war, but a boundless end in itself, pursued even at the risk of losing a war on account of it. Dethroning all gods ever worshiped anywhere, Nazism assumed the vacated throne in order to presume to decide what peoples had a right to live and what

3. The criticism here merely hinted at is more fully developed in my *Encounters between Judaism and Modern Philosophy* (New York: Basic Books, 1973), chap. 4.

peoples did not. And the decision was both made and executed in a terrifyingly contemporary framework. For the first time in history, murder became an industry whose products included human hair and soap made of human bodies. An ancient Midrash asks what became of the fear of God when the Romans destroyed Jerusalem, and it answers that it is because this fear still exists that Israel, now scattered helpless among the nations, is not destroyed by them. After Auschwitz, this answer has become impossible.

The Nazi Holocaust hurls at all contemporary mankind the demonic assertion that if there is no God, everything is permitted. No contemporary man—secularist or religious—can ignore that challenge. We cannot say that Nazism is safely past; the world still gives Hitler posthumous victories. Nor can we say that it affects only its immediate victims. When the bomb fell on Hiroshima (and not into the sea), and when a shot killed Martin Luther King in Memphis, or, for that matter, when Gomulka stirred Polish antisemitism against the pitifully few survivors of the Nazi slaughter, Hitler must have laughed in hell.

In May 1967, the worldwide Jewish community had a moment of truth that revealed clearly, if only momentarily, what has remained otherwise obscure and ambiguous, or even wholly concealed. Jewish students dropped their studies and rushed to Israel. Elderly gentlemen of modest means mortgaged their homes. Tactful Jewish spokesmen abandoned tact and screamed, at the risk of alienating Christian friends. Faced with the fact that the state of Israel was in mortal danger, the worldwide Jewish community became, for a moment, wholly united in its defense. More precisely, time-honored divisions—between Orthodox and liberal, Zionist and non-Zionist, religious and secularist—lost for a time their significance, to be replaced by a new division between Jews willing to stand up and be counted, and Jews who (whatever their reasons, excuses, or ideologies) stood aside.

What caused this unexpected and unprecedented response to an unexpected and unprecedented situation? Not "nationalism"; among those standing up to be counted were non-Zionists and even anti-Zionists. Not "religious sentiment";

the response transcended all religious-secularist distinctions. Not "humanism"; not a few Jewish humanists stood aside when Jewish—rather than Arab or Vietnamese—children were in danger. The true cause cannot be in doubt. For a whole generation Jews had lived with the Nazi Holocaust, racked by grief and true or imagined guilt. For a whole generation they had not known how to live with the fact that Jews had been singled out for murder by one part of the world and that the other part had done little to stop it. When in May 1967 the same words issued from Cairo and Damascus that had once issued from Berlin, Jews were divided not into Orthodox and liberal, religious and secularist, Zionist and non-Zionist, but into those who fled (and were revealed as having fled all along) from being singled out by the first Holocaust and those who responded to it (and were revealed as having responded all along) with a resolve that there must be no second Holocaust.

In what terms shall we understand this response? Much too puny are all categories that do justice to but relative commitments such as group loyalty or the "values" of a half-remembered tradition. Indeed, *all* past categories are inadequate, even when they do justice to absolute commitments, if only because religious categories exclude the secular, and secularist categories, the religious. Nothing less will do than to say that *a commanding Voice speaks from Auschwitz; that some Jews hear it while others stop their ears; and that among Jews hearing it are secularists who hear no more and believers who identify its Source.* No redeeming Voice is heard, or ever will be heard, at Auschwitz. *But Transcendence is found at Auschwitz in the form of absolute Command.*[4]

III

What does the Voice at Auschwitz command? In a recent, pre-Six-Day-War symposium on "Jewish Values in the Post-Holocaust Future," I replied: "The authentic Jew of today is

---

4. See Professor Harold Fisch's letter cited above, chap. 3, p. 41.

forbidden to hand Hitler yet another, posthumous victory."
This commandment I specified as follows:

> We are, first, commanded to survive as Jews, lest the Jewish people
> perish. We are commanded, second, to remember in our very guts
> and bones the martyrs of the Holocaust, lest their memory perish.
> We are forbidden, thirdly, to deny or despair of God, however much
> we may have to contend with him or with belief in him, lest Judaism
> perish. We are forbidden, finally, to despair of the world as the
> place which is to become the kingdom of God, lest we help make it
> a meaningless place in which God is dead or irrelevant and every-
> thing is permitted. To abandon any of these imperatives, in re-
> sponse to Hitler's victory at Auschwitz, would be to hand him yet
> other, posthumous victories.[5]

Even as I wrote these words I realized their fragmentariness
and their temporariness. Jewish survival is a duty, and indeed
after Auschwitz, in itself a monumental act of faith; yet it is not,
as it never has been, an ultimate end in itself. Jews may not
despair of the world, but after Auschwitz they know no
longer—and not yet—how to hope for it. Jews may not deny the
God of Israel, yet after Auschwitz even many believers know no
longer—and not yet—how to affirm him. We must remember
the martyrs of Auschwitz; but we cannot yet do so without remembering Hitler along with them. Jewish tradition, however,
would require that his name be wiped out rather than remembered, for to remember him forever would give him a victory
forever, leaving the earth defiled and unhealed.

Since Auschwitz, Jews are singled out by an evil at once
wholly demonic and wholly modern. They can survive as Jews
only if they accept rather than flee from this singled-out condition, transfiguring victimization by the modern demons concentrated at Auschwitz into testimony against them everywhere.
But they will have the strength for such testimony only if they
hear the commanding Voice of Auschwitz. Like Israel in June
1967, the Jewish people as a whole will be saved by "the com-

5. See above, chap. 2, pp. 23–24.

mandment which the Lord of history [has] ..., so to speak, pronounced at Auschwitz."[6]

When the Roman world waned, ancient paganism perished, but Judaism was renewed and Christianity originated. Is our modern crisis as radical as the ancient one? Is our question, too, what will perish and what will be renewed or transfigured? In the age of Auschwitz, Hiroshima, and the shot that rang at Memphis, perhaps Transcendence speaks to us all primordially through the Voice of Command. Perhaps to have any hope for renewal we must listen to that Voice, lest the demons unleashed by a mechanizing age destroy us.

It may be objected that in a postreligious, secular age, one cannot hear such a Voice. But perhaps our crisis is far deeper than is generally imagined in that secularity, as well as religiosity, is in question. And perhaps we shall all be saved by a commanding Voice which can be heard by secularists as well as believers, revealing to both, and most clearly so in the places of the most extreme human degradation, that man is created in the divine image.

6. Ibid.

9. *Demythologizing and Remythologizing in Jewish Experience: Reflections Inspired by Hegel's Philosophy*

I

THERE ARE three reasons for my choice of this topic.

1. At one time the distinction between *lumen naturale* and *lumen supernaturale* would have enabled a Jewish philosopher to participate in a Catholic philosophical conference simply *qua* philosopher. That this distinction, while not rejected, has become questionable today is indicated by the very theme of this conference. Hence, philosophical integrity obligates me to speak to you as a Jewish philosopher. I could avoid this obligation only if I believed that there were such a thing as "religion-in-general." This, however, I believe to be an empty abstraction.

2. The Catholic and Jewish religious worlds are both in crisis, but the two crises are not the same. I will not presume to speak of the first; I must say a few words of the second. Since 1933 the Jewish people have been in an unprecedented war for existence itself—and the end is not yet in sight. The one deci-

Reprinted from *Myth and Philosophy: Proceedings of the American Catholic Philosophical Association*, vol. XLV, Washington, 1971, pp. 16–27. For the overall interpretation of Hegel's philosophy behind this paper, see my *The Religious Dimension in Hegel's Thought* (Bloomington: Indiana University Press, 1968; Boston: Beacon, 1970).

sive event in this war has been the Nazi Holocaust; the other, the rise of the first Jewish state in two thousand years. I cannot predict the future. But I am bold enough to predict that there will be but two alternatives. One will be true peace for the state of Israel—the final defeat of Hitler. The other will be the destruction of the state of Israel. After twenty years of reflection on this latter harrowing possibility, I say without hesitation that it would mark the end of the Jewish people after nearly four thousand years of existence.

3. The above assertions, if true, are of unquestionable religious significance if only because the survival of the age-old divine-Jewish covenant is inextricably bound up with the life or death of the Jewish people. Within the contemporary Jewish world, political events have, therefore, an immediate religious significance, and it is not surprising that the remythologizing, which is the subject of my philosophical thought, is in evidence in Jewish life on every side. Indeed, it is becoming increasingly difficult to say which form of contemporary Jewish life is "religious" and which is "secularist."

The above comments make it clear that it is not for philosophical reasons alone that I think little of the philosophical tradition that regards any and all religious myth as simply false, and itself as its appointed critic. Any such view is philosophically presumptuous and thus unphilosophical; it also shows a monumental and indiscriminate contempt for mankind's entire religious tradition. Is it believable that the storytellers and imagemakers of the Divine have been, one and all, wholly unaware of the fact that they were "only" telling stories and making images? Does not on the contrary the most elementary justice to the facts of religious life disclose that the more profoundly men have experienced the presence of the Inexpressible, the greater has been their need to express it, together with an awareness that the expression is perforce inadequate? Expression has been necessary, at any rate, when, as in Judaism and Christianity, the Divine manifests itself as initiating a divine-human relation. Expression has here been necessary. This fact, however, has not diminished the awareness that the expression is inadequate. Thus in Judaism the storyteller knows that he tells "only" a story, and this is called Midrash. The mythmaker knows that he makes "only" a myth—and a myth of this sort is called symbol. All this becomes inescapable for a Jewish philosopher who lives in an age in which old Midrashim are coming to new life and, indeed, new ones are being born.

II

We turn from philosophic blindness to at least partial philosophic sight when we consider the thought of Immanuel Kant. Kant limits reason so as to leave room for faith. The result of this act is a demythologizing and a remythologizing. Kant destroys what he calls "literal anthropomorphism." He reinstates what he calls "symbolic anthropomorphism." This latter philosophical act has three interrelated aspects, two negative, one positive. (1) Philosophically unacceptable anthropomorphisms are eliminated. (2) Philosophically acceptable anthropomorphisms are shown to be "only" symbolically and not literally true, and the status of such truth is pointed to if not fully developed. (3) Finally, philosophically acceptable symbolic anthropomorphisms are shown to be not only acceptable, but also necessary. They are necessary for two reasons: first, the philosopher cannot rise above the symbolic or religious truth to a higher conceptual or philosophical form of truth; second, the man cannot dispense with symbolic anthropomorphisms; without them his existence remains incomplete.

That the Kantian wisdom is, nevertheless, incomplete, is shown in the following passage from Hegel's *Philosophy of Religion:*

> I am to make myself fit for the indwelling of the Spirit. This is my labor, the labor of man; but the same is also the labor of God, regarded from His side. He moves toward man and is in man through the act of raising him. What seems my act is thus God's and, conversely, what seems His is mine. This, to be sure, runs counter to the merely moral standpoint of Kant and Fichte; there the Good

always remains something yet to be produced, . . . something that ought to be, as if it were not already essentially there. A world outside me remains, God-forsaken, waiting for me to bring goodness and purpose into it. But the sphere of moral action is limited. In religion the Good and reconciliation are absolutely complete and existing on their own account . . . and the question is only, concerning me and over against me, that I should lay aside my subjectivity and take and have a share in the work which eternally completes itself.[1]

In the passage cited, Hegel refers only to the Christian religion. (We shall soon show that its central point applies to the Jewish religion as well.) Our present purpose is to show the limitations of Kant's achievement. Kant permits a symbolic affirmation of the Divine; he rejects the possibility of a divine-human relation or (which in practice is the same thing) permits it only in the infinite future; and—this is shown by Hegel—the ground for this rejection is the elevation of moral-human autonomy to an absoluteness which makes the outcome, instead of the conclusion of an open contest, a foregone conclusion. In contrast, Hegel's philosophy takes upon itself the task of taking all religious existence as it takes itself before undertaking such tasks of demythologizing and remythologizing as may be philosophically necessary. We must here confine ourselves to key points in what is necessarily a vast undertaking.

The first of these is what may be termed Hegel's phenomenological understanding of authentic religious existence as such, insofar as he considers so abstract and general an understanding to be possible. He discovers three internally related components—feeling, representation, and cult.

(a) Feeling may be considered as the aspect of involvement. To feel, or at any rate to feel religiously, is to be geared to the felt in one's totality, i.e., not in abstraction from one's singularity but rather in one's singularity.

1. G. W. F. Hegel, *Werke* (Berlin: Duncker & Humbolt, 1840–47), vol. XI, pp. 222 ff. That this Christian (or post-Christian) statement would require a partial modification in the context of Judaism will emerge in part in the following discourse—and also that the point fundamental for our present purpose remains unaffected.

(b) Without content, however, feeling can have no religious specificity and, indeed, not be religious at all. The content, however, depends on the object to which the feeling is geared. To say that this object must be higher-than-human or even, as it were, absolutely high, is not sufficient, for this would yield no more than the "feeling of absolute dependence"—a feeling which the Christian shares with the dog.[2] The object must have specific content, and this content Hegel terms "representation."

If feeling is involvement or at-oneness with the felt, "representation" is the element of otherness of the Divine which, indeed, since the human is finite and the Divine infinite, is a radical otherness. This radical otherness, to be sure, clashes with the necessity of specific content; this clash is resolved, however, in religious representation itself in that, while being specific and therefore finite, it testifies to its own inadequacy and points beyond itself to the Infinite. Religious representation, in short, is symbolic.

(c) While feeling and representation require each other, they would both lack existential seriousness without the "labor" of cult. Religious feeling would remain a mere pious "fog"; representation, mere ideas of irrelevant gods, with reality lacking in both cases. Cult acts out the difference of the divine-human nonunion which is yet a union, and so transfigures that relation as to produce—depending on the religion—a kind of actual union.

(d) But cult requires feeling and representation as much as these in turn require cult. Without feeling, cult is external observance. Without a represented God, it is meaningless reality and purposeless labor. *Every genuine religion, then, is a totality of existence in which the inwardness of feeling is united with outward action and external occurrence, through a representational meaning that permeates both.*

To the brief phenomenological account just given, two points must be added which are but two aspects of one. First,

---

2. I am referring to Schleiermacher and Hegel's famous derogatory comment on his most famous doctrine.

Hegel rejects every form of philosophical reductionism, so that the existence just described must be taken as it takes itself, i.e., not as a human projection but rather as a divine-human relationship. Second, if philosophy is to presume the task of taking religion in terms other than it takes itself, it cannot presuppose its capacity for this task but rather bears the onus of proof.[3]

We take a giant leap from the first key point to a second. Hegel considers Christianity to be the "absolute" religion. One central reason for this view is that Christianity is what he terms doubly representational. In the already cited passage he writes:

> I am to make myself fit for the indwelling of the Spirit. . . . This is my labor, the labor of man; but the same is also the labor of God, regarded from His side. He moves toward man and is in man through the act of raising him. What seems my act is thus God's and, conversely, what seems His, mine.

Elsewhere he states:

> Grace enlightens the heart of man, it is the divine Spirit in man, so that man may be represented as passive in relation to its activity, i.e., it is not his own activity. In the Notion, however, this double activity must be grasped as single.[4]

These passages suffice to identify a doubly representational religious existence. Doubly representational feeling is a togetherness of being-gripped by the Divine and free commitment. Doubly representational representation is a complex of symbols in which the Divine, its infinity notwithstanding, is involved with the human, and the human, its finitude notwithstanding, is an active partner in a divine-human relationship. Hence cult is a double labor in which God and man both are at work and known to be at work.

If Hegel confines doubly representational religious existence to Christianity, it is because he considers Christianity the

3. On this section, see further my *Religious Dimension*, pp. 116–27, 154–55.

4. Hegel, *Werke*, vol. XII, pp. 117 ff.

realization of what he calls "the identity of the Divine principle and the human."[5] But we shall shortly show that the Divine-Jewish covenant (which does not accept the identity of the Divine and the human) nevertheless manifests itself as a doubly representational religious existence. And we may stress at this point that whereas Christian thinkers may recognize their religion as doubly representational in Hegel's sense, Hegel has had no significant Christian theological followers who affirm, and develop philosophically along his lines, his identity of the divine principle and the human.

We turn to the third key point. Hegel does not confine himself to a phenomenological description of doubly representational religious existence. He seeks philosophically to transfigure its religious "form."

> In the Notion, this double activity must be grasped as single.

This single passage suffices to sum up the entire project of Hegel's philosophy of religion, if indeed not his philosophy as a whole. Together with the foregoing, it also suffices to disclose that this project is not, so far as religious existence is concerned, a demythologizing but rather a transmythologizing. Under no circumstances may philosophy, as self-appointed judge, reduce what to religious existence itself is a Divine-human relation to a mere human projection. On the contrary, it may transform the "doubly" representational religious existence into a "single" Notion only if it can prove itself capable of becoming a single self-activity of Thought which can only be described, not as human, but rather as human-divine.[6]

We shall here refrain from inquiring either into the nature of Hegel's transmythologizing activity or into the reasons why he considers it possible. We shall merely consider its effects upon religious existence itself. Hegel writes:

---

5. See my *Religious Dimension*, chaps. 5 and 6.
6. This obligation remains, *mutatis mutandis*, even in left-wing Hegelianism, that of Marx included, inasmuch as—to use Feuerbach's formulation—it can reduce "theology" to "anthropology" only if, at the same time, it can also "elevate" anthropology to theology.

The language of representation differs from the language of the Notion. Further, man not only to begin with knows Truth by the name of representation. *He is also, as living man, at home with it alone.* The task of philosophic science, however, is not to write its figurations into . . . abstract realms only. *It is also to show . . . their existence in actual Spirit. But that existence is representation.*[7]

The import of the passage is clear. Even if the philosopher *qua* philosopher can rise to the single thought-activity of a transmythologizing divine-human Thought, he continues to exist, *qua* man, on the human side of a doubly representational divine-human relationship. *Hence the task of philosophy is not only to transmythologize but also—if it can muster the power—to remythologize as well.*

We turn to the fourth key in Hegel's thought that presently concerns our purpose. Since, by virtually unanimous contemporary philosophical consent, a rise of philosophical thought to Divinity, and hence Hegelian transmythologizing, is impossible, we ask: what, according to Hegel, would result if philosophical thought were confined to human finitude? Hegel writes:

The experience . . . that I cannot help myself by means of reflection, that I cannot, in fact, take my stand upon myself at all, and the circumstance that I still crave something that stands firm—all this forces me back from reflection and leads me to adhere to the content in the form in which it is given.[8]

In other words, philosophical thought, if unable to transmythologize, becomes merely "reflective" and demythologizes. Since, however, it transcends reflective finitude sufficiently to recognize the reductionist falsehood of such mere demythologizing, it points beyond reflection back to a

---

7. *Berliner Schriften*, ed. Hoffmeister (Hamburg: Meiner, 1956), pp. 318 ff. (Italics added).

8. Hegel, *Werke*, vol. XI, p. 147.

religious immediacy which now, however, becomes (to use Kierkegaard's term) immediacy after reflection.

We can thus sum up our present concern with Hegel with the following overall conclusion. *Whether or not Hegel's transmythologizing thought-activity is possible, a remythologizing is necessary by which doubly representational religious existence is reinstated.*

Before showing the Midrash of Judaism to be the expression of a doubly representational religious existence we give *prima facie* plausibility for this undertaking in a passage from Martin Buber's *I and Thou*. That Buber should have been influenced on this issue by Hegel is out of the question. That he was immersed in Jewish (though not primarily midrashic but rather biblical and Hasidic) religious literature is unquestionable. From this self-immersion result these words:

> I know that "I am given over for disposal" and know at the same time that "It depends on myself." . . . I am compelled to take both to myself, to be lived together, and in being lived together they are one.[9]

This passage, nourished by Jewish religious experience, tersely reproduces in its entirety Hegel's doctrine of double representation (which is nourished by Christian experience). There are, however, two decisive qualifications, and these, as already hinted, contemporary Christians might share. First, Hegel's "absolute" religion, or "divine-human identity" is unacceptable. Second, his philosophical transmythologizing is impossible.

III

In turning from this *prima facie* confirmation to Midrash itself we do far better to cite strategically chosen Midrashim than to speak of Midrash-in-general. Three Midrashim must here suffice:

9. Martin Buber, *I and Thou* (New York: Scribner's, 1958), p. 96.

Rabbi Azaryiah and Rabbi Aḥa in the name of Rabbi Yoḥanan said: When the Israelites heard at Sinai the word "I" [i.e., the first word of the ten Commandments]; their souls left them, as it says, "If we hear the voice . . . any more, then we shall die" (Deut. 5:22). . . . The Word then returned to the Holy One, blessed be He, and said: "Sovereign of the universe, Thou art full of life, and Thy law is full of life, and Thou hast sent me to the dead, for they are all dead." Thereupon, the Holy One, blessed be He, sweetened [i.e. softened] the Word for them."[10]

Rabbi Sim'on bar Yoḥai said: . . . "Only when Israel does God's will is His heavenly place secure." . . . Nevertheless, Rabbi Sim'on bar Yoḥai also quoted "This is my Lord and I will praise him" (Exod. 15:2), and he said: "When I praise Him, He is glorified, and when I do not praise Him, He is, as it were, glorified in Himself.[11]

"Ye are My witnesses, saith the Lord, and I am God." (Isa. 43:12). That is, when ye are My witnesses, I am God, and when ye are not My witnesses I am, as it were, not God.[12]

The first Midrash shows why Hegel did not consider Judaism to be a doubly representational form of religious existence—and that he was mistaken. Hegel accepts the traditional Christian view that the Sinaitic revelation is law without grace. The Midrash tells the tale of this view, explores its radical implications, and overcomes it. A divine commandment devoid of grace would be humanly unperformable, and indeed, a divine Presence revealing itself as commanding is paradoxical. For *qua* present the divine Infinity destroys the human community in its finitude: "they are all dead." But *qua* commanding it requires a human response—which is possible only if the human community is alive even in the moment of divine Presence. This paradox is resolved by the Midrash in the second descent of the Divine which, "sweetening the Word," makes

---

10. *Midrash Rabba, Song of Songs*, V 16 #3, trans. M. Simon (London: Soncino Press, 1961), pp. 252 ff. I have expounded this Midrash more fully in my *God's Presence in History* (New York: New York University Press, 1970; New York: Harper Torchbook, 1973), pp. 14 ff.

11. *Sifre on Deuteronomy*, Berakhah 346, 144a.

12. *Midrash Rabba*, Psalms, on Psalm 123:1.

the divine commandment capable of human performance. For Pelagius, divine grace is merely an event subsequent to the human failure to perform the divine commandment. For Augustine, it redeems man from the commandment itself. In Judaism, grace is manifest in the gift of the commandment itself which, bridging the gulf between two incommensurables, makes a human community partner in a divine-human covenant.

The second and third Midrash show that both the paradox and the grace that resolves it do not vanish into the dead and irrelevant past but remain in the life of the covenant itself. On the one hand, the primordial divine commanding grace has established a truly mutual relationship. Hence the bold words that the heavenly place is not secure, and indeed God not God, unless Israel performs its labor which (as Hegel has stressed) is "the labor of man." Yet since the pristine paradox and the grace that resolves it both remain, these affirmations are true only "as it were": they are stories which are known to be "only" stories—and yet must be told. And the divine-human incommensurability which remains, even as the relation is mutual and real, is fully explicated when Rabbi Sim'on bar Yohai affirms that, on the one hand, God does need human glorification and, on the other, is "glorified in Himself."[13]

The second Midrash thus seems to express a fuller and richer truth than the third. If nevertheless we place this latter third, and indeed cite it at all, it is because it takes cognizance, if only implicitly, of a grim possibility inherent in Jewish religious existence, and possibly unique to it. Both Midrashim take cognizance of the possibility and actuality of Jewish infidelity to the covenant, and the second Midrash finds security against this cognizance in the knowledge that God, if not glorified by Israel, is "as it were, glorified in Himself." But what if the people Israel failed to witness, not because of infidelity, but because of nonexistence? The Midrashim were all written after 70 C.E., the greatest catastrophe in all of Jewish history prior to

---

13. On the above see further my *Quest for Past and Future* (Bloomington: Indiana University Press, 1968; Boston: Beacon, 1970), especially chaps. 2, 7, 13, 14.

the Nazi Holocaust. The Christian covenant is with the individual and the church, and *in extremis* can fall back on the doctrines of the holy remnant and the invisible church. No such ultimate recourse is possible when the covenant is with a flesh-and-blood people. The rabbis who lived through the catastrophe of 70 C.E. had to reckon with the possibility that there might be no covenant because there would be no people—not because of Jewish infidelity but rather because of Roman massacres. Thus, *in extremis,* the last word cannot go to the Midrash which makes God "glorified in Himself." Is he glorified in himself if his people are dead? Such religious smugness, if not obscenity, is avoided in the third Midrash. Remaining, as it were, open-ended, it implicitly contains a whole host of religious possibilities, such as protest, defiance and even despair.

IV

We turn to a final key point in Hegel's teaching which has hitherto had to be postponed. What if religious representational existence were demythologized in our time, not by a possible and necessary philosophical criticism, but rather because, for one cause or another, religious life itself had withered away? We have shown that Hegel's philosophical thought does not demythologize religious representation but rather reinstates it. We must now add his admission that such a philosophical reinstatement is possible only if religious life is still extant. The power of philosophy, Hegel realistically concedes, does not extend to either reviving a dead religion or creating a new.[14]

With this admission it may well seem that demythologizing has, after all, the last word, and that our entire discourse has been an anachronistic exercise. We may have refuted with Hegel's help the philosophical presumption that all myth and symbol are mere superstition, and that philosophical criticism is their appointed judge. We have done nothing to refute the

14. See especially Hegel, *Werke,* vol. XII, pp. 354 ff.

voices on every side which assert that the Divine no longer speaks, and hence that all myth and symbol are dead.

We shall not here inquire into these broad, sweeping and indiscriminate affirmations. We must testify, however, that they run directly counter to contemporary Jewish experience where it is most self-exposed to contemporary Jewish history. Two events have happened to the Jewish people in this generation, more momentous than the fall of Jerusalem in 70 C.E. ever was. The rabbis then confronted the possibility that the Jewish people might die. At Auschwitz this people in fact died. The rabbis dreamt of salvation and resurrection after catastrophe. Such a salvation and resurrection has, in fact, become actual in Jerusalem in our own time.

It would be absurd to look for explanations, religious or otherwise, of these events—an enterprise in any case contrary to the whole midrashic tradition. We can and must ask, however, whether, in response to these events, Jewish existence has remained in the demythologized condition which is so widely and so confidently proclaimed to be the universal modern fate. And what casts doubt on these confident proclamations is that not only old Midrashim have assumed new life. New Midrashim have been born. They are still being born. They will continue to be born.

Some might ask for a philosophical theory of the new Midrashim to which I refer. Those have not understood what has been said. Present Jewish existence has lived and is still living the events of Auschwitz and Jerusalem. It cannot detach itself from these events, much less rise above them, and philosophical reflection only points back to an immediacy in which the stories themselves are told. They are "only" stories, and known to be so; yet they must be told, and their telling is a testimony in which Buber's "I am given over for disposal" and "It depends on me" become one "in being lived."

In Elie Wiesel's *Night*, the work of a man who was in Auschwitz as a fourteen-year-old boy, we read the following:

One day when we came back from work, we saw three gallows rearing up in the assembly place, three black crows. Roll call. SS all round us, machine guns trained: the traditional ceremony. Three victims in chains—and one of them, the little servant, the sad-eyed angel.

The SS seemed more preoccupied, more disturbed than usual. To hang a young boy in front of thousands of spectators was no light matter. The head of the camp read the verdict. All eyes were on the child. He was lividly pale, almost calm, biting his lips. The gallows threw its shadow over him . . .

The three victims mounted together onto the chairs.

The three necks were placed at the same moment within the nooses.

"Long live liberty!", cried the two adults.

But the child was silent.

"Where is God? Where is He?", someone behind me asked.

At a sign from the head of the camp, the three chairs tipped over . . .

I heard a voice within me answer . . . :
"Where is He? Here He is—He is hanging on this gallows . . ."[15]

I heard my second and third stories in 1970, when together with my wife, I went with a group of survivors on a pilgrimage to the murder camp of Bergen-Belsen—and then to Jerusalem.[16] When we arrived at Hannover, the city nearest to Belsen, it rained. The leader of our group told us: "We have revisited this place of our suffering many times. It always rains. God weeps. He weeps for the sins he has committed against his people Israel."

And then, by a mere brief airplane ride, we leaped over the eternities that separate Bergen-Belsen from Jerusalem. There, a friend told us how one day at six A.M. he went to the Western Wall, and there, at the most sacred place of the Jewish people, he met an old Jew, who greeted the stranger, saying, "My friend, I have a *simhah*, a celebration! Celebrate with me! Have some schnapps and some cookies!" Having accepted the invita-

15. Elie Wiesel, *Night* (New York: Avon, 1972), pp. 75 ff.
16. See below, chap. 10.

tion, our friend some days later returned to the Wall at the same time, only to be greeted by the same old man in the same way. And so it went three or four times. Finally, our friend could no longer restrain his curiosity and asked the old man: "My friend, what kind of celebration is this? A wedding? A Bar-mitzvah? What *simhah* can last for weeks upon weeks?" The old man replied, "I am a survivor of Auschwitz. Also, I am a Cohen, descendent of priests and, as you may know, a Cohen has the duty, privilege, and joy of invoking the blessing of God on his people but a few times a year. In Jerusalem, however, he may bless the people every single day. And since I must be at work in my kibbutz at eight A.M., I come here every day at six A.M. to fulfill my duty and my privilege. This is my *simhah*, my celebration. It will last as long as I live."

Part Three

THE CENTRALITY
OF ISRAEL

10. From Bergen-Belsen to Jerusalem

I

IN JULY 1961, *Commentary* published a symposium on the state of Jewish belief. About fifty rabbis, theologians, philosophers, and others were asked to contribute, myself included. When looking at that symposium again about a year ago, I was shocked and scandalized (which had not been the case at the time)—not by the questions that were included, one or two of which I have now forgotten, but rather by those that were omitted. No ques-

Originally delivered in Jerusalem in July 1970 at a meeting of the late President Shazar's Study Circle on Diaspora Jewry. The lecture was followed by a discussion involving the late Arthur D. Morse, Piotr Rawicz, Manès Sperber, Alfred Kazin, and President Shazar himself. The whole evening was marked by the experience of Bergen-Belsen to which, under the great leadership of the late Josef Rosensaft, all above participants (except for the President), together with a group of survivors, had just made a pilgrimage.

While the lecture was adapted for publication from the tape, an effort was made, so far as was possible and seemed desirable, to preserve the spoken word of the occasion and thus the occasion itself.

The entire proceedings were first published (in Hebrew translation) by the Institute of Contemporary Jewry in the publications of the Study Circle on Diaspora Jewry held in the home of the President of Israel (5th Series) in 1972, and a revised English version was published in 1975 by the Institute of Contemporary Jewry in cooperation with the Cultural Department of the World Jewish Congress.

tion was asked either about the Holocaust or about the state of Israel.

Today this would no longer be possible. These sins of omission, if committed by *Commentary*, would provoke strong and bitter protests. Nor would *Commentary* itself commit them. Its editors would not dream today of raising some such fashionable subject as the so-called "God-is-dead" theology (now itself already dead, and never a Jewish subject), while at the same time ignoring the two events in our time that have jolted all things Jewish, religious belief included, as few other events in all of Jewish history.

What has happened to Diaspora Jewish consciousness to make this tremendous difference? The answer is obvious: the Six Day War. In the terrible weeks preceding and during the Six Day War two things leaped at once into the North American Jewish consciousness—the all too real threat of a second Holocaust in a single Jewish generation, and the immense anguish and guilt of the first Holocaust which had been festering beneath consciousness all these many years, repressed but not forgotten.

In this audience, composed of survivors and Israelis, I must begin with two questions. How does one who is not a survivor dare speak of the Holocaust? And how does one who dwells safely in Toronto, Canada, speak to Israelis? Please consider my words as representing a viewpoint of one who is outside—but involved and, I think, representative.

The task of a philosopher is to think as comprehensively as possible, formulate as precisely as he can, and put his conclusions down on paper. After a great deal of thinking about the watershed in Jewish consciousness produced by the Six Day War, I wrote down the following statement: *Only three epoch-making events have happened to the Jewish people since the fall of the Second Temple, and two of them have occurred in this generation: the Emancipation, the Nazi Holocaust, and the rise of the first Jewish state in nearly two millennia.*

When a statement like that is put down on paper, it should no longer be a random feeling, an irresponsible emotional reaction, the mere expression of a mood, but a responsible assertion.

Hence, I weighed and questioned it again and again, and tested it from many angles. And I realized that it is true: We, the Jewish people of today, have been cursed and blessed as perhaps no generation of Jews since Sinai itself. Two epoch-making events in a single generation! Rare is the generation of men anywhere that experiences even one.

What does it mean to live in the midst of an epoch-making event? Try to imagine what it must have been like to live in Paris during the French Revolution. Nobody went about ringing bells, saying, "Hear ye, hear ye, the French Revolution has broken out!" What did people see? Some buildings were burned, others stormed—events not uncommon in North America today. Empirically observed, burning buildings do not by themselves constitute epoch-making events. Then what *does* constitute such events? And how do the people involved *recognize* them for what they are? To the first question the vague answer must here suffice that somehow everything is transformed. In answer to the second, it must be admitted that perhaps many or even most people do *not* recognize that everything has somehow changed. But one must also insist that *until they do—until the epoch-making event is not only recognized but also responded to*—the event itself remains incomplete. To take the most momentous event in our own history—what if at Sinai itself there had been thunder and lightning, or even the voice of God, but no Jewish recognition and response? Or what if the first generation had said *Na'asseh V'nishma'* ("We shall do and hear") but the next had forgotten?

How long does it take to respond? It depends. In the case of the first epoch-making event mentioned above, the Emancipation, one would have to reply, "Very long indeed," and we shall find later on that the response is not complete even now. Yet the beginnings of a response must surely come at once, unless the event *itself* is to be lost forever. To turn to the events of our own time, I can think of few possibilities more tragic than that these should pass us by—and leave no impact on future Jewish generations. What if the Holocaust had happened and the next generation forgot? What if the state of Israel had arisen and Jews throughout the Diaspora went on with business as usual?

Yet here I come to you as a witness from North American Jewry; perhaps not from the majority—when have we ever thought in terms of majorities?—but from what may be called the community of the committed. These consider this an age of urgency, and precisely in response to the two epoch-making events in contemporary Jewish history.

That, of course, brings us to the first and most agonizing question of all. One can repeat the words, "Remember Dachau!" But how does one remember? How does one express the inexpressible, respond to the incomprehensible? To raise these questions in the presence of survivors makes someone like myself who is not one of them, wish to sit down and not say another word, which is what I almost did the first time a group of survivors asked me to speak about it. And yet, if *only* survivors can remember and respond, then the event will die with them. *And this must not happen.* So we must dare.

And so we went to Bergen-Belsen. We saw the biblical words on the memorial, "Earth, cover not the blood shed upon them," in the midst of acres of peaceful, beautiful grass which did just that. What a terrible, intolerable, unacceptable contradiction! And it seemed as if the earth itself must explode all that beautiful grass, refusing to cover the horror done by human criminals, and unable to still the anguish suffered by the human victims. And there one stands and endures the contradiction, in helpless anger, pain, and guilt.

There is no escape for us from this helpless endurance. A pagan might escape from it, and indeed it is perhaps the essence of paganism to deny all uniqueness—the uniqueness of crimes and the uniqueness of anguish, as well as that of acts of holiness and moments of joy—and to assert that the rhythm of nature covers it all. Yet a Jew knows about memory and about uniqueness. He knows that the unique crime of the Nazi Holocaust must never be forgotten—and, above all, that the rescuing for memory of even a single innocent tear is a holy task.

This much, at least, we must demand that Christians share with us Jews, for Christians, like Jews, know about uniqueness. When the ancient pagans heard the message of the dying and risen Christ they replied that they had known all along that the gods keep dying and rising, dying and rising. But the Christians replied in turn that the Christ, having risen, would die no more. (This is what theologians refer to as the "scandal of particularity.") Thus we might expect—indeed, must demand—that whatever response Christians may find themselves able to give to the Nazi Holocaust, they will in any case refuse refuge in a paganism that denies all uniqueness and lets the grass of nature cover it all.

Yet precisely this sort of denial abounds in North America on every side. The scandal of the particularity of Auschwitz and Bergen-Belsen is evaded by all sorts of comparisons, and that these comparisons *are* evasions is clear when one considers the comparisons actually made. Even when Hiroshima, Dresden, or Vietnam are mentioned in this connection, it would be far better that each tragedy should be viewed in its own terms; the speedy generalizations I have in mind avoid the particularity of each. What is more, far more indiscriminate comparisons and analogies are being made. Indeed, in an article widely reprinted in the North American student press, a lecturer, Jewish himself incidentally, has seen fit to compare the situation of the student on the American campus with that of the victims of Auschwitz. Here is an extreme case, not only of flight from the scandal of the particularity of the Nazi Holocaust but also of Jewish self-hatred.

That the Nazi Holocaust was unique needs no proving to the present audience: indeed, its members might quite justifiably resent such a proof, as if it were not evident that something quite different from the tragedies mentioned occurred when Eichmann diverted trains sorely needed by the Nazis for military purposes in order to send Jews to their death. Evil as a means to an end is one thing, evil for evil's sake, even at the risk of self-destruction, quite another. We have been told of the "banality" of Eichmann's evil, and I will not go into the merits of this assertion. For the one thing that matters is obvious—that when Eichmann declared that he would jump laughing into his grave, knowing that he had murdered millions of Jews, he gloried in the very opposite of the banal, a demonic, groundless exaltation of death and destruction which is ultimately inexplicable.

As rational beings we find it difficult to accept this last-named conclusion. More specifically, the academics among those present here who are devoting their lives to the study of the Holocaust surely try not only to discover and preserve the records of what happened but also to explain how such an incredible crime was possible; and we must indeed be quite relentless in our inquiries as to how Christian, German, and European antisemitism provided conditions without which the Holocaust could not have happened. Yet even in his ordinary research the historian is always tempted to explain away what he seeks to explain. In the case of the Holocaust, each explanation is false, if not downright obscene, unless it is accompanied by a sense of utter inadequacy. And when one has just come from Bergen-Belsen, all the explanations one has ever heard or read about seem to vanish like smoke.

Yet evasion, and evasion-by-explanation, seems a possibility even when one is present in this hell. At Belsen we were handed a memorial book which contains addresses given by German political leaders at previous rallies of remembrance. Doubtless these were all well intended; yet most were quick to draw lessons and to resort to categories that obscured rather than shed light on the uniqueness of the crime. The sense of inexplicable horror was missing.

II

Perhaps we must not be harsh in judging this kind of escapism. (Who among us can *wholly* avoid it?) Still, we must recognize it for what it is—and in the case of Jews no less than of non-Jews. An article of mine on the Holocaust was criticized by a Jew in Washington who wrote that Auschwitz was only half the story, and that the other half was Vietnam. The obvious reply was, of course, that I had not written about Vietnam because Vietnam had not been my subject, and that the least that one might demand is that Auschwitz be considered as a story in itself. This Jew, though safe in Washington, was running away from the Holocaust.

One cannot be so sure that the same is true of those young Jews in North America who care very deeply about Vietnam and not at all about the Holocaust. Certainly what they *say* is entirely different. They say, "Why bother with ancient history?" and it is at least true enough that this "history" cannot be as alive to them as to those of us who lived through it. (Once on a Vietnam protest march the first thing I heard was a youngster saying to me, "Don't you think this is the most wicked war in all of history?" and I felt like leaving right then and there but didn't—the youngster didn't know.) Still, with all due regard for the much-publicized generation gap, we must ask whether we can take at face value what these young Jews are saying. Is the Holocaust really ancient history to them? Or is it a case of un- conscious escape from the singled-out Jewish condition—an escape that may move from self-abnegation to self-hatred? If the first were the whole truth why is it that of the many who protest against the Vietnam war few protest on behalf of Soviet Jewry, and fewer still come out firmly and boldly in behalf of Israel? Now we have even Jews supporting al-Fatah. (Someone has shrewdly observed that this is the Jewish equivalent to trying to "pass for white.") I must confess that I detect traces of uncon- scious Jewish escape even in those young Jews who confront the Holocaust but react chiefly through accusations against the older Jewish generation—as if the primary (albeit, to be sure, not exclusive) guilt does not lie elsewhere.

So among Jews as well as non-Jews there is escapism. If the kind I presently speak of has a particular hold, it is because it looks innocuous, indeed, highly moral. *It is escapism into "universalism."* At Auschwitz Jews were singled out as Jews— and among the next generation there are those, who, in their own minds universalists, in fact seek escape from the singled- out Jewish condition. In reacting in this manner, they inter- nalize the hostility, if not of our implacable enemies, at least of our dubious friends. The survivors here taught me that while at

Belsen our enemies tortured and murdered them as Jews, our friends, the moment they arrived, honored them as Frenchmen, Belgians, Dutchmen, and the like. Those who erected the International Memorial at Belsen put on inscriptions in many languages, but forgot Hebrew and Yiddish—and did not mend this error until the survivors themselves protested. Escapism into universalism *looks* innocuous, but is not. It is not universal. Not only does it induce Jews to fight for all sorts of causes except Jewish ones. It also produces in Jewish hearts and souls "identity crises" which after the Holocaust are particularly tragic.

There are other forms of escapism, which derive not from Jewishness but are escapism nonetheless. I myself for many years compared the Holocaust to prior tragedies in Jewish history, avoided the fundamental differences, thus reaching the comforting conclusion that Judaism and the Jewish faith are not called into question in a unique, unprecedented way. Yet there *is* a radical, fundamental, shattering difference. Prior to the Holocaust, Jews died for their faith, believing that God needs martyrs; Negro Christians died for their "race," finding comfort in a faith not at issue. *The more than one million Jewish children murdered by the Nazis died, not because of their faith, nor for reasons unrelated to the Jewish faith but rather on account of the Jewish faith of their grandparents.* Had these latter not raised their children as Jews, then their remote offspring might have been among the Nazi murderers; they would not have been among their Jewish victims. *Like Abraham of old, European Jews sometime in the nineteenth century brought a child sacrifice, by obeying the mere minimum commandment of the Jewish faith of raising Jewish children; only unlike Abraham they did not know what they were doing—and there was no reprieve.*[1]

As before, I am quoting a statement put down after much thought. Only this time the problem is not whether the statement is true. The problem is whether the truth is not so terrible

---

1. See above, p. 30 and p. 47 n. 1

that, rather than be uttered, it should be concealed with the utmost care forever after. For what possible effect can the disclosure of this truth have except to make Jews flee from their Jewish condition lest their remote offspring be doomed to a second Mauthausen or Buchenwald? What else can the result be except that Jews may voluntarily disappear in one way after Hitler's attempt to make them disappear in another?

III

Yet in these extreme straits we all, I think, can make a radically astonishing, wholly liberating discovery. For twelve long years the world had been divided into those bent on the murder of every Jewish man, woman, and child on earth, and those lukewarm or indifferent. For twelve long years the world had conspired to make every Jew wish to flee from his singled-out condition in total disarray, and in every way he could. Yet to this unprecedented threat to Jewish survival and sanity the Jewish people have responded with a reaffirmation of their Jewishness which, however, fragmentary and inadequate, has been, under the circumstances, little short of miraculous.

Thus, the terrible truth I have referred to makes us view contemporary Jewish existence in a revolutionary perspective. For twenty years we have told ourselves: How miserable is bourgeois Jewish life in America! How puny a response to the Holocaust is UJA! How are we to resurrect our spirits even in the light of the great and heroic Israeli enterprise, after the European tragedy? All this is true. Yet out of the darkness of despair there arises a revolutionary question: *Where in the entire world of today is there a faith and a faithfulness that can compare to that of the Jew who, however inadequately, reaffirms his Jewishness after the Holocaust?* Where are witnesses comparable to the Jew who stays committed to his Jewishness, who in this very act says No! to the demons of Auschwitz, and who stakes on this No! his own life, the lives of his children, and the lives of his children's children? The result of entering into the terrible darkness of Auschwitz, for all those of us who emerge reaffirming our Jewishness, cannot but be *a love for our people of which we should otherwise be incapable—and an end to all Jewish "identity crises" forever after.*

I once heard Josef Rosensaft say that the Jew now has a second *Sh'ma Yisrael:* Never again a Belsen or an Auschwitz! It is true. The survivors live by this. So do all Jews who face up to the Holocaust and persist in their Jewishness. Indeed, it would appear that all the old divisions between us—religious and secularist, Orthodox and non-Orthodox, Diaspora Jew and Israeli—are now superseded by a division between all those Jews who, in one form or another, run away, and those who face up to the forces that denied the Jew the right to existence itself, and who thus, by the simple act of reaffirming their Jewishness, defy the devil himself.

Where have Jews—rich and poor, learned and ignorant, pious and secularist—found all these years the strength for that monumental defiance and testimony? Indeed, where did Jews at Belsen itself, knowing full well that the devil had come there as an antisemite rather than a racist, gain the strength to reject Jewish self-hatred, and instead to sing Yiddish songs, tell Jewish stories, and remain totally unwavering in their Jewishness? How was it possible that there was a total Jewish liberated self-acceptance in the midst of the most extreme and incomprehensible Jew-hatred that the world has ever known?

Elie Wiesel has dared to compare Auschwitz to Sinai itself and added that we are not listening. We may shrink from such a comparison and yet must take it seriously. For to the questions I have raised there seems no answer except that a Commanding Voice speaks to all of us, and indeed spoke at Auschwitz and Belsen itself, bidding us to affirm our Jewishness and in this very act say No! to the No! of the Holocaust; to live despite and because of death; to sing despite and because of the mourning. And the fundamental division between Jews after the Holocaust of which I spoke divides those who listen, however fragmentarily, from those who stop their ears. The words *Am Yisrael Chai* have always signified joy and defiance. Today they signify radical surprise as well. Whether from the lips of religious or secularist Jews, the words have become sacred.

IV

And so we came from Belsen to Jerusalem. A staggering trip. Twenty-five years ago, an eternity between them. Today, a trip of a few hours. The eternity between them remains, and we must retain it in our souls lest we blaspheme. Yet there is truth also in the connection. Jerusalem by itself produces radical astonishment. The astonishment is inescapable when Auschwitz is juxtaposed with Jerusalem. And juxtapose the two we must, however much we may tremble at the thought of abusing Jerusalem for cheap comfort. For the whole Israeli nation is collectively what each survivor is individually: a testimony *in behalf of all mankind* to life against the demons of death; a hope and a determination that there must be, shall be, will be no second Auschwitz; and on this hope and this determination every man, woman, and child in Israel stakes his life.

In Israel one hears again and again the statement: "I am not religious." The visitor from abroad, and above all he who has come from Belsen, is astonished by *the religious quality of the "secularist" Israeli Jew.* The hope and courage in the midst of fear (and of circumstances warranting fear), the fidelity to a millennial history in a world that has yet to learn that Jewish history did not end two thousand years ago, the commitment to the renewal of a people against overwhelming odds—what are these qualities but religious by all except narrow standards? Add to this the incredible fact that Jerusalem came to new life after Auschwitz, and there remains a radical astonishment that is beyond all adequate utterance and is the innermost source of religious life. You who live with the epoch-making event called "Israel" may be tempted to deny this in your inevitable daily struggles and conflicts. To the visitor (who is spared these struggles and comes upon Israel suddenly) more than poetic truth attaches to the pictures of "secularist" and Orthodox Jews embracing in front of the Wall.

V

And so we shall return to our homes in North America—for the time being at least, for in these stirring times few of us can say with certainty whether the pull and the love of Israel may not become irresistible. We must ask: What response to the epoch-making events in contemporary Jewish history is required of us in the Diaspora? Here we come back to the first above-mentioned epoch-making event, the Emancipation, and my assertion that it is still incomplete. Only a few years ago this assertion would have struck most North American Jews as absurd, for until quite recently it has been easy to be a Jew in North America—certainly easier than anywhere else. After all, in America it is (or used to be) as difficult to be against "religion" as against motherhood; religious pluralism is a true part of the American genius, and since Hitler it has been hard to be for antisemitism and even to be against Zionism. Since the Six Day War, however, Jews in America, perhaps for the first time, are being *tested;* it takes *something* to stand up for one's Jewishness—and the key issue is Israel.

I am sure you realize that Arab propagandists in the United States and Canada have been increasingly effective ever since their discovery that Shukairy's talk about Jewish genocide in Israel was not well received. The surprising fact, however, is not their change in propaganda but rather its amazing success—a success surely as surprising to them as it is shocking to us. I am sorry to have to tell you that when a Jew in the United States or Canada nowadays asserts that the existence and security of the state of Israel is not negotiable, he is likely to be told that there is "another side" to this story, or that non-Jews must be "free to criticize the policies of the state of Israel." Not one of these people would confuse the right to criticize the policies of, say, Canada or Russia or Greece with the right to call the existence of these states into question. Hence after much painful searching of mind and soul one is driven to the inescapable conclusion that even the Western world has not yet fully accepted the sovereign existence of Jews in a state of their own; or, to put it otherwise and more bluntly, that in most if not all cases "anti-Zionism," in the year 1970, is antisemitism. A Christian friend of mine, Roy Eckardt, has defined antisemitic statements, 1970 style, as beginning, "Israel has a right to exist but . . ."

So Jews in North America are being tested in these trying times. I am happy to say, however, that while many fail or waver, others are rising to the challenge in impressive numbers. Is it because of the Holocaust that they do not waver in their support of Israel? Or, on the contrary, is the fact of Israel bringing the long-repressed memory of the Holocaust to our consciousness? In either case, it is not true that the memory of the Holocaust becomes dimmer as the event recedes in time. The opposite is the case. Perhaps twenty-five years had to pass before we found some power to respond.

The long-delayed power to respond is now beginning to confront us in the West with an ineluctable imperative—to complete the hitherto incomplete event of Jewish emancipation. We all recall the fatal post-French Revolution emancipation slogan: "To the Jews as men we give everything, to the Jews as Jews we give nothing." Today it is not difficult to detect the antisemitism in this formula, and to perceive the Jewish "identity crises" which must result when Jews themselves accept the validity of that formula. (How can one split oneself up so as to be a "man abroad" and a "Jew at home"?) With this detection there goes, in the age of Auschwitz and Jerusalem, the duty to reject this formula with all its implications. Our response today must be: For more than a millennium and a half the nations of Europe oppressed the Jewish people—how did they dare attach conditions to our freedom when at last they repented of their sins? *Only the as yet incomplete emancipation of the Jewish people as Jews will make our liberation complete; and since no one ever hands out freedom as a present, this event requires a total Jewish self-liberation.* Our sages tell us that the saddest part of our slavery in Egypt was that our forefathers had become used to it.

The times are ripe for Jewish liberation and self-liberation in North America, and this is doubtless in large measure because of the Black struggle, in many ways similar, for total liberty. At the same time, there are differences as well, and I fear that Christians are not nearly so ready to listen to Jews in this matter as whites are ready to listen to Blacks—partly because whites and Blacks are both Christian, and partly because while there can be no doubt about dark skin there continues to be doubt, among Jews and non-Jews alike, as to whether Jews are a people. The fatal Emancipation slogan is still with us. Hence some of our militant young Jews have coined the slogan: "Zionism is the liberation movement of the Jewish people."

This slogan arouses some misgivings, for it is, of course, once again a borrowed one, and the whole point of radical Jewish liberation is that Jewish existence must no longer be defined and justified in terms borrowed from alien sources. Yet the best of our young people are clearly aware of this when they make use of this slogan. Thus they do *not* mean, at one extreme, that Zionism is for the persecuted Jews of Poland and Russia only; nor, at the other extreme, that Aliyah alone can emancipate the Jews of North America. They *do* mean that their Jewishness must be liberated from the definitions and sufferance of others, and that in this age the crucial test of their own emancipated condition is an uncompromising commitment to the secure survival and flourishing of Israel. It is not long ago that such a commitment seemed to be a merely vicarious Jewishness. Today, it frees our own Jewishness from all false, externally imposed "identity crises." Even at its minimum it is a commitment to Jewish survival without "ifs" and "buts." To the question still being heard, "What is the point of mere Jewish survival?" we reply, in the words of Milton Himmelfarb, *"After the Holocaust, let no one call Jewish survival 'mere.'"*

One hears a great deal today about "alienated" Jews in North America, with "identity crises" for which psychiatrists seem to have no cure. In Israel one probably hears far less about North American Jews who are increasingly determined to live with nothing less than an undiluted, unapologetic, joyous Jewishness. On my own campus *yarmulkahs* have become a common sight, as have protest marches on behalf of Soviet Jewry. My university has just initiated a program of Jewish studies, with a response exceeding our fondest expectations. The genuine Jewishness manifest in these phenomena cuts across traditional barriers such as old and young, Orthodox, Conservative, and Reform, and even religious and secularist. It reveals, as it were, a secular holiness which has crept by stealth, as will the Messiah, into our midst. Here are Jews who have learned that, in the age in which Auschwitz has happened and Jerusalem has become Jewish, no self-respecting Jew outside Israel can *remain* outside unless he is *totally* liberated from the definitions and the sufferance of others.

Most decidedly such Jews would not have appeared on the American scene were it not for the existence of Israel. Yet, mysteriously in an age in which so many things Jewish are mysterious, the relation of giving and receiving seems to be mutual. One of your distinguished scholars, after a recent visit with us, told us that he had had to come to North America in order to rediscover the sacredness of Israel. Perhaps your recognition of the Jewish strength you give us, serves in turn to reinforce your own Jewish strength. As for the Holocaust, it lives in us all. A hundred and fifty years ago the great Jew, Heinrich Heine, concluded sadly that Jewish survival was a lost cause. We all must sometimes wonder whether the odds against Jewish survival are not too great. Even in such moments of weakness the children of the Holocaust make us reject Heine's conclusion. Jewish survival has become holy even for "secularists"—and the holy is not negotiable.

One asks what Jews a thousand years from now will think of our own Jewish generation. One asks so vast a question with fear and trembling—so deep is our involvement with our here and now, and so uncertain is the future of the whole human race. Even so, one thing is sure. Among ourselves, only the professional historians have statistics about those Jews who defected after the catastrophe of the destruction of the Temple two thousand years ago; every one of us remembers those Jews who did not defect, whose faith and steadfastness is the cause of our own existence, and who invoked in that dark time the biblical words, "I shall not die but live, and declare the works of God." Surely Jews a thousand years from now will not remember the alienated and defecting Jews but rather those who renewed their Jewishness in whatever form they could in the midst of the crisis of our own time. Surely they will say, "Those were the Jews who at that time said, 'I shall not die but live'; those were the Jews who declared the works of God."

11. Jewish "Ethnicity" in "Mature Democratic Societies": Ideology and Reality

I

The general purpose of this conference is to examine Judaism and the Jewish experience, with a view to drawing out their relevance and significance for contemporary men and institutions, both within and without the Jewish community.

The general program of this conference is in startling contrast to the ideas suggested to me for treatment in my own contribution. I quote in part as follows:

> Emphasis [is] to be placed on the anomaly of maintaining group identity in a secularized, universalist culture. Is there a conflict between maintaining strong ethnic ties and membership in a society dedicated to civic unity? What is the rationale for supporting the "people of peoples" conception in mature democratic societies? Is maintenance of an ethnic subculture a genuine ideal or a merely temporary necessity? What about conflicts arising from possible tensions between ethnic loyalty and devotion to the common good? Ethnic loyalty and the ideal of universal brotherhood? . . . What is to

Originally published under the title "The Survival of the Jews" in *The Center Magazine*, November-December 1973, pp. 15–28. I have restored my original title. The paper was delivered at a conference on Jews and Judaism sponsored by the Santa Barbara Center for the Study of Democratic Institutions.

be said in reply to those who reject the claims of ethnicity in favor of a larger loyalty, either to the nation or mankind in general? What case can be made for the continued existence of ethnic subcultures when members of the group are offered free access to the general culture?

The first statement invites us to consider Judaism and Jewish experience freely and in their own right, unencumbered by defensive looks to the right or the left, and indeed to assume, possibly rashly, that in their unadulterated uniqueness Judaism and Jewish experience may have universal significance at this time. The second statement, in contrast, is thoroughly defensive. It does look to the right and the left. And it assumes, without a shadow of doubt or a murmur of protest, that terms such as "general culture," "common good," and "mature democratic society" are *absolutely* normative; hence that it is in such corresponding terms as "ethnicity," "subculture," and the like that Jewish existence must be both classified and justified if it can be justified at all. And this procedure is so certain of its validity that the *Jewish* "subculture" is not so much as mentioned.

I was urged to feel free to reject some or all the ideas suggested to me for treatment. If I do not make use of this freedom, it is because the conflict between the first and the second statement seems to me to reflect with total accuracy the current conception of the Jewish community in the Western world, both on the part of society at large and on the part of Jews themselves. On the one hand, there are in this age of Auschwitz and a Jewish Jerusalem many signs indicating that the old Jewish defensiveness is crumbling, that present Jewish experience has a unique message to the world which only waits to be spelled out, and indeed that there are some (though not many) in the non-Jewish world who can hardly wait. On the other hand, the old defensiveness is still a deadening weight in the Jewish community, while the outside world (which has caused or occasioned the defensiveness in the first place) has as yet little awareness of what it has been doing. The task of either side to rid itself of the old stance is rendered all the more difficult by the fact that our conceptual frameworks are, virtually without exception, themselves part of that stance. In asking without prejudice what Jewish existence is today, and may and should be tomorrow, we shall have to separate ideology from reality, and in so doing often grope for as yet nonexistent concepts.

II

In 1955 Will Herberg's *Protestant-Catholic-Jew* predicted the impending disappearance of all or most "ethnic" groups in the United States in what was not, as had hitherto been generally assumed, a single but rather a "triple melting pot." To be sure, according to Hansen's law "what the son of the immigrant had wished to forget the grandson wished to remember.[1] However, he would and could not recapture his grandfather's Norwegian, Polish, or Yiddish linguistic culture but only his religion, and this latter merged him with other Americans of the same religious identity. Hence, there were emerging three ways, increasingly equal in legitimacy, of being American—the Protestant, the Catholic, and the Jewish—each all the more legitimately American because the old "European" antagonisms had been left behind.

Few prophecies have ever been so quickly and thoroughly confounded. Protestant and Catholic Blacks have ignored their fideistic differences in behalf of their common liberation. Puerto Ricans, Mexicans, and Indians are beginning to follow their example. And, Hansen's law or no Hansen's law, even third-generation "Middle America" is rediscovering "ethnicities" that had been sociologized out of existence. As for Jews—whose formerly "passionate Zionism" had supposedly since 1948 dissolved itself into a "vague, though by no means insincere friendliness to the state of Israel"[2]—they have discov-

---

1. Will Herberg, *Protestant-Catholic-Jew* (New York: Doubleday, 1955), p. 273 et passim.
2. Ibid., p. 205.

ered ever since the Six Day War a love for Jerusalem whose
intensity they had not hitherto suspected, and this love has now
spilled over into support for the oppressed Jews of the Soviet
Union, in which militancy is shown not only by the Jewish
"counter-culture," but also, unexpectedly, by the notoriously
defensive "Jewish Establishment." Indeed, even Yiddish is
experiencing a revival of sorts. The murdered language of the
murdered millions, this once secular language is becoming as
sacred as the memory of those who had spoken it.

Why have the predictions of a serious and in many ways
sound work been so quickly confounded? We need not look far
for an answer. The book said much that was and remains true,
but also what people at the time, including and perhaps above
all the author, wanted to believe. Christians wanted to believe
that the age-old but un-American Christian hatred of the Jewish
people was not so much Christian as merely "European." Jews
wanted to believe that their Judaism was as closely related to
apple pie as the Protestantism and Catholicism of their friends
and neighbors. In short, the book mixed ideology with insight,
and in so doing ignored, belittled, or papered over real tensions
in North America. Blacks and Puerto Ricans were admittedly
unassimilated; but this admission did not upset or even shake
the triple melting pot.[3] Admittedly, too, antisemitism had not
yet wholly vanished in North America; yet it was considered
insignificant enough to produce on the part of the author an
attitude of condescension toward organized Jewish efforts to
combat it.[4] Indeed, astounding though it is in retrospect,
neither Nazism nor the state of Israel were important enough to
deserve a listing in the index, and (unless this reader has
missed it) the Holocaust was not so much as mentioned. No
wonder such ideologizing of yesterday has found its nemesis
today in a plethora of "ethnicities" and "particularisms," the
ironic climax of which is that not a few of them rival Herberg's

---

3. Ibid., pp. 127–29.
4. Herberg actually confuses "defensiveness" with "defense"—as if antisemitism in America existed only in the Jewish "minority consciousness" and
not outside it.

theological perspective with theological (or pseudotheological) perspectives of their own.[5]

The fate of Herberg's book (and of the ideologizing beliefs that it articulates) must give us pause. The swiftness of contemporary events may in any case overwhelm our own present concern with "ethnicity" as speedily as they did Herberg's "triple melting pot." We may at least guard against this danger by means of a resolute effort to eliminate ideologizing from our perceptions and judgments. In Herberg's own case, the ideologizing was doubtless inspired by a desire to classify Jewish existence completely but decently in the light of categories provided by the modern world, and this desire was satisfied by the thesis that the open society of immigrant-America had succeeded where the closed society of tradition-ridden Europe had thus far largely failed. Could it be that our current, diametrically opposite concern with Jewish "ethnicity" is equally shot through with ideologizing, and, paradoxical though it may seem, that its mainspring is exactly the same?

It will gradually emerge that such is precisely the case with virtually all the ideas suggested to me for treatment in this paper. For the present it suffices to assert that it is certainly true of a good many current manifestations of Jewish "ethnicity" in the American Jewish community, of which some on the campus are the most widely advertised. This is true whenever Jewish "particularism" is considered acceptable in America only because particularism-as-such is considered acceptable; and whenever only because all "ethnic" groups should rise against "the system" Jewish "ethnics" may and should do likewise. Herberg's fideism had assimilated "Jew" to "Protestant" and "Catholic" beyond the bounds of legitimacy.[6] Much current

5. Vol. 9 in the series *New Theology*, Martin E. Marty and Dean G. Peerman, eds. (New York: Macmillan, 1972), has the following subtitle: "Theology in the Context of the New Particularisms—Nation, Tribe, Race, Clan, Ethnic Group, Gender, and Generation."

6. The most glaring example is the assertion that "the People Israel" is "the equivalent in Judaism" to "the Church" in Christianity (p. 272), an assertion which is in no way redeemed from absurdity by the theological context in which it is made. The statement was made exactly ten years after the most devastating revelation in all of history that Christians may choose martyrdom as

Jewish "ethnicism" in America follows a totally parallel course, thus paradoxically compromising or even submerging precisely that Jewish uniqueness that it seeks to preserve.

Such an outcome is inevitable so long as Jewish existence in the modern world is authenticated, not directly—that is, in terms of its intrinsic capacity to speak in and to the modern world—but only indirectly—that is, in terms of standards provided by the modern world whose absolute validity is presupposed. So long as it is assumed without a shadow of doubt that the Jewish people must appear *unilaterally* before the bar of the modern world and some set or other of its standards, we shall misdefine our topic into some euphemism such as "the Jewish problem" or "the Jewish question,"[7] phrases shot through with evaluation; we shall give answers shot through with defensiveness and ideologizing; and, to the extent to which this is true, it will not make too much difference what the answers are.

III

This unilateralism has been with us ever since the Age of the Emancipation—ever since the men of the French Revolution proposed to give to Jews "as men" everything, and to them "as Jews," nothing. This proposal had two hidden assumptions. One was that Jews were an anachronism as Jews, and on trial as men. The other was that the faith of Jews could fairly be judged, and their humanity be properly put on trial, by a civilization that had oppressed them for nearly two millennia.[8]

---

individuals, whereas Jews (when they are free to choose at all) are faced with the grim fact that their own choice involves their children and their children's children. In fairness it ought to be added that in 1955 not many Jewish theologians were able to confront the Holocaust.

7. There are, to be sure, Jewish problems. However, "the" Jewish problem is either a figment of antisemitic ideology or the product of antisemitic activity. In either case "the" problem is antisemitism.

8. This paragraph partly quotes a passage from my *Encounters between Judaism and Modern Philosophy: A Preface to Future Jewish Thought* (New York: Basic Books, 1973), p. 4. The book tackles some philosophical aspects of the problems outlined in this section.

The French post-revolutionary proposal is a fact. The assumptions concealed in it are a matter of militant hindsight knowledge. Neither then nor thereafter was the emancipating modern world—whether in its Christian, nationalist, liberal-secularist, or communist forms—ever willing or able to consider seriously the possibility that it had no right to qualify the emancipation of its erstwhile victims; that, on the contrary, any *genuine* emancipation of the Jewish people required, as its dialectical counterpart, a deep self-examination if indeed not self-transformation on the part of the emancipators. As for the Jewish recipients of Emancipation, they were, if they did not distrustfully reject it, for the most part too intoxicated with the promise (as well as too powerless outwardly and thus inwardly as well) to protest against its qualification, or in many cases even to notice it.

This qualification in the modern emancipation of the Jewish people was to do deep and lasting damage to the moral health of modern Jewry. No less importantly, it manifested profound weaknesses in the moral strength of the modern world. To grimmer manifestations of both we shall turn in a while. For the present, two illustrations may suffice, one taken from the right, the other, from the left.

When in the 1880s a wave of antisemitism swept Germany (much to the dismay of German Jews who had believed themselves at long last to be accepted even in Germany), the foremost German philosopher of the time, Eduard von Hartmann, laid aside his philosophical tomes long enough to compose a pamphlet in defense of the Jews. In short, a friend.[9]

---

9. That his was a dubious friendship is shown by Hugo Bergmann, "Eduard von Hartmann und die Judenfrage in Deutschland," *Leo Baeck Yearbook* V (London: East and West Library, 1960), pp. 177–97. Thus, e.g., Hartmann does not hesitate to assert that the emancipation of German Jews had an "implicit" condition, and that Jews had failed to live up to that condition simply by persisting in "feeling Jewish tribal solidarity" which was a "rival" to the German national feeling (p. 185). Thus, he differed from the antisemites of his day only in his view that German Jews needed more time to get rid of their Jewish "feelings"; in his hope that they would succeed in so doing; and in his clearly expressed opinion that the antisemites hindered this process when it should be furthered.

Yet this friend expressed one reservation. If faced with the choice of saving the life of a fellow German who was not Jewish, or a fellow Jew who was not German, the professor confessed to being in doubt as to whose life a German Jew would save. And the German-Jewish periodical reviewing the pamphlet in effect replied: "*Aber Herr Professor,* how can you doubt it! Of course we would save the life of the fellow German!"[10]

From right-wing nationalism we turn to left-wing universalism. Rosa Luxembourg had three strikes against her. She was a Pole, a woman, and a Jewess. Nevertheless, with her outstanding character and intellect she became the leading leftist in Germany during and after the first World War, until her murder at the hand of rightist gangsters. Yet this outstanding person wrote to a Zionist friend from prison as follows: "Why do you pester me with your Jewish sorrow? There is no room in my heart for the Jewish troubles." According to the historian Jacob Talmon who reports the episode, she then goes on to speak eloquently of the Chinese coolies and the Bantus in South Africa. Talmon laconically concludes: "Twenty-five years later, after the Germans had occupied it, there was not a single Jew left alive in Rosa's native Zamosc."[11]

Ideally, von Hartmann's Jewish reviewer should have rejected the inhuman choice with which he was presented, and in so doing he would have been a faithful Jewish witness against the fatal kind of modern single-loyalty nationalism that was to produce the World War I, then escalate into Nazi totalitarianism, and in the process nearly destroy the modern world. Ideally, too, Rosa Luxembourg's heart should have been large enough to include concern for all suffering peoples, her own included, regardless of the dictates of leftist ideologies. Yet, neither Jew can legitimately be criticized in hindsight. For the modern world on both right and left singled out Jews for excep-

---

10. Ibid., pp. 186 ff. The actual tactic of the reviewer was to evade Hartmann's question and instead to assure him that German Jews disliked Polish Jews.

11. J. Talmon, "The Jewish Intellectual in Politics," *Midstream,* January 1966, p. 10.

tionalist demands, requiring, on the right, that Jews be more German than Germans and more French than the French, and, on the left, that Jews, and Jews alone, be or become men-in-general. Both these exceptionalist demands were, of course, remnants of premodern antisemitism, too effectively disguised and transformed, however, to be easily recognized as such by either society at large or Jews themselves. The result was that countless Jews on both right and left fought bravely against antisemitism, while at the same time unconsciously submitting to it.

Has America been different? This question, traumatic in the Jewish mind ever since a once-civilized European country exploded in an unprecedented orgy of Jew-hatred, permits no simplicist answers. On the one hand, the land of immigrants offered Jewish immigrants a home on terms more equal than tradition-bound Europe; unencumbered by medieval traditions, it was largely unencumbered by medieval antisemitism also. (Hence Herberg's "triple melting pot" and our current classifications of Jewish "ethnicity" within schemes of American "ethnic pluralism" each contain a measure of truth.) Yet on the other hand, America too has exacted its price. To be sure, the price seemed a just price—that of becoming American—which all had equally to pay. Yet some were more equal than others, and the fact that this inequality remained ideologically disguised was to have drastic consequences.

The official doctrine of the United States of America is and largely remains the Enlightenment propositions that all are created equal, that each is to count as one and none as more than one, and that man is essentially man-in-general. American man therefore is general at least vis-à-vis all the "European" immigrant differences. That this doctrine, certainly not without reality, was nevertheless shot through with ideology from the start was not fully uncovered until late in this century, when the general *Homo Americanus* was revealed as being in fact a particular man, namely, paradigmatically a White Anglo-Saxon Protestant and derivatively one making every effort to become as WASP-like as possible. It is not without historical logic or justice that this revelation should be largely thanks to the militancy of the Blacks, that is, the one group to which total assimilation was impossible and, moreover—such is the power of ideology—which in the collective proposition that all men are created equal had been systematically forgotten if not excluded.

This mixture of reality and ideology in America has produced numerous characteristically American tensions and confusions—and very special ones in the American Jewish community. Thus, on the one hand, one may doubt whether any European Jewish community to this day walks as uprightly as the Jewish community in America did virtually from the start. Yet, on the other, one may also doubt whether any Jewish community cast away as quickly and recklessly vast parts of its Jewish heritage, mistakenly believing itself to be merely Americanizing it when in fact it emasculated or even unconsciously Protestantized that heritage. To this day, one may observe the paradoxical contrast between the vigor of the United Jewish Appeal (without doubt the greatest American Jewish collective achievement) and what has been called the wasteland of American Jewish educational institutions. Here is tension resulting from the mixture of reality and ideology. There is also confusion coupled with the tension. This is manifest in the unsurpassed Jewish commitment to the American separation of state and church, conjoined with considerable courage brought to the defense of altogether legitimate political Jewish interests—a conjunction that encourages the ideology that the community thus acting is either not acting *politically,* or else that it is not acting politically *as a community,* but merely as a collectivity of individuals most or all of whom happen to be Jewish.

A sociologist has recently given a portrayal of "the ambivalent American Jew" in which the Jewish community appears as perhaps more torn between the extremes of "integration" and "survival" than any other group of Americans.[12] American Blacks can only be black, and therefore can be first-class Americans only as Black Americans. Italian immigrants may "resist

12. Charles S. Liebman, *The Ambivalent American Jew* (Philadelphia: Jewish Publication Society, 1973), especially pp. 23–41.

acculturation" more strongly than Jews in the first generation, but since Italy is for them only of the past, this resistance tends to vanish in subsequent generations. The Amish, like the Jews, continue to resist acculturation; yet unlike the Jews, "they do not insist that, concurrently with their separateness, American society close its eyes to their distinctiveness in economic, political, and social considerations." In short, we learn that American Jews want to be, first, unlike the Amish, fully accepted; second, unlike the Blacks, accepted not in their "ethnic" distinctiveness, but simply as American individuals; third, that unlike the Italians, they consider their distinctiveness as somehow of the future as well as the past, thus aiming at group survival. Hence they are more "torn" between the poles of "integration" and "survival." They are also, our author observes, characteristically "denying the very existence of the tension."[13]

Since it thus seems that American Jews manifest in an extreme and therefore possibly paradigmatic form tensions common to many groups of Americans, it may therefore appear natural that a conference purportedly devoted to Judaism and Jewish experience should ask one contributor to address himself to such general questions as the possible conflict between "ethnic devotion" and "the common good"; reply to those who "reject the claims of ethnicity in favor of a larger loyalty, either to the nation or to mankind in general"; and make a "case" for the "continued existence of ethnic subcultures when members of the group are offered free access to the general culture."

Yet one should be lacking in reflection if one undertook to answer the questions instead of subjecting their very terms to a close scrutiny. Would the maintenance of a White Anglo-Saxon Protestant group identity—say, the Episcopal Church of the United States, or the United Church of Canada—be considered an "anomaly" in our "secularist universalist culture"? Would any decent person today, with Blacks rather than Jews in mind, dare to imply that a "common good" could *be* common unless it did full justice—or such justice as were possible—to the needs and legitimate demands of Black Americans? Is the very term

13. Ibid., pp. 23, 24, 27.

"subculture" not suspect precisely to the degree to which the corresponding term "general culture" represents an ideological distortion of what is in fact the dominant culture?[14] We need not question the questions any further (a task that could easily be accomplished) in order to suspect that they are asked of no other group of Americans with equal intensity, if indeed at all. The questioners consist of two groups. One, heirs of the French revolutionaries, continues to attach conditions to the liberation of the Jewish people. The other, heirs of Rosa Luxembourg and von Hartmann's Jewish reviewer, continues to be victimized by some version or other of the proposal that Jews "as men" are to be given everything, and Jews "as Jews," nothing.

There is, to be sure, a difference between Europe and North America. Frenchmen and Germans typically expected Jews to outdo themselves in gratitude for ceasing to be persecuted, that is, if right-wing, to excel all others in patriotism, and, if liberal or left-wing, to be the one and only group of men-in-general. (Contemporary Soviet Russia, the multinational nation *par excellence*, expects Jews alone to exist in the limbo of "mankind.") In contrast, North America expected Jews merely to privatize whatever part of their religio-cultural heritage they wished to preserve, while at the same time promising that everyone would count publicly as one and none as more than one. It is no wonder that Jewish immigrants responded enthusiastically to both the expectation and the promise, and to the extent to which the promise and the expectation were and could be realities Jewish emancipation in America has been a success. However, they were also (perhaps inevitably so) shot

---

14. Norman Podhoretz writes about his student experiences, respectively at the Jewish Theological Seminary and at Columbia University, as follows: "The demand being made on me as a student of Jewish culture was concrete, explicit, and unambiguous: 'Become a good Jew!' The demand being made on me as a student of Western Culture, by contrast was a seductively abstract and ideologized: 'Become a gentleman, a man of enlightened and gracious mind!' It is not that Columbia was being dishonest in failing to mention that this also meant 'Become a facsimile WASP!' In taking that corollary for granted, the college was simply being true to its own ethnic and class origins; and in nothing did this fidelity show itself more clearly than in the bland unconsciousness that accompanied it." *Making It* (New York: Random House, 1967) pp. 49–50.

through with ideology. Did the separation of state and church make a *total* end to Constantinian Christian imperialism? Had the New World rid itself *entirely* of the antisemitism of the old? It is surely not only the American idea but also a well-founded fear of "group prejudice" that makes American Jews demand to be treated simply as Americans. And it is surely this fear, together with the knowledge that Jewishness is not and cannot be either purely "private" or purely "religious," that gives rise to the tension between "integration" and "survival." And it is this mixture of ideology and reality in the American and the American Jewish mind that gives rise to the denial of "the very existence of the tension."

Many decades ago Martin Buber, here as elsewhere ahead of his time, criticized the modern world for having emancipated the Jewish people only as individuals and not as a people. His criticism remains valid to this day. However, the time is now ripe for the emancipation of the people. For the Nazi Holocaust has made this a moral necessity. And the rise of the first Jewish state in two millennia has made it a spiritual and political possibility.

IV

To refer to the Nazi Holocaust as a repudiation of the Jewish emancipation is an insult to the Middle Ages and the understatement of the century. Nevertheless this understatement is not without a measure of truth. A veritable gulf may yawn between the medieval proposition that the only good Jew is a dead Jew or a Christian,[15] and the Nazi proposition that the only good Jew is a dead Jew.[16] Nevertheless, the two propositions are logically and historically connected. For just as medieval Christendom slandered, persecuted, and expelled Jews as Jews, so it was precisely as Jews—not as species of the genus "minority" or "inferior race"—that Nazism murdered

15. A deliberately hyperbolic formulation by the Christian theologian C. Rylaarsdam.
16. Hitler is reported to have recognized one good Jew—the Viennese writer Otto Weininger, whose Jewish self-hatred was so extreme as to make him commit suicide in his early twenties.

them. And it was because German liberals, leftists, and decent conservatives were prepared to defend German Jews not as Jews but only as either men-in-general or Germans-in-general that their opposition was ineffective if indeed it was not shot through with fraudulence.[17] (Did those suggesting the ideas for this paper mean to include the Federal Republic of Germany among the class of "mature democratic societies"? If so, could anyone in all seriousness expect the Jewish remnant surviving in that country to subordinate their merely "ethnic" loyalties to the "larger loyalty" to that "nation"?)

Our present concern, however, is with the behavior, not of Nazi Germany but rather of the democratic societies which opposed it. No amount of ideologizing can conceal the fact that these responded to the Nazi assault on the Jewish people with an ambivalence that delighted and encouraged the Nazi criminals. One democracy, Great Britain, sabotaged quickly and unnecessarily her own great promise toward Jews as a people—the Balfour Declaration—and at the same time compensated for this sin by decency toward them as individuals, i.e., a rescue policy at home generous by the standards of the time. Another democracy—my own Canada—pursued a stingy immigration policy, and while the policy itself was secret, it was no secret that antisemitism contributed to the stinginess. The most powerful democracy of all was before, during, and even after the war the greatest refuge for Jews fleeing from the gas chambers, at least until the founding of the Jewish state. Yet not only were the fixed immigration quotas never changed in behalf of Jews fleeing for their lives, they were not even filled. (In 1956, ways were found, quota or no quota, to admit Hungarians fleeing from political persecution, but rarely for their lives.) More important for our subject, any attempt on the part of pro-Jewish Americans to introduce a *Jewish* quota in response to the need (in addition to German, Polish, and all the other quotas) would have been rendered counterproductive by anti-Jewish Ameri-

---

17. The phenomenon of antisemites hating Jews as Jews and of "democrats" defending them as men was also discovered in post-World War II France by Jean-Paul Sartre in his *Anti-Semite and Jew* (New York: Schocken, 1948).

cans. On January 14, 1939, President Roosevelt cabled to his representative at the Vatican, Myron Taylor, as follows:

> The fact must be faced that there exists in Central and Eastern Europe a racial and religious group of some seven million persons for whom the economic and social future is exceedingly dark. While the Intergovernmental Committee has *wisely treated the German refugee problem as being one of involuntary emigration regardless of race, creed, or political belief,* it must be frankly recognized that the larger Eastern European problem is *basically a Jewish problem.* Acute as the German problem is, it is, I fear, only a precursor of what may be expected if the larger problem is not met before it reaches an acute stage, and indications are rapidly increasing that such a stage may be reached in the near future.[18]

Two weeks later, Hitler promised "the annihilation of the Jewish race in Europe," a promise he was to keep. The annihilated Jews were mostly Polish—but the United States' Polish quota was small.

Especially poignant was the Wagner-Rogers Bill and its fate. In 1939, Senator Robert Wagner of New York introduced a special bill in the American Congress which would admit twenty thousand German refugee children over a period of two years. To be sure, these children would be additions to the quota, not, however, a burden on the taxpayer, for "within a day after the plan was announced, four thousand families of all faiths had offered to adopt the children." Yet tremendous support from many sides was countered by a virulent opposition so openly anti-Jewish that Senator Wagner was forced to repeat over and over during the following months that "almost half the youngsters to be admitted would *not* be Jewish." Wagner closed his initial appeal with the Biblical words: "Suffer little children to come unto me and forbid them not; for of such is the Kingdom of Heaven." In July 1940, the United States heeded that injunction and admitted ten thousand British children fleeing from food shortages, bombs, and a possible Nazi invasion. A

18. Arthur Morse, *While Six Million Died* (New York: Random House, 1967), p. 256. (Italics added.)

year later, however, the door was shut to the German children—more than half of whom, after all, *were* Jewish—who were seeking refuge from certain death. The Wagner Bill was withdrawn.

> The ladies of the Grand Army of the Republic and the philosophers of the American Legion had triumphed. They had won their war against the children. The aliens had tried to breach the mighty Republic, but the patriots had withstood their assault.[19]

During the war, some Jews serving in the Dutch Legion and training in Canada requested that their families be offered asylum in Canada until the war was over, and the Dutch government offered to pay for their maintenance and arrange for their repatriation after the war. However, the Dutch Minister in Ottawa reported to his government as follows:

> The chief criterion for admission to Canada is race. The United States, where the criterion for entry is country of birth, has been swamped with Jews and other undesirable elements. It is a fact that Jews, having once obtained permission for their families to join them, if only temporarily, are exceedingly difficult to get rid of again.

The historian Jacob Presser who reports this episode adds: "This remarkable document was dispatched on May 26, 1943, the very date that Amsterdam witnessed its worst anti-Jewish raid, the day on which the invader had no difficulty in 'getting rid of' thousands of such 'undesirable elements.'"[20]

So much for the ambivalence of the great democratic societies at the time of greatest Jewish need. Let us now test some of the ideas suggested to me in the light of the conditions prevailing at that time. Were American or Canadian or British Jews acting "anomalously" when they sought to save their brethren from Hitler? On the contrary, they were surely acting

---

19. Ibid., pp. 252 ff., 254, 258, 269.
20. Jacob Presser, *Ashes in the Wind: The Destruction of Dutch Jewry* (London: Souvenir Press, 1968), p. 286.

anomalously—that is, contrary to moral decency—when their will and their courage was sapped by the *mistaken belief* that such behavior would be anomalous, or by the *correct belief* that it was *in fact* considered anomalous by the self-styled "patriotic" enemies of the Wagner Bill. Was Jewish "ethnicity" at that time smaller than any "larger loyalty" whether that of "the nation" or "mankind"? In 1939, fully 83 percent of Americans opposed an increase in the United States' immigration quotas, and a mere 8.7 percent called for a larger quota, a figure subdivided into 6.3 percent of the Protestants, 8.3 percent of the Catholics, but 69.8 percent of the Jews.[21] Who represented "the nation"? If it was the 83 percent, in what except a quantitative sense was their loyalty "larger"? And who among the Jews were loyal to "mankind," the 69.8 percent not deterred by the "patriots" in their concern for human lives by the fact that these lives were mostly those of Jews, or the 30.2 percent who were intimidated or else did not care? And who represented "civic unity"—Senator Wagner and his friends in their uphill struggle, or those who *claimed* to represent civic unity, waved the American flag, and left the children to their doom? America *had* to have civic unity then, but it was Senator Wagner and his friends who were forced to compromise. As for American Jews, they were abandoned to their grief—and their European relatives, to death.

The end of the war found many displaced persons from Germany, Poland, Hungary, and other lands, most of whom were allowed by the occupying forces to return home. But to few of the pitiful Jewish survivors of Bergen-Belsen, Mauthausen, and Ravensbruck could Germany, Poland, and Hungary ever be home again. Still, a few trickled back, especially to Poland, until a pogrom in a Polish town called Kielce, caused by a rumor that Jews had killed a Christian child for his blood, put an end to that trickle. The rest were left behind in camps like Bergen-Belsen, often for years, until someone kind enough might consent to take them out. The war was over. The truth about Hitler's genocide against the Jewish people was known.

21. Morse, *While Six Million Died*, p. 261.

Yet the world, the democratic societies included, still viewed the survivors as either men-in-general, or Poles, or Germans, or Czechs in general. Nothing had changed.

One thing, however, had changed. The Jewish inmates of Bergen-Belsen had fought for their lives against the Nazi enemies. They now meant to fight for their Jewishness vis-à-vis their democratic friends. We have already mentioned that these friends erected a monument at Bergen-Belsen with inscriptions in virtually all European languages, but none in Hebrew or Yiddish.[22] The survivors of Bergen-Belsen did not rest until Hebrew and Yiddish were added to all the other languages—in the center of the monument, where they belonged.

These men, women, and children of Bergen-Belsen were among the first *fully* emancipated Jews in the modern world. Before them the Warsaw Ghetto fighters had fought their hopeless battle against the enemy who denied their very right to exist. Their fight now necessitated the next battle for the right to exist *as Jews*, with apologies to no one. In neither case was emancipation a gift bestowed by the world. Both were acts of *auto*-emancipation.

At the same time, a spontaneous movement originated among the European Jewish survivors—*Brichah*, or flight from blood-soaked Europe, preferably to Palestine.

> Brichah . . . saw it as the supreme moral right of Jews, after what had happened to them in the war, to move toward Palestine or, at any rate, out of the lands of their oppression. Military regulations by foreign armies were not binding upon them, and for once, after a long obedience to others, the Jews would obey only their own institutions, which were at that time clandestine. The moral right of the non-Jew to tell the Jews what to do and where to go or stay had lapsed, and it was in this light that all problems of legality were approached. Foreign as this concept may have been to Jews from Western democratic countries, it was accepted unquestioningly by those hundreds of thousands who were connected with Brichah or with other manifestations of an independent Jewish nationalism . . . [non-Jewish] friends may not have fully comprehended this in its

22. See above, pp. 135–36.

theoretical formulation, but they evinced humane understanding for the position in practice. Such an attitude, it must be added, was found almost only among American officers—the French, British, or Russians showed no sympathy whatsoever for this point of view.[23]

Just as a direct line leads from the first act to the second and third, so a direct line leads from the three to the founding of the state of Israel.

V

There are those (the present writer included) prepared to argue that the Nazi Holocaust is quite sufficient to make "maintenance of a [Jewish] ... subculture a genuine ideal" rather than "merely a temporary necessity." (The terms used, though, seem grotesquely inadequate.) The crime is without equal in the annals of history. So is not only the suffering but also the heroism (physical and spiritual) of countless of the victims. Most of their traces were destroyed with Teutonic efficiency. To preserve the remaining traces forever after is a holy duty for the survivors, their children, and their children's children. Uncannily, a folk tradition exists even now which refers to the murdered millions, whether religious or not, equally as "holy ones." Their memory is itself holy, as is the Jewish survival without which it cannot live.

But there are others who assert or take for granted that this is another age—that gone without a trace are not only the Nazi criminals of yesterday but also the self-styled American "patriots" and their counterparts in other democratic societies. Those taking history so lightly must admit, if nothing else, that no event as momentous as World War II ever vanishes without large historical consequences. One of these relevant for our purpose is the rise of the nonwhite world against colonialism, intertwined with the demand of Black Americans for real, in-

23. Yehuda Bauer, *Flight and Rescue: Brichah* (New York: Random House, 1970), p. 266.

stead of merely ideological, liberation. The other is the rise of the state of Israel from the ashes of Treblinka, Dachau, and Buchenwald.

These two facts are of course generally recognized, as is the further fact that between them they are largely responsible for (or have sparked off) most or all the self-affirmations that are today, rightly or wrongly, classified as "ethnic." Whether or not this classification *is* right requires several further tests in which, this time, the very term "ethnic" is called into question. If applied to American Jews the term "ethnic" must certainly include today a commitment to the autonomy and security of the state of Israel. Let us therefore proceed to test the ideas suggested for this essay in the light of this commitment.

Who, in 1947, represented that "mankind" which commands the "larger loyalty"—the United Nations when it voted the state of Israel into existence, or that same organization when it raised not a finger against seven Arab armies which attacked Israel the day after the British left? Who represented the American "nation" still commanding a larger loyalty—though possibly not quite so large—than Jewish "ethnicity": President Truman, when he was the first head of state to recognize Israel, or those inside and outside the State Department who imposed an arms embargo that would apply to the Jewish Yishuv in Palestine but not to Jordan, Egypt, or Syria? As for those Americans (incidentally, not all of them Jewish) who resorted to arms smuggling in order to save the state recognized by their own president—were they patriots or traitors? Was breaking the law, in this case, "loyalty" or "disloyalty"? The sociologist already cited finds it "ambiguous" when American Jews "support the state of Israel financially, politically, and emotionally, when such support must surely raise the specter of dual national loyalty, if not downright disloyalty to America; but they are outraged by the idea that the State Department discriminates against the Jews in its personnel policies."[24] At least in the light of the conditions prevailing in 1947 and 1948, one may well ask whether this behavior was not exactly right, and *considered*

24. Liebman, *The Ambivalent American Jew,* p. 25.

ambivalent only by anti-Jewish Americans, on the one hand, insufficiently emancipated Jews, on the other.

But perhaps the turmoil surrounding the founding of the Jewish state too has now become a thing of the past, with the result that Jewish Americans who wish to preserve "ethnic" ties with the Jewish state now have, or should have, such ties in a manner exactly analogous to that, say, of Greek Americans to Greece, and Portuguese Americans to Portugal. Yet, however altered in form, the world's ambiguity toward the emancipation of the Jewish people survives. That the Arab world has not yet ceased to deny Israel's very right to exist is a subject beyond the scope of this essay.[25] Not beyond its scope is the fact that to this day the world submits to Arab intransigence whenever it equates Israel's right to exist with a presumed Arab right to destroy her. Greece is criticized for her fascist regime just as Portugal was criticized for her repressive colonialism in Angola, and Canada and the United States are asked to be nicer to their native Indian populations. Zet the *existence* of neither Greece nor Portugal is (or was) called into question; nor is it ever suggested that all except tenth-generation Americans and Canadians should go back to their native countries and return effective control to Indian survivors of all the white massacres. An analogous suggestion about Israel, in contrast, creates serious consideration or even enthusiasm. After all, why not let the Palestine Liberation Organization replace the "racist" Jewish with a "secular Palestinian" state in which Muslims, Christians, and Jews would live amicably together? (It is true, as the P.L.O. "National Covenant" states, this noble end requires the expul-

25. See below, p. 226 ff. We suggest in passing, however, that this *truly* anomalous refusal to accept a Jewish state *on any terms whatever*, coupled with the *totally* intransigent attitude toward *any kind* of exchange of refugees, may well have its ultimate grounds in Muslim theology. Just as the basic Christian objection to a Jewish state is that the "new" Israel has superseded the old, so the—in principle milder—Muslim objection is that while Jews may be subjects in a Muslim state, the very thought of Muslim subjects in a Jewish state is intolerable. Such ideas are still very much alive, see e.g., *Arab Theologians on Jews and Israel: Extracts from the Proceedings of the Fourth Conference of the Academy of Islamic Research*, introduced and edited by D. F. Green (Geneva: Editions de l'Avenir, 1971).

sion of almost all the Jews and the reduction of the miniscule remainder to minority status.) The mind taking such proposals seriously is the same mind that, ever since the French Revolution, has proposed to give to Jews, "as men," everything, and to them, "as Jews," nothing. And when those not emancipated from such a cast of mind urge Jews, whether from London, Paris, or Toronto, to dissolve their "narrow" Zionist or Israeli "particularism" into "pure universalism" they deserve the reply: "After you, Sir!"

For the true meaning of the Emancipation slogan and all its subsequent varieties is no longer in doubt—Jews must either disappear as Jews or else continue to be tolerees even in the modern world. However, this proposal is itself no longer tolerable. As for the state of Israel, it has served notice by its very existence that it would no longer tolerate it. Yet it is precisely this notice that the world finds hard to accept, or even to forgive. Here lie the roots of the still persisting ambivalence toward the Jewish state.

Returning to our question, we therefore conclude that at least so long as Israel's right to exist continues to be questioned, American Jews are not in the same moral position as Americans of Portuguese, Greek, or genuinely comparable "ethnicity." Can it be considered a "lesser" loyalty than either to "the nation" or to "mankind" to oppose *absolutely* the dismantling of the state that has made an end to centuries of Jewish homelessness? (While a repetition of Masada cannot be ruled out, Israel has made as certain as possible that there can be no second Auschwitz.) Who represents "the nation" today—the heirs of Senator Wagner and President Truman, or the heirs of the ladies of the Grand Army of the Republic and of Truman's enemies in the State Department? And can the United Nations be said to represent "mankind" when its recent president condemned white African racism but dismissed Soviet antisemitism as an "internal affair" of the Soviet Union? The shades of Eduard von Hartmann and Rosa Luxembourg continue to becloud the mind, not only in societies that are insufficiently emancipating, but also among Jews who are insufficiently emancipated.

Thus, for a second time, the questions treated in this essay have turned out to be themselves questionable. Still a third test is required, however, and this will be decisive: it will break through the old, outworn, defensive stance and bring to view outlines of a positive Jewish self-affirmation in the modern world.

VI

Is maintenance of an ethnic subculture a genuine ideal or merely a temporary necessity?

Item: After the post-World War II pogrom in Kielce few except such Jews as were both thoroughly Polonized and thoroughly Communist remained in Poland. This did not prevent a vicious campaign against them in the wake of the Six Day War, which in turn led to the forced exodus of most of the remainder.

Item: The Soviet Union today permits every linguistic culture self-expression, including that of the recent German enemy: Jewish culture alone is forbidden.

Item: The President of Algeria urges all members of the Organization of African States to sever all links with Israel or, if that is not possible, at least to freeze or suspend these relations *until the liberation of all of Africa as well as all the Arab world.* (Italics added.)

These three items (chosen at random) suggest two Jewish counter-questions to the above questions: (1) How long is temporary? (2) Are "temporary necessity" and "genuine ideal" mutually exclusive alternatives?

The first (particularly with the third above item in mind) may be disposed of quickly and wryly—"until the messianic days, and then all 'necessity' will in any case vanish." The second counter-question requires a closer scrutiny. Antisemitic campaigns directed against assimilated Jewish Communists in Poland may make it "necessary" *for them* to reaffirm some sort of Jewishness. On their part, *American* Jews will find it "necessary" to respond to these persecutions with an "ethnic" Jewish self-affirmation only if they *identify* with these strangers at least in attitude if not in action, and this involves commitment on their part to an "ideal." (This is pointed out quickly enough by those who disagree with this ideal, and Eduard von Hartmann might even have found it treasonable.) Correspondingly, a *Havurah* on an American campus may wish to affirm its "ethnic subculture" as a pure ideal unsullied by any "necessities." Yet, while a purely spiritual self-expression in prayer, meditation, and study might earn the affection of many religious groups, it would be lacking in Jewish legitimacy, and indeed be tantamount to a betrayal, unless it also made the "necessities" of Jews in Iraq and Syria, Russia and Israel, its own.

The alternatives, "temporary necessity" and "genuine ideal," then, fail to do justice to Jewish realities. Do they fail elsewhere as well? May the question owe its seeming innocuousness to its generality—a generality that flattens out *differences* between types of "ethnic subculture," which cannot, and in justice may not, be flattened out? Let us look at this list, by no means complete, but sufficient for our purpose:

1. Groups such as the Amish, who want the right to preserve their "subculture" without wanting, or demanding, the right to participate significantly in the "general culture."

2. Groups such as Norwegians and Swedes who did not flee but freely came to America and its "general culture," yet also freely choose to perpetuate as a "subculture" their old-country heritage.

3. Polish, Hungarian, and Irish refugees who meant to leave behind persecution and hunger but not necessarily their cultural heritage.

4. Blacks who did not come at all but rather were forcibly brought as slaves.

5. Indians who were the original settlers but whose originally general culture was reduced to a subculture where it survives at all.

6. WASPs whose culture became the dominant culture that gradually became sufficiently liberal to assimilate other cul-

tural elements, and to be partly taken, partly mistaken, for the general culture.

7. Jews who came, minimally in flight from persecution to individual freedom, and maximally in search of a full collective Jewish life under conditions of total emancipation.

Why are types of groups so different lumped together? In point of fact, the dynamics of "acculturation" work differently for some or all of them. In point of ethics, they both ask for, and are entitled to, different kinds of justice and, indeed, the flattening out of this difference is *already* an act of injustice, or at least renders more difficult the justice that needs to be done. Before which bar is the American or Canadian Indian to justify his "ethnic subculture" either as a "temporary necessity" or as a "genuine ideal"? This alternative may seem to question the validity of the melting pot ideology. In fact, it presupposes its validity, *if only because it flattens out the differences between what is termed "ethnic subcultures."* Is the maintenance of "ethnic subcultures" a mere temporary necessity? In that case the "general culture" is the sole embodiment of "genuine ideals." Or is their maintenance a "genuine ideal"? In that case the "general culture" may seem to be subject to a certain challenge. However, this challenge can hardly be genuine *so long as "ethnic subculture" means simply what the "general culture" is not.*

This silent presupposition of the melting pot is nicely illustrated by a recent definition of "ethnic" as "a human collectivity based on the assumption of common origin, real or imaginary."[26] Who is an "ethnic" here? In Europe, everyone. Even in neighboring Canada, English-Canadians and certainly French-Canadians would fall into the category. Only in the United States would there be a sharp dichotomy between ethnics and non-ethnics, the latter consisting of all who had assimilated to the dominant culture, the former consisting of all unassimilated groups, *indiscriminately lumped together.* That such a definition is parochially American is not its main fault,

26. Andrew Greeley as cited by Ronald I. Rubin, "The New Jewish Ethnic," *Tradition*, Winter 1973, p. 6.

and no fault at all if the self-limitation to America is deliberate. As the foregoing has endeavored to show, its main fault is the flattening out of differences. One may safely say that the current "revolt of the ethnics" is a protest against real or imagined injustices. The *doing* of justice requires careful discrimination between *kinds* of injustice, as well as between *real* injustice and such as is *merely imagined*. To this end, it would be best if such terms as "ethnic subculture" were either abandoned, or at least not given greater significance than they deserve.

VII

In a conference dedicated to America, one would at this point have to explore the kinds of "ethnic" self-affirmations in America *in their differences*, consider their respective claims and the conflicts between them, and ponder in the light of all these factors the unique history and destiny of America as a nation. Proceeding from such sociological inquiries to philosophy, one would have to separate reality from ideology in the American Enlightenment philosophy by weighing the claims of pluralism, and to reflect on how unity and plurality can be reconciled. In such an effort, this writer would wish to update the Hegelian idea of mediation which would, in effect, balance the one-sided American *"E Pluribus Unum"* with a creative, ever-challenging, albeit never unproblematic, *"In Pluribus Unum."*

In a conference devoted to Judaism and Jewish experience we must explore instead the maximal hopes that brought Jews to the North American continent. We can do no less, for, as we have shown, any conditional or qualified emancipation of the Jewish people is no longer either morally possible or physically necessary—the first not after the Nazi Holocaust and the silence of the world; the second not after the rise of a state in which Jews can be both unambiguously Jews and unambiguously free. David Ben-Gurion has said that a full Jewish existence is possible nowhere outside Israel. Whether or not he is right still remains to be seen. His statement in any case shows that the democratic societies are on trial, vis-à-vis the Jewish people no less than, in different ways, vis-à-vis Blacks, Indians, and many others.

It is not likely that any of these groups will receive full emancipation simply as a *gift* even in the most mature democratic societies. Nor is this, in every case, fairly to be expected. (Black Americans cannot be but black. But have American Jews the right to emancipation as Jews unless they want to remain Jews?) In addition to emancipation, there is need for Jewish auto-emancipation. We have referred to the auto-emancipation of the Jews of Warsaw, Bergen-Belsen, Brichah, and Israel as accomplished facts. Why, in the friendly atmosphere of America, do we find instead Jewish "ambivalence" between the wish for "integration" simply "as Americans" and "survival" as Jews?

Here one might cite the official American doctrines of state and church, or of each publicly being equal and difference being private, and the like. But our current "revolts of the ethnics" in any case suggest that these doctrines intermingle ideology with reality. We must now show, in addition, that any special American Jewish *emphasis* on these doctrines has ideological roots of its own.

The American separation of state and church embodies the modern principle of the secular state. Any special Jewish attachment to this principle is surely motivated by the specter of a "Christian state" which would inevitably reduce Jews to second-class citizenship. That each should count for one, regardless of background or origin, is a moral principle of democracy. Any special Jewish commitment to this principle is surely motivated by the fear of antisemitism. Both fears, we wish to stress, are well grounded. But rather than expect more of principles than they can furnish, would it not be preferable to articulate the hidden fears, and to fight on its proper terms a fight that needs no apology? To choose this course would, in effect, be to demand that the democracies *complete the emancipation of the Jewish people,* and to express faith in their capacity to do it. It would also be an act of American-Jewish auto-emancipation. They would still be committed to Jewish "survival." They would continue to seek "integration." There would be, however, an end to "ambivalence." For the American Jew would seek integration, no longer "simply as an American," *but as an American Jew.*

Let us give two illustrations. The American Jewish community has generally been especially vocal in opposing, on grounds of principle, state aid to parochial schools. This has brought it into a conflict with the Catholic community, the more so as increased financial burdens have come to threaten the quality if not the existence of the American Catholic school system. Moreover, there has arisen an internal Jewish conflict as well, for Jews, alarmed by the threat to their survival, have rapidly built a Jewish school system. The result has been not only a Jewish-Catholic conflict incapable of mediation, but also, in many cases, a Jew in conflict with himself. *Qua* American he is opposed to all aid to parochial schools, the Jewish included. *Qua* committed to Jewish survival he sends his five children to a Jewish school, and in the middle between these extremes is bankruptcy.

What if the issue were joined on terms from which ideology were eliminated? It is not likely that either Catholics or Jews will abandon their commitment to the secular state. But liberating the principle from an absoluteness whose hidden source (in the case of Jews) is fear of antisemitism, American Jews could balance this commitment with two others—that America needs a good Catholic school system, and *that she needs a good Jewish school system as well.*

A brief glance at the situation in Ontario may shed some further light. The Canadian Province has two school systems, a "public" and a "separate" (Catholic) one. When the system was founded, few children went to school beyond grade 10, and there were very few Jews. Now, however, the Catholics ask for full support, while the Jewish schools which have burgeoned still have no support whatever. The situation, of course, is different from that in the United States. Yet no one will maintain that Ontario is a lesser democracy, and that the present injustice is not that the Catholic system receives public support, but that the Jewish system does not receive it. As for the "ambivalent" Jews of Ontario, some went so far in a recent election campaign as to favor continued (if not extended) support for the Catholic school system, while opposing any aid whatsoever to the Jewish school system.

Our second example is the current controversy over admission policies to United States colleges. This has produced a tragic clash between Jews and Blacks—tragic because it is between two (albeit differently and even oppositely) disadvantaged groups.

At present the clash is largely seen in ideological terms. Insisting that the merit system delays their liberation, Blacks in effect demand a quota system whose chief victims would be Jews. Insisting that the merit system alone is just (as well as necessary for academic standards), Jews demand its perpetuation, maintaining that the lowering of academic standards would be no true help to Blacks. To the extent to which the conflict is ideological it is frozen; moreover, the truly privileged groups are apt to stand by—one is tempted to add, with a smile.

All this might change if the ideological aspects of the tension were exposed and removed. Blacks (already with a stake of their own in academic standards, at least in such fields as medicine and engineering) would modify their demands when facing the fact that one group of Americans, itself disadvantaged, would have to pay the major price for them. On their part, Jews can bring this fact to light only by the insight and admission that, paradoxical as it may seem, they have a *collective* stake in a system in which *individual* merit alone counts.

Ever since the Emancipation, if counting as one at all, Jews did count as one only if their merit was greater than that of others. Their traditional love for learning apart, they were driven into superior and even unnatural efforts by the proposition that Jews can be equal to others only if their work is better. On their part, Blacks were driven into inferior efforts or even unnatural indolence by the proposition that *no amount* of effort would give Blacks equality. Hence the above assertion that Jews and Blacks confront each other as oppositely deprived groups.

Their common realization of this fact would make the pres-

ent conflict capable of mediation between them. More important still, neither side would permit the truly privileged groups
to stand outside. As for the Jewish side, it would be involved in
this mediating process not as a collection of American individuals who happen to be Jewish but whose Jewishness is not to
count, but rather as American Jews.

VIII

Two weeks after the great Nazi pogrom of November 1938,
known as *Krystallnacht*, Mahatma Gandhi wrote an article in
which he expressed his sympathy for German Jews but attacked
Zionism.[27] Jews "should make that country their own where
they are born and where they earn their livelihood," and resist
with "soul-force" the "godless fury of dehumanized man," a
strategy that would enable the German Jews to "score a lasting
victory over the German Gentiles in the sense that they [would]
. . . convert the latter to an appreciation of human dignity." As
for the "cry for the national home," it was not only unjust to the
Arabs but also offered "a colorable justification for the German
expulsion of the Jews." Even for the Jews living and toiling
there, the true Palestine "of the Biblical conception" was not a
"geographic tract." It was "in their hearts." So completely did
one of the saintliest and politically most astute men of this century misunderstand Jewish existence in our time.

In a long reply dealing with many matters (including the
nature of Nazism, the issue of "dual loyalty," and the Arab-
Jewish conflict), Martin Buber wrote as follows:

> Zion is the prophetic image of a promise to mankind; but it would
> be a poor metaphor if Mount Zion did not actually exist. This land is
> called "holy"; but it is not the holiness of an idea, it is the holiness
> of a piece of earth. That which is merely an idea and nothing more
> cannot become holy; but a piece of earth can become holy just as a
> mother's womb can become holy.

27. Reprinted in *Two Letters to Gandhi*, from Martin Buber and J. L.
Magnes (Jerusalem: Rubin Mass, 1939), pp. 39–44.

Dispersion is bearable; it can even be purposeful, if there is some-
where an ingathering, a growing home center, a piece of earth
where one is in the midst of an ingathering and not in dispersion,
and whence the spirit of ingathering may work its way into all the
places of the dispersion. When there is this, there is also a striving
common life, the life of a community which dares to live today
because it may hope to live tomorrow. But when this growing center
. . . is lacking, *dispersion becomes dismemberment.*[28]

In one respect, Buber's vision, unrealistic and perfectionist
in some ways, has inevitably been pushed still further beyond
reach by the darkness which was descending upon the Jewish
people even at the time of Buber's writing—a darkness whose
effects are still with us. Even so, the wonder is not that the
actual Zion (and through it "dispersed" Jews everywhere) has
not come closer to Buber's vision but rather that neither has
despaired of it.

In another respect—this underestimated by Buber—his vision has been surpassed. *Israel has acted to complete the
emancipation of the Jewish people,* and she has done so by
challenging at its roots "the Gentile problem"—a "teaching of
contempt" which has assumed many forms through the centuries but which originated in, and continues to be fed by, a
two-thousand-year-old attempt to theologize the Jewish people
out of existence.

The result is that while "dismembered" Jews may feel
threatened by the boldness of the Israeli presence, "dispersed"
Jews everywhere have become less at war with themselves,
more wholesome, more human, more Jewish. The "spirit of
ingathering" has helped produce "the life of a community
which dares to live today because it hopes to live tomorrow."
Israel is a daring witness to the world that the Jewish people
lives and will live tomorrow.

It has thus become possible to ask, if not yet to answer, the
question: What would a *truly* emancipated Jewish existence be
in the modern world?

28. Ibid., p. 7. This part of Buber's letter is reprinted in *The Writings of
Martin Buber,* ed. Will Herberg (New York: Meridian, 1956), p. 281.

Jews are now free to open themselves to long-delayed challenges. Having sealed his heritage off from the modern world to preserve it lovingly, one Jew must now contend with his "cruel" God (Job 30:21) who has become suddenly and inexplicably a "Man of War" (Exod. 15:3). The other, having embraced the modern humanistic promise of freedom and dignity for all, love among all, and persecution nowhere, must now contend with a faith in man and human organization which did not allow for the underground man who has come up from hell. Perhaps when they emerge from their struggle they will speak to each other what has never been spoken before.

12. *The Theo-Political Predicament in the Contemporary West: Reflections in the Light of Jewish Experience*

I

> Then the men of Israel said unto Gideon: Rule thou over us, both thou and thy son and thy son's son also; for thou hast saved us out of the hand of Midian. And Gideon said unto them: I will not rule over you, neither shall my son rule over you; the Lord shall rule over you. [Judges 8:22]

This statement marks the beginning, or at any rate the most radical first statement, of the theo-political predicament in Jewish experience. It is a predicament that persists unto this day, not only in Jewish experience but also in that of the Western world. I shall attempt to shed some light on their interrelation.

The gods of ancient Greece, being finite, can be political without any trouble. Athene is the goddess of Athens and of Athens only, and when later the Greek gods become transformed gods of the Roman Empire, they are in due course re-

Reprinted from *Religious Education*, vol. LXXI, no. 3, May-June 1976, pp. 267–78. Originally delivered at the Bicentennial Celebration Convention of the Religious Education Association, devoted to the topic "Civil Religion in America."

placed by Roman emperor gods. Correspondingly, the God of mystics, West and particularly East, whose infinity is immediately experienced, is for that reason indifferent to the all-too-finite political realities of men. In contrast with both these possibilities, Gideon's statement is a *prima-facie* absurdity because it binds the infinite God of the universe to a finite flesh-and-blood community. Unless this *prima-facie* absurdity is to be dismissed at once as insanity, it is necessary to recognize what I call the *tension of the hyphen*—the tension between God and politics.

This tension has certainly marked biblical Jewish experience. Gideon may reject the very idea that Israel shall have a king of flesh and blood. Yet, soon after him the prophet Samuel, on the one hand, delivers the most anti-monarchical speech in all of human history while, on the other, he yields to the people's demands for a king who *is* of flesh and blood. This, however, does not destroy the tension of the hyphen, so that now Israel has abandoned the idea of divine kingship. The king, to be sure, is human. He is not, however, above divine judgment and criticism. Hence the tension between king and prophet persists in ancient Israel until kingship itself is, at least temporarily, destroyed. Even thereafter the tension of the hyphen does not vanish from Jewish history. Thus as late as in the eighteenth century the Hasidic Rabbi Levi ben Yitzchak of Berdichev interrupted the sacred Yom Kippur ritual to address words something like the following to God. "The British have a king and he protects them. The Russians have their Tzar, and he may not do much for the poor, but after a fashion and up to a point at least he protects his people too. We, your people, have only you as a king. Why then do you not protect us?"

It may seem that Christianity transcends the theo-political predicament of Judaism because first, unlike in Judaism, redemption is already actual; second, because it is simply universal, that is, not tied to any particular flesh-and-blood people but rather to mankind as a whole. However, the most superficial glance at the history of Christianity shows that, since God in Christianity is not the Lord of disembodied souls but rather of flesh-and-blood human beings, the predicament is merely altered. Hence Christianity either is involved with the political order, or, if it is indifferent and simply other-worldly, then in due course this indifference to political realities provokes protests such as those all too familiar today.

What I have called the tension of the hyphen implies the following consequences: (1) short of the eschatological fulfillment there can be no perfect relationship between the theological and the political aspects of the relation. There is always a predicament relating these two aspects, a predicament that necessarily involves difficulties. (2) All solutions, in their nature inadequate, occur in historical contexts, that is, they are to be understood as responses to specific challenges. (3) The responses (which have to be judged each on its own terms and also within the historical situation in which they are made) quite naturally range over a full spectrum, from disastrous at one extreme to solutions of extraordinary viability at the other extreme, to responses in the middle that have only ephemeral significance, incapable of lasting. As examples of disastrous responses I would list within Judaism the embracing of all false messiahs, the most recent example of which is that of Shabbtai Zvi in the seventeenth century. Within Christianity I would list Constantinianism, to say nothing of the response of those "German Christians" who thought it was possible or even desirable to be Christians and Nazis at once. (Mention must also be made of the Concordat between the Vatican and Nazi Germany without which all recent history might have taken a different course.) Among ephemeral responses I would list within Judaism that of Gideon, which, we have already seen, had to be abandoned by Samuel shortly after. Within Christianity a good example might be those early Christian communes which, as "extremist" as Gideon himself, were unable to come to terms with flesh-and-blood history.

What concerns us most are the viable responses. Within Judaism one might here list the response of waiting and working in exile for redemption, a response that has shown extraordinary power to persist through the most varied circumstances, from the destruction of the second Temple until the Nazi Holocaust. Within Christianity I would stress what brings us closer to our present subject, namely, the option for secular liberal democracy not despite but because of a commitment to religious conscience.

If one abstracts from the historical context, it may well seem that secular liberal democracy falls outside the range of the tension of the hyphen altogether, that it has broken that tension, and indeed this break seems to be enshrined in the American separation of state and church. However, there is today a suspicious togetherness in our present concern with "civil religion," when at the same time both liberal democracy and Western religious (that is, Jewish and Christian) traditions are in a state of crisis. I suggest—and this is the major assumption of my essay and the critical aspect of its contribution to the current debate concerning civil religion—that if one understands our present situation in a historical context, then one will understand the option for secular liberal democracy as itself motivated by the religious (Judeo-Christian) tradition; that is, as one particular response within history to the challenge of the theo-political predicament.

Negatively, the option for secular liberal democracy is an option against medieval Constantinianism, and against the so-called "Christian state" as being an oppressive state. Positively, it is inspired by the distinction between *private* (whether religious or anti-religious) conscience and *public* (i.e., political) action. It is the distinctly Judeo-Christian insistence on the privacy of religious conscience that demands the secular state. And it is the transformation of the religious into political values that adds two dimensions to the two dimensions that permeate every viable society. Hence we find in secular liberal democracy a togetherness of the perennial social values of unity or order and justice, and the values specific to the biblical tradition of liberty and equality. (Only if man is understood as created in the image of God is liberty as well as equality understood to be a value. This commitment, one should specifically state, may persist if the original inspiration has become obscure or even perhaps if it has vanished altogether.)

These four values, taken together, make up the intrinsic values of secular liberal democracy in the West. It ought to be added that they are not a harmonious system but rather in tension with each other. In any society there is a tension between unity or order and justice. Justice can never be complete on account of the requirements of order, just as order can never be complete or perfect without doing violence to justice. The tension becomes more complex still when the two values just referred to (liberty and equality) are added. These are in tension with each other as well as with the other two values already mentioned. Hence the tensions of secular liberal democracy are always so great that its enemies deny that it has any power to survive at all.

The fact is that secular liberal democracy has shown an extraordinary viability. However, in this century its crises have been so great that its enemies have confidently predicted its imminent demise and even its friends have wondered whether its viability has not come to an end. It is instructive to note that this crisis in the political sphere coincides with a crisis in the religious sphere.

II

If what has been said is correct, the only fruitful way of understanding, and hope of responding to, our contemporary crisis is by viewing it in its historical context. I will view our crisis first from the standpoint of Western experience and then from that of Jewish experience, in the hope that each will shed light on the other.

The first great challenge in this century to the viability of the modern Judeo-Christian option for secular liberal democracy was the first World War. This may be called the War of Absurdity. The political aspect of the absurdity was expressed in famous slogans. The world was to be made safe for democracy, yet an ally of the democracies was Tzarist Russia. It was to be a war to end all wars, yet the greatest of the democracies bowed out of the League of Nations, and what remained of that League was left without ideals. The theological aspect of the absurdity was that God was invoked by both sides, a trauma from which Christianity has not recovered to this day.

The second great crisis was World War II. This was correctly described by Arthur Koestler at the time as a war in behalf of a half-truth against a total lie. This crisis too had its political and its theological aspects. As for the political, the half-truth of the democracies was shown even before the war began, when there was only a half-hearted defense of the ideals of democracy against what was or should have been known to be absolute evil, Nazism. The defenders of democracy lacked passion. Their Nazi enemies were full of passionate conviction. Thus when the war began, the men of Munich who had betrayed Czech democracy had poor credentials when they went to war on behalf of semifascist Poland. As for their American brothers, they would or could not come to the aid of the embattled democracies until they themselves were directly under attack. As for the theological aspect of the crisis, before America entered the war, pacifist clergymen preached reconciliation with or even love for Hitler, and needed reminders from such very few prophetic figures as Reinhold Niebuhr to the effect that Hitler's victims were worthier objects of their loving attention. On its part, the German confessional church responded to World War II as its predecessors should have responded to World War I, i.e., by refusing to underwrite religiously what was then the German state. In the end, for the most part the opposition consisted of trying to give unto Caesar what belongs to Caesar but not giving unto him what belongs to God. Only very few figures, of whom Dietrich Bonhoeffer is the most notable (and even he only when the time was late), recognized that the throne of Caesar was then occupied by the anti-Christ. And he responded to this fact, unprecedented within Christendom, not as a Christian witness within the sphere of religious testimony but as a political plotter against Hitler's life. Until today it is not clear whether he took this step because or in spite of his theology.

The third crisis, of course, is our own. And it may be best understood as the nemesis of our half-truth in the crisis of

World War II. We then fought racism abroad, but the fact that we were practicing it at home has long come to haunt us. We then espoused freedom, being ourselves all the while involved in colonialism. And equality is an ideal that rings hollow when, as is universally manifest today, the world is rent by the most basic inequalities of all, between the rich and those so poor as to be on the brink of starvation.

The current political crisis of the West (which, bringing as it does our own half-truth to consciousness, inevitably leads to radical self-doubt) has once again a theological counterpart. Persisting Constantinianism, for all our commitment to secular liberal democracy and the right to privacy of religious conscience, has permeated all along the missionary efforts of the Christian option for secular liberal democracy, with the result that the current doubt in *all* missionary efforts comes close to affecting the Christian substance. And the basic failure of World-War-II-Barthian neo-orthodoxy—its radical separation of the Word of God and the word of man—has now found a nemesis in a variety of theologies, many of them mutually incompatible, which have one common denominator, radical this-worldliness. Among these one might include the theologies of hope, liberation, and politics, and also our present interest in "civil religion."

It is an essential part of a deep crisis that while one is in the midst of it one does not know a way out. One may attempt, however, to understand it and thus gain a perspective and perhaps thereby hope. For this reason it is valuable (what I have proposed in any case to do) to view the same crisis we have hitherto viewed in the light of Western experience, the experience we all share, in the light of Jewish experience.

The first and foremost thing to say about Western liberal democracy, from the standpoint of Jewish experience, is that for the first time since the year 70 C.E. the Jewish people was offered hope of a Diaspora which would no longer be exile. In view of current confusions it is important to stress that this hope was seen not only by those Jews who saw the democracies bring an end to many centuries of Jew-hatred and who therefore proposed henceforth to be German, French, British, or American citizens of the Jewish faith, but also by those who considered antisemitism a force so deep as to make such a project dubious if not impossible. Theodor Herzl, to be sure, was shocked by the Dreyfus trial into the vision of a Jewish state. However, he not only envisaged this future state as a liberal state but also showed his faith in liberal democracy in the hope that the founding of a Jewish state would mark the end of antisemitism everywhere. To this day, Jews have a deep attachment to secular liberal democracy, and all its successors in the political arena (of which the Communist pseudo-secular state is the most notable) have proved themselves long since, so far as Jewish experience is concerned, to be false gods.

In view of this hope and faith in liberal democracy, which persists among Jews to this day, it is therefore all the more noteworthy that the three crises already described have a special Jewish dimension.

If World War I was the War of Absurdity for Western democracy, for Jews it represented an absurdity that tore them apart. Patriotic Jews in both camps were fighting each other, and what is more, they were doing so in the name of Judaism. In the light of hindsight it may be strange that Jews should have been fighting for the Central Powers with deep patriotic fervor. Yet none other than Sigmund Freud declared that his whole libido was with Austria-Hungary. More important still, Hermann Cohen, without doubt the greatest spirit among liberal German Jews of the time, declared that whereas undoubtedly Western Jews enjoyed equal rights to a degree that German Jews still lacked, it was nevertheless the case that all Jews (not only the Jews of Germany) ought to be on the side of Germany since, as he held, there was a spiritual kinship between Judaism and "Germanism." In retrospect it would be difficult to find a more tragic statement coming from the Jewish community of World War I. To illustrate the absurdity still further, one nation in the Allied camp, Great Britain, proposed through its Balfour Declaration to end Jewish homelessness by making a Jewish homeland possible, while at the same time another member of the same camp (Tzarist Russia) was the main cause of making such a homeland necessary.

But the absurdities of World War I pale in comparison to the stark horror of World War II. The West was fighting in behalf of a half-truth against a total lie. From the viewpoint of the Jewish people, the total lie expressed itself as the determination to murder every available Jewish man, woman, and child. The half-truth on the other side expressed itself in weakness of opposition to the crime of the century. Prior to the beginning of the war, those Jews who were able fled for their lives from the Nazis. Yet, while at that time the Nazis were willing to let them go, the democracies were only half-willing to receive them. After the war began, the Nazis no longer let Jews go, but murdered them. On their part, the democracies maintained that the saving of Jewish lives had to wait until the war was won. But gradually it became clear that once the war was won there would be few Jews left to save.

This shocking experience has had two theo-political effects upon the Jewish people. First, since secular as well as religious Jews were murdered without discrimination, Jews would never be able again to define themselves as a "religion" only. (An Israeli philosopher has rightly observed that Franz Rosenzweig, who died in 1929, was the last great Jewish thinker who would ever be able to think of history as waiting until he would have decided whether or not he wished to remain a Jew.) The second effect was that the events were bound to make religious Jews doubt God and secular Jews doubt man and all his institutions, liberal democracy included.

While nothing since World War II, and possibly nothing conceivable, can ever match in depth the crisis which World War II represented for the Jewish people, nonetheless the crisis of today is more traumatic still in one respect. In the wake of World War II the Jewish people, collectively speaking, did the one thing possible as an alternative to total and final despair. They set out to break the millennial unholy connection between hatred of Jews and Jewish powerlessness, by founding a state of their own. (For my part, I shudder to think how great the worldwide spiritual demoralization of the Jewish people would be today had they not taken this momentous step.) Yet this state, which ought to be universally viewed as a monumental expression of faith in the future arising from the very depths of despair, has become today the object of a new, differently named, antisemitism whose effective center is nothing other than the United Nations, i.e., the organization founded by the victors over Nazism in the wake of their victory.

In view of the current worldwide slander of Zionism and its effects (which show no signs of diminishing), it would not be surprising if the Jewish people were now prey to a final failure of nerve; if, so far as his central objective was concerned, Hitler were to win the posthumous victory.

The last named developments have been on the way at least since 1967 when, prior to the Six Day War, the Jewish people was confronted with the specter of a second Holocaust within a single generation and there was silence in the Christian churches a second time. Since that time, Jewish-Christian dialogue (in which I myself have been engaged ever since I can remember) has gotten into difficulties. For some time now I have been thinking about a parable which I will tell you, but the conclusion of which occurred to me only in connection with the present essay.

Two friends walk on a way through the forest engaged in discussion. Suddenly one of them falls into a swamp and he shouts, "Help!" The other, however, does not hear and wonders why his friend has broken off the conversation. To this parable (which I think applies to Jewish-Christian dialogue at least since 1967) I must now add that the one who shouts "Help" keeps shouting louder and louder. Not only does he need help himself, but he must also warn his friend. If his friend does not take care he too may fall into the swamp. And the swamp is the same.

The Jew of our time, as a result of his experiences in this century, is a witness to his friend (the Christian insofar as he is committed to liberal secular democracy), a witness who warns him lest he fall into the swamp. The swamp is an all-too-understandable failure of nerve which must nevertheless be resisted. A generation ago there were those who predicted that the wave of the future was with the totalitarian dictatorships and that the democracies were doomed. We *would* have been doomed had we listened to their voices. One asks: what if the wave of the future has been merely delayed, and at long last the barbarians are at the door? The question is a serious one, all the more so since the Western democracies, haunted as they are by the half-truths in their past, are currently engaged in a process of masochistic self-flagellation. Yet fatalism concerning our future must be resisted.

How shall we resist it? In many ways the Western world seems comparable to the Roman Empire in its time of decline when the barbarians overwhelmed it, Christianity was born, and Jews alone survived. But there are also decisive differences. Why did the Jewish people, despite their tragedies, survive the fall of the Roman Empire? Because they alone had in their political reality a transcendent religious inspiration. The modern West differs from ancient Rome in that, having conquered paganism, it has, potentially at least, escaped the power of fate. Like Judaism it has in its political dimension a transcendent religious inspiration. *This transcendent source may be a source of renewal.*

III

To believe in the possibility of renewal is not to be without fear of catastrophe. For the Jew of today, the togetherness of hope and fear is nowhere more acutely expressed than in his focus on the state of Israel. As we have said, in response to the Holocaust the founding of the state was the sole possible alternative to total and final despair after four millenia of unbroken history. The foundation of the state of Israel was an expression of courage, hope, and faith in the future. This is not to say, however, that there was and is no fear. The fear need not be spelled out. One knows it when one reads the newspapers. And yet the fear is countered with a determination that may and should be an inspiration to the Western world.

A generation ago Roosevelt proclaimed that we have nothing to fear but fear itself. This was an obvious half-truth. That a great deal more than fear was to be feared is evident today to us all. We therefore do well to listen to the Israelis who could never delude themselves in this manner. For other nations the fears have concerned territory, defeat, sickness, poverty. The fear of the state of Israel since its inception has concerned existence itself. Israelis have had no alternative but to face this fear, a fear that is now coming to haunt us all. And yet they have not fled from it but rather confronted it. Hence I find myself, again and again, compelled to speak of the religious quality of the so-called "secular" Israeli. His secular self-reliance has an inspiration that, however indefinable or even unutterable, transcends the realm of the probable and certainly the realm of the useful and the calculable.

Hence, as we are threatened by failure of nerve and tempted to listen to self-fulfilling prophecies concerning a supposed wave of the future, we do well to listen to the testimony of the Israeli (who has become the spearhead of the whole Jewish people). The Israeli would be lost if he believed in waves of the future. So would the Jewish people. So would the Jewish people have been lost at virtually all times in their history. The Israelis, the Jewish people, those still believing in the future of the Western democracies and of the continued viability of the option for it, can do no better than listen to, and make their own, what was once a Hasidic saying and became an Israeli song during the Yom Kippur War when all seemed lost and yet defeat was never considered for a moment. It is an utterly realistic song. It is a song of the utmost profundity. And it is a song that epitomizes what faith can be in the contemporary world: "The world is like a narrow bridge. But what matters above all is not to be afraid as one walks across it."

13. Israel and the Diaspora:
Political Contingencies and Moral
Necessities; or, The Shofar of
Rabbi Yitzhak Finkler of Piotrkov

The Termini of Jewish History

WE ALL RECALL the great, terrifying biblical tale of Abraham's sacrifice of Isaac. In Jewish tradition that tale assumes world-historical significance, and is referred to as the "binding" of Isaac, to indicate that there was a reprieve, that in this particular case the shedding of Jewish blood was averted, and a ram sacrificed in Isaac's stead.

Not surprisingly, the ancient rabbis think highly of that ram. Concerning one of them, Rabbi Hanina Ben Dosa, there is a current scholarly controversy as to whether or not he lived to see that great shedding of Jewish blood—the destruction of the Jerusalem Temple in the year 70 C.E. Rabbi Hanina told a story, a Midrash, about that ram. It was so holy that no part of it went unused. Its ashes subsequently became part of the inner altar of the Temple. Its sinews were made into strings of David's harp; its skin, into the girdle of Elijah's loins. Finally there were the horns. What about those ram's horns? One of them—so Rabbi Hanina Ben Dosa concluded his Midrash—was used at Mount

Originally delivered as Yaacov Herzog Memorial Lecture at McGill University, Montreal, on November 27, 1974, and subsequently published as a pamphlet by the sponsors.

Sinai. And the other, somewhat larger, will be blown in the End of Days, so as to fulfill the saying of the Prophet Isaiah, "And it shall come to pass in that day that a great horn will be blown." (Isa. 27:13).[1]

In Jewish historical tradition and religious imagination the ram's horn, or shofar, has many uses. Its best known and most regular use, during the Rosh Hashanah festival and at the end of Yom Kippur, is to arouse the worshipers to repentance. But it is also used to warn of danger and to arouse to battle, just as it is an expression of grateful relief when the danger has passed. Sometimes it is used to arouse men; at other times, to arouse God. Only one thing is always the same: *the shofar always arouses,* or as Maimonides in a rare flight into poetry put it, it is meant to awaken the sleepers from their sleep.[2]

What then of those two horns of the ram that was sacrificed in Isaac's stead? The left, blown at Sinai, ushered in Jewish history, whereas the right—somewhat larger—will mark its eschatological end. The Jewish people exist between these two termini and are defined by them, and in 1921 the greatest theological work within the Judaism of this century, Franz Rosenzweig's *Star of Redemption,* was still able to assert that nothing decisive has happened or can happen between these two poles.

Rosenzweig died in 1929. Less than four years after, events began to take their course which, though most people today pretend that they are over and done with, continue to have world-historical effects. As for the Jewish people, to attempt to forget would be to attempt the impossible. And so distant has Rosenzweig's vision become from us that is impossible for the Jew of today to hear authentically either the shofar of Sinai or the shofar of the End of Days without also hearing yet a third shofar—the shofar of Rabbi Yitzhak Finkler of Piotrkov. *Whatever the political contingencies of history between Sinai and the End, there exists now a new moral necessity, for the Jewish people and indeed for the world.*

1. *Pirke Rabbi Eliezer* XXXI, quoted in S. Y. Agnon, *Days of Awe* (New York: Schocken, 1965), p. 67.

2. *Hilchot Teshuvah* III.4, quoted by Agnon, ibid., pp. 72 ff.

Piotrkov

Let me tell you about the city of Piotrkov. I look at the map, and find that it is located some hundred miles to the south of Warsaw. I look next at the recently published Jewish encyclopedia, for I want to know about the Jewish population, and I find some very precise statistics. In 1917 the Jewish population of Piotrkov was 14,890. Four years later it had dropped, for reasons one may guess, to 11,630. And then a sentence leaps at you from the pages—on October 28, 1939, the first Nazi-established ghetto was set up in Piotrkov. Thereafter the Jewish population began to rise, for reasons which are only too obvious. By April 1942, it had risen to 16,469: the statistics are still quite precise. In October of the same year it had risen dramatically: it had leaped to 25,000. The figure is no longer precise. There was no longer time to worry about statistics, and a few hundred Jewish lives more or less no longer mattered so much. And then a second sentence leaps at you—in a single week in October 1942, 22,000 Jews were deported to Treblinka, to be murdered.

I look at my atlas to find out about Piotrkov today. It tells me that its population is roughly 58,000. There is no mention of Jews in Piotrkov. It is not necessary. After the Nazi murderers and a vicious post-Nazi Polish antisemitism which persists to this day, it would be surprising if there were a single Jew left in Piotrkov.

Rabbi Yitzhak Finkler

Let me tell you about Rabbi Finkler. I find out about him in a memorial book. After the great catastrophe, reverent survivors all over the world composed a large number of memorial books to commemorate the saintly victims who otherwise would be as though they had never been. The memorial book about Piotrkov tells me that Rabbi Finkler was a man of conscience. When the Nazis came and said to the Jewish community council, "Register young Jews for work, it will be good for them—they will get more food," Rabbi Finkler said, "No, you do not have the right to make such decisions for someone else!"

Then the Nazis asked for volunteers and said to Jews, "You, you, and you—report for work, it will be good for you!" And Rabbi Finkler said, "Let *no one* go voluntarily! Do anything, everything. Disappear, hide, lie down, anything—but don't volunteer!" Thus Rabbi Finkler is credited by his chronicler not only with great moral integrity but with a political shrewdness and uncanny foresight that are almost superhuman.

One therefore wonders whether in this case, as in so many others, the chroniclers in their pious anguish do not exaggerate the virtues of their dead—until one comes to a passage which has the ring of utter authenticity: the piety of Rabbi Finkler. Throughout the ordeal he studied and prayed, a source of comfort and strength to all. More seriously, he obeyed the commandments. This is more serious, at a time of such hunger, observing the dietary laws. So we find it quite plausible and indeed inevitable that during the one-and-a-half years which he spent in a forced labor camp before Treblinka, he suffered more than others, not only spiritually but physically, because of the unaccustomed labor—and above all, the hunger.

The Third Shofar

Then came Rosh Hashanah, and Rabbi Finkler and his followers were deeply worried because they did not have a shofar. A shofar which to blow, so as to let it arouse them to penitence for their sins. So they sold their bread for money, gave the money to a Polish Gentile who had access to the labor camp, and asked him to buy a shofar outside. The Pole made a mistake and came back with a calf's horn, the only kind of horn not permitted, reminiscent as it is of the golden calf and the time of Israel's great sin. By then Rabbi Finkler and his pious ones were full of anxiety, for Rosh Hashanah was already near, but they sent out the good-natured Pole again and he finally came, just in time, with a genuine ram's horn. And, thus, the chronicler finishes: "They blew the ram's horn on Rosh Hashanah and a prayer rose heavenwards, together with the sound of the Shofar. It threw itself before the throne of Divinity saying 'tear up the evil decree.'"[3] But alas, the evil decree was not torn up—*and this is why the shofar of Rabbi Yitzhak Finkler still resounds on earth and in heaven, and will never be silenced until the End of Days.*

Anyone who knows Jewish liturgy understands the reference of the chronicler. Of all the prayers of the awesome festival, the most awesome is one supposedly composed by a medieval martyr, the *Untanne Tokef.* It projects what might happen in the year to come. Who will grow richer, who poorer? One does not know. Who will live and who will die? It is unknown. Who will die at his time, and who before his time, and among the latter who will die of hunger and who of thirst, who by fire, by the sword, by strangulation or the plague? And, after all this, the grim but utterly realistic catalogue ends with the tremendous affirmation that "repentance, prayer and good works will tear up the evil decree."

Try to picture Rabbi Yitzhak Finkler in his last days, his last hours, in the last minute of horrified recognition which surpassed all possible foresight. There can be no question as to how he behaved. Most assuredly he said to himself and to his pious ones: If the evil decree was not torn up in our case, although it surpasses all evil decrees ever, it is because we did not repent enough, because we did not pray enough, because we did not do enough good works. That is what *he* said. But it cannot possibly be what *we* can say. We must cry out to God and men: if not for him and his like, then for whom? If not for these righteous ones and these saintly ones—then when will the evil decree ever be torn up? And this is why for all those who come after and hear that shofar—be they Jews, be they Gentiles, be they Diaspora Jews or Israeli Jews—there is now a new moral necessity amidst all the contingencies of human existence, that *the course of history, or in any case the course of Jewish his-*

---

3. *Piotrkov Trybunalski, Sefer Zikaron,* publ. by the Landsmanschaften of Piotrkov in Israel, the U.S., Great Britain, France, and Argentine, n.d., pp. 855–61.

tory, must be so altered that such as Rabbi Yitzhak Finkler will never again be the helpless victims of the great hatred.

Of Those Who Did Not Hear

We ask: who listened then; who listened at the time when Rabbi Finkler blew his shofar? I will forbear today to ask questions about God. There are too many questions about man. And the first statement to be made may seem to be a ridiculous statement, a redundant statement, a totally superfluous statement; the Nazis did not listen to that shofar.

Of course they did not listen. We all know that. But then a question must be asked. The human species, supposedly created in the image of God, includes S.S. men. It includes Himmler and Heydrich, Eichmann and Hitler. The question therefore is *why* they did not listen.

We do not know.[4] However, we know very well how they would have behaved if by chance they literally had heard Rabbi Finkler blow his shofar. If any member of the Nazi apparatus had been physically present, he might have murdered Rabbi Finkler on the spot for the unforgiveable crime of practicing Judaism on holy Aryan ground. As an alternative, he might have called in a few comrades for some fun and games. Some of the Nazis were familiar with Jewish theology. They knew that the shofar is supposed to avert the evil decree. Let's put this to a little test. Come Rabbi Finkler, blow the horn! Blow it, let us say, twelve times, and we'll have twelve Jewish babies and a little target practice after every sound! Or maybe, to vary things, throw a baby here and there up into the air, and catch him with a bayonet! Amusement and theology, all in one!

---

4. The mountainous literature attempting to answer this question confirms this statement. Accounts which *do* give explanations of Nazi behavior are either offensively glib or unconsciously circular (such as in the use of the unexplained terms mania, madness, psychosis, and the like). And those accounts which inch closer to an understanding succeed by virtue of a deep sense of shock, horror, and intellectual humility.

Contrary to traditional Jewish practice, we must dwell on the deeds of the wicked ones in order to emphasize that not only was Nazism evil, it was an evil unprecedented under God's sun, and that its central target was *both* the Jewish people and the Jewish faith. Moreover, its shadow is still over us. When the ancient Syrians attacked the Maccabees on the Sabbath, it was a case of pragmatic cynicism; unwilling to fight on the Sabbath, the Jews were caught unawares. When the Nazis customarily rounded up Jews on their holiest days—Jews whom they could equally have rounded up on any other day—it was, so to speak, a case of diabolical idealism. It served no practical end. It was desecration for desecration's sake. And if this point needs to be made with great emphasis, it is because since that time we have become more and more accustomed to desecration for desecration's sake, particularly if its victims are Jews. UNESCO never raised any questions about the desecration of Jewish cemeteries and synagogues when Jordan occupied the Old City. (Now, when there is no desecration whatever in the Old City, UNESCO expels Israel, after the Jordanian desecrators have joined with the Polish antisemites to sponsor the motion.) When the Yom Kippur War was launched almost no one really asked—almost no one to this day really asks—why it was launched on Yom Kippur. Indeed, I myself believed at first that it was comparable to the case of the ancient Syrians, a case of pragmatic cynicism: the Jews got caught unawares. But then one realizes that this is the one day on which Israeli soldiers can easily be reached: in the synagogue. More important still, more significant to anyone who knows Israel's highways, it is the one day in the year on which the highways are clear and not crowded with traffic. So why is it that to this day no one is really bothered, let alone appalled, by the date on which the Egyptians and the Syrians attacked? No, the Nazis did not listen to the shofar of Rabbi Finkler of Piotrkov, and the effect is still with us.

Did the world listen? Let us consider the testimony of that most gentle of Zionist statesmen, Chaim Weizmann. He visited the United States in 1940 when that country, in his words, was "violently neutral" and any mention of the Jewish tragedy was associated with "war mongers." He writes: "It was like a nightmare which was all the more oppressive because one had to maintain silence. To speak of such things (as the danger to European Jewry) in public was 'propaganda'."

In 1943, Weizmann came to New York again, and to speak of war then was no longer propaganda. In Madison Square Garden he made this statement:

> When the historian of the future assembles the bleak record of our days, he will find two things unbelievable; first, the crime itself, second, the reaction of the world to the crime. . . . He will be puzzled by the apathy of the civilized world in the face of the systematic carnage of human beings. . . . He will not be able to understand why the conscience of the world had to be stirred. Above all, he will not be able to understand why the free nations, in arms against a resurgent, organized barbarism, required appeals to give sanctuary to the first and chief victims of that barbarism. Two million Jews have already been exterminated. The world can no longer plead that the ghastly facts are unknown or unconfirmed.[5]

Among the two million already dead was Rabbi Yitzhak Finkler of Piotrkov.

Of Some Who Heard

Let us turn to some who listened. It is a relief, it is a great joy; under the circumstances one might almost say it is a miracle, to be able to report that some *did* listen. In 1946 David Ben-Gurion appeared before the Anglo-American Committee of Inquiry, a committee composed of men who, after the tragedy had been revealed, took seriously the possibility that there might have to be a Jewish state. Ben-Gurion tried to explain why Jews had come to Palestine. He spoke, of course, of those who came because of persecution. But he also asked why some

5. Quoted in Walter Laqueur, *A History of Zionism* (London: Weidenfeld & Nicolson, 1972; New York: Schocken, 1976), pp. 550, 551.

came who were not persecuted. Why did some come from
friendly, free countries? Ben-Gurion replied in part as follows:

> They came because they felt it was unendurable that they should be
> at the mercy of others. Sometimes the others are excellent people,
> but not always, and then there is discrimination, and they did not
> like it. As human beings with human dignity, they did not like it,
> and they did not see how they can change the whole world, so they
> decided to return to their own country and be masters of their own
> destiny. I want to give you an example of moral discrimination.
> Gentlemen, I do not know in Europe a more tolerant, a more liberal,
> a more fair-minded people than the English people in their own
> country. . . . There was recently in the House of Lords . . . a debate
> on the Jewish problem. . . . It was on the seventh of December
> 1945, and in that debate the Archbishop of York in very strong
> language condemned antisemitism as un-Christian. . . . He also ex-
> pressed deep concern over the sufferings of the Jewish people. . . .
> He then began talking about the Jewish attacks on or criticism of the
> policy of His Majesty's Government in Palestine, meaning the
> White Paper policy of 1939, and the attacks being made by Jews
> on both sides of the Atlantic, and he said these significant words:
> "It (meaning this criticism) is being resented and may easily lead
> to a most dangerous reaction." Well, Jews are not the only people
> who are criticizing or attacking the White Paper policy. In 1939,
> the White Paper policy was described, not by a Jew, but an Eng-
> lishman, a pure Englishman, a Gentile, as a "mortal blow to the
> Jewish people." The name of that Englishman, gentlemen, is Win-
> ston Churchill. We agree with this description. It was and is a mor-
> tal blow.
>   Well, gentlemen, when a people receives a mortal blow from
> somebody, would anybody ask them to lie down and take it
> silently—*a mortal blow?* Would anybody resent this criticism, this
> attack on the mortal blow? This was said by Mr. Churchill in 1939
> when our people in Europe were still alive. Since then tens of
> thousands of human beings, of babies—after all, Jewish babies are
> also babies—have met their death because of that policy. . . . Is it
> surprising that we as human beings should criticize or attack this
> policy? I am sure His Grace understands that. He is a great person-
> ality, he knows the mind of his people, and said this may lead to a
> most dangerous reaction. We receive a mortal blow; we must be

silent. If not, it may lead to a dangerous reaction. Where? Not in Poland, but in that most liberal and tolerant country—I say this with the greatest respect—England.[6]

This is what Ben-Gurion said in 1946. And there were men and women throughout the world then who listened and understood. They understood that, whatever the political contingencies of the world (then very uncertain, perhaps far more uncertain than today), *there were certain moral necessities that had gradually but inescapably become clear in the development of the Zionist movement from Theodor Herzl to David Ben-Gurion; and that among these was a Jewish state.*

The State of Israel as a Moral Necessity

The most obvious factor that had made a Jewish state necessary was, of course, the Holocaust. But in view of worldwide, well-oiled Arab and communist propaganda it is necessary to remind ourselves at this time that this was by no means the only factor. The well-known critic, Robert Alter, lists the following additional factors. First, there was the series of murderous assaults by armed Arab mobs on the Jewish populace of Palestine beginning in 1921, long before a Jewish state existed when, except for organized Arab terror, there might well have gradually developed a binational state, a secular democratic state, and all the rest that we hear of today. Second, there was the British mandatory abrogation of even the humanitarian aspects of the national home by cutting off Jewish immigration at the precise time that Hitler was preparing the gas chambers. Third, there was an absolute refusal on the part of the Arabs to cooperate politically with Palestinian Jewry or to consider any binational alternative. Fourth (if one had been in the United Nations in November 1974 and listened to Yassir Arafat's address

6. Quoted in *Israel through the Eyes of Its Leaders,* eds., Naamani-Budavsky-Katsh (Tel Aviv: Meorot, 1971), pp. 7 ff.

and the Assembly's reaction, one would have thought this had never happened) there was the total unwillingness of the Arabs of Palestine to agree even to the admission of a hundred thousand survivors of the gas chambers, coupled with the promise that those would be the last Jews to be admitted.

These are the facts, or some of the facts, that made a Jewish state a moral necessity. What is more, that state has become a moral necessity, not only for the Jews of Israel but for all Jews throughout the world, or at least for those who remember, understand, and are lent courage by their duty. For no matter where they live, *it has become a duty for Jews in this century not to tolerate "moral discrimination" any longer.* They owe this duty to the memory of their martyrs. They also owe it to the countries in which they live, lest these countries have even the slightest resemblance to the Nazi criminals. However, they shall find the strength to fulfill this duty only because of the heroic example of the state of Israel. This means no less than that the state of Israel has become the spearhead of the whole Jewish people. (All attempts to separate Israel and the Diaspora are attempts either of self-hating or cowardly Jews, or of our enemies.) It may even be said that, after what has happened in this century, in a certain respect the state of Israel is a spearhead of all mankind. The world is somewhat less dark today because after the Holocaust there arose a state of Israel, a state in which Jews are "masters of their own destiny." There were many who understood this at the time. Among them were Winston Churchill, Harry Truman, and our own Lester Pearson.

A Generation After

Who listens today? To ask this question is to engage in a melancholy enterprise. I have quoted Chaim Weizmann as of 1943. His description then was correct. His prediction, however, could not have been more mistaken. If one looks through the history books of our time (except for those specifically dedicated to the Holocaust), one finds the Holocaust either not mentioned at all, or buried in footnotes.[7] And if one looks in these books for a sense of puzzlement, let alone outrage, at the callousness then shown by the world toward Jews looking for a place of refuge, one quite naturally finds very little—quite naturally, for since then callousness has become a worldwide phenomenon which we take for granted. (As I said, the effects of Nazism are still with us.)

A statesman more cynical than Weizmann might have predicted such developments. However, not even the most cynical statesman or historian of the forties would have predicted that the time would come when a great and revered historian would equate, in any respect whatsoever, the Israeli survivors of Nazism with the Nazis themselves. Arnold Toynbee did this first in 1954. In 1961 he repeated the equation in this city, when he compared the behavior of Israelis toward Arabs with that of Nazis toward Jews.

Yaacov Herzog (in whose memory this lecture was given) challenged Toynbee to a public debate, thereby showing courage, a commitment to freedom of speech, and a belief— precarious in this age—that truth will prevail. Very much a gentleman, Toynbee accepted. The debate is now available on two long-playing records.[8] To hear it, hear it repeatedly and listen carefully, instructs and surprises. The first thing that surprises is the gentleness and nobility of Yaacov Herzog. He did not ask, as a less tolerant man might have asked: Where are the Israeli gas chambers? Where are the cattle trains? Where is the murderous anti-Arab ideological propaganda? Where is the desecration for desecration's sake of Muslim holy places? Herzog did not ask any of these questions. Instead, by simple probing, he elicited the statement—so remarkable that I had to listen to the record twice to believe it, hearing it four times in all, for the

7. See Henry Friedlander, *On the Holocaust: A Critique of the Treatment of the Holocaust in History. Textbooks Accompanied by an Annotated Bibliography* (New York: ADL, 1972), pp. 3–30.

8. CBS Records, CP 13–14. See also Yaacov Herzog, *A People That Dwells Alone* (London: Weidenfeld & Nicolson, 1975), pp. 21–47.

statement itself was made twice by its author—(this is Toynbee speaking)—"what the Nazis did was nothing peculiar." As he went on it became clear that for him the Holocaust crime did not differ in kind from the sort of crime to civilians that happens as the result of passion or hate in any war. Yaacov Herzog then asked the logical next question, "If this is true, then why single out Israel for comparison with Nazism?" and after a certain amount of breast-beating on behalf of the British, Toynbee had nothing more to say. What about the Russians—white or red? What about the English in Ireland? Or the French in Algeria? Or the Arabs in the Sudan? Or American and Canadian behavior toward Indians? Nothing. Toynbee evaded the question. And, as far as I can see, Yaacov Herzog was satisfied to let the facts speak for themselves.

But what did the facts actually say? What was this altogether extraordinary equation of Nazis and Israelis, by a man who, after all, is not one of Goebbels's ex-henchmen now operating as a "second world" democrat in East Berlin, or as a "third world" democrat in Cairo? You listen to it a few times—and the answer is clear. *Once this obscene equation is permitted the world's guilt is wiped out. The slate is clean. There is no moral necessity as far as the Jewish people are concerned. The shofar of Rabbi Yitzhak Finkler of Piotrkov is effectively silenced.*

Listen to the record again, and you realize beyond all doubt that Toynbee did not perform this equation with any such calculation in his mind. He performed it in innocence, whatever one may think of such innocence. This is evidenced by his obviously genuine surprise that his equation should have upset the Jewish community. However, the same excuse cannot be given for many others who have traded on this evil identification ever since. These include some Christian spokesmen, many Arab leaders, sundry "third world" ideologists, and especially those who are above all suspicion of innocence, but rather calculate every step before setting the propaganda machine into motion—high level Soviet politicians. The first time Federenko made that obscene equation in the United Nations, every single member of that august body should have walked out; yet not one of them did. And, so far as its relationship to Israel as well as the Jewish people is concerned, the United Nations has sunk lower and lower ever since, until now (as the distinguished Christian theologian, Roy Eckardt has put it) the United Nations has become "the operative centre of world antisemitism."[9]

This point had already been reached when the P.L.O. was invited to speak and before Yassir Arafat ever opened his mouth. For no member of the United Nations can plead ignorance of the Palestinian National Covenant first formally announced in 1968 and reconfirmed as recently as 1974. This document openly demands two things: the destruction of the state of Israel and the expulsion of all Jews who have immigrated to Palestine since 1917.[10] Thus it is *already* clear that, once Israel is equated with Nazi Germany, anything goes.

And then Arafat actually appeared at the United Nations, gave his speech, and had most of the delegates cheering. Wildly.

One reads that speech and almost believes it oneself. It is an extraordinary, a masterfully well-written document. What makes it so compelling is the wholesale theft of virtually every significant Jewish symbol: The desert blooms—now it is the Arabs that have made it bloom. The Nazis (this is familiar by now)—the Israelis are the Nazis. The Arab terrorists, why, they are just like World War II resistance fighters; in other words, the anti-Nazis. And then finally comes what is at once the mas-

9. A. Roy Eckardt, "The Devil and Yom Kippur," *Midstream*, August–September 1974, p. 69.

10. Article 19 and 20 of that document declares both the Balfour Declaration of 1917 and the U.N. resolution of 1947 as null and void, thus declaring *any* Jewish State as null and void. Article 22 equates "Zionists" with Nazis. Article 4 affirms an "innate" Palestinian personality which is hereditary (surely not only the most irredentist but also among the most racist affirmations currently alive), while article 20 denies that Jews are "one people with an independent personality." Article 6 is terse: "Jews who were living permanently in Palestine until the beginning of the Zionist invasion will be considered Palestinians." This Article leaves some—not much—room for interpretation: What Jews are to be expelled from the "secular democratic Palestinian state"—those coming after 1917, or merely those coming after 1947?

I see no reason for not taking this chilling document seriously.

ter stroke of propagandistic genius, the dead give-away, and the unforgivable sin against the truth. *The Six Million.* Yes, you heard right—the six million. By dint of some mathematical calculations no one can understand, but not accidentally one may be sure, it is six million Arabs or their symbolic equivalent that have undergone martyrdom at the hands of the Israelis. So the process begun with the identification of Israelis with Nazis, obscene from the start, is complete. The perversion has become a system.

There is a grim logic in the fact that Arafat, the brave Arab underground resistance fighter against Israeli Hitlerism, is the spiritual heir (and, incidentally, a physical relative) of the Mufti of Jerusalem. (He died recently, with many Arab dignitaries present at the funeral to praise his memory and his heritage.) The Mufti was Hitler's honored guest in wartime Berlin. He issued calls to the Arabs such as "kill the Jews wherever you find them. This pleases God, history and religion. This saves your honor. God is with you."[11] He visited Auschwitz and probably Maidanek as well.[12] And he not only had a share in implementing the "Final Solution" but was personally responsible for the Nazi murder of at least four thousand Jewish children.[13]

Of course neither Arafat nor his supporters wish to be associated at this particular time with the Mufti and his wartime loyalties and activities. The propaganda requirements of the moment are otherwise. Moreover, coupling these two will doubtless be considered unfair play by many well-meaning liberals who rightly look for someone to represent the Palestinian Arabs, and (largely because of Arab terrorism) cannot at this

11. Quoted in Joseph B. Schechtman, *The Mufti and the Führer* (New York: Yosseloff, 1965), p. 151.

12. Ibid., pp. 152 ff.

13. Ibid., pp. 157 ff. According to Dieter Wisliceny, an Eichmann aide who ought to know, "the Mufti had repeatedly suggested to the various authorities with whom he was maintaining contact, above all to Hitler, Ribbentrop, and Himmler, the extermination of European Jewry. He considered this as a comfortable solution of the Palestine problem." (Quoted by Schechtman, ibid., pp. 159 ff.) Schechtman's book is fully documented and deserves close study.

time find someone else. Yet the P.L.O. itself does not disguise the fact that, whereas the tactics may have changed, the strategy has not. And when one remembers the children of Ma'alot and Kiryat Shmoneh—does anyone still remember them?—one wonders whether even the tactics have changed that much. It was Hitler who taught the Mufti that Jewish children grow up to be adults, and that this is enough reason to kill them. (Or did the two inspire each other?) Perhaps what has changed is merely the vocabulary. And a code word for the destruction of the state of Israel and the subjection of surviving or remaining Jews to minority status—the celebrated "secular democratic Palestinian state for Jews, Muslims and Christians"—was enough to bring the majority of the U.N. delegates cheering to their feet. Among them was one Canadian. He could not restrain his enthusiasm.

Some voted against this travesty. They were not many. A generation ago Lester Pearson had been a major figure working toward the creation of the state of Israel. When during the past few weeks decisive moves were made aimed at the destruction of that same state, Canada, on two of the three crucial votes, abstained.

Those of us old enough feel as if we were back in the thirties. Ever since the Yom Kippur War one hears it said here and there that if only Israel would somehow "go away" there would be peace in the world. (One distinguished American clergyman actually said that Israel "might have to die" to prevent World War Three.)[14] In the thirties Chamberlain tried but failed to secure "peace in our time" by sacrificing one small democracy. Western statesmen will succeed no better in this goal today by sacrificing another. As for Canada, she may yet rise to greatness, though the hour is late. Once Lester Pearson won Canada's only Nobel Peace Prize by creating a scheme that stopped war and, he hoped, would keep Israel's would-be destroyers perma-

---

14. The Rev. David Stowe, a top executive of the United Church of Christ, in conversation with Gerald S. Strober (See Strober's "American Jews and the Protestant Community," *Midstream*, August–September 1974, p. 52).

nently away from her. There is no reason why Canada should not stop hiding behind equivocations and restore the Pearson tradition.[15]

Israel and the Diaspora

Under the grim circumstances just described it is not surprising that the Jews of the Diaspora should be gripped by a certain failure of nerve. They too have become uncertain as to where in this world of political contingencies moral necessities lie. I am not referring to assimilationist, let alone self-hating Jews, who never did perceive any moral necessity unless it was related to people other than Jews themselves. The trauma of today is that there is a failure of nerve among some of the most committed. Ever since the Yom Kippur War we have heard statements such as "we in Canada or the United States cannot be vicarious Israelis" and "Israel is not all of Judaism." Also, there has been a flurry of spiritual activities, even including the creation of new journals.

In themselves, such statements and activities are unexcep-

15. Canada's ambassador to the U.N. made a fine speech refusing to prejudge who was the legitimate representative of the Palestinian Arabs—and then boosted the P.L.O. by failing to vote against it. Essentially the same doublethink is contained in a letter to me by Mr. Pierre Elliot Trudeau's secretary explaining Canada's position, in response to a telegram protesting the Canadian abstention.

After Arafat's address The Hon. Allan J. MacEachen was the only Foreign Minister who cared sufficiently to travel to the U.N. to address the General Assembly. In his address he said: "The claim of the P.L.O. to represent the Palestinians is . . . one which, in our view, is not for Canada to decide. It is a question which remains to be resolved by the parties directly involved in the course of their continuing efforts to work toward an agreed peace, and *Israel in our view is a principal deciding party.*"

Obviously no country can decide who represents another country. But no less obviously every country has the right and indeed the duty to *extend recognition to, or withhold it from,* groups of people *claiming* to represent another country. Since in this case the Canadian Foreign Minister stated that Israel would have to be "a principal deciding party" and Arafat had just reiterated the P.L.O.'s unaltered aim to destroy Israel, it was clearly Canada's duty to vote *against* granting observer status at the U.N. to the P.L.O., instead of, by abstaining, strengthening the P.L.O.'s stature and prestige.

tionable. What must cause surprise and suspicion is their tim-
ing. Could it be that what is at work here is, so to speak, a
spiritual hedging of bets, purportedly for the sake of Judaism?[16]
If so, let it be said loudly and clearly that this is not the time for
the Diaspora to back away from what continues to be the
spearhead of the Jewish people and a spearhead of all
mankind—the embattled state of Israel. Are there today, once
again, good Jews, devoted Jews, who try to hear the shofar,
either of Sinai or of the End of Days, but at the same time wish
to reassert the view that nothing decisive has happened or can
happen between these two termini of Jewish history? Are there
Jews, too, who no longer hear the shofar of Rabbi Yitzhak Finkler of Piotrkov, or even seek to silence it? If so, the attempt must
fail.

Israel and Judaism

Let us consider the present state of Jewish eschatological
expectation. On the liberal and left-wing this is now as always
thought of in terms of a this-worldly messianic universalism, a
future condition in which every people is free, just, and fulfilled. However, Rabbi Finkler's shofar arouses one to the realization that, unless something new and particular is added to
this "universalism" in this projected fulfillment of all the peoples, the *Jewish* people alone will either have disappeared or
else, once again, be at the mercy of others. Thus this form of
left-wing or liberal theological internationalism reveals itself
as a form of escapism.

A different form of escapism is found on the Orthodox right.
An American Jewish theologian asserts that nothing evil hap-
pened to the children of Auschwitz, that they are all happy with
God in Heaven. This is not a use of traditional Jewish belief in
the "world-to-come," but rather an abuse. And it is apt to make
Marxists of us all. For Marx religion was the opiate of the

---

16. See my article in *The Yom Kippur War: Israel and the Jewish People*, ed.,
Moshe Davis (New York: Arno Press, 1974), pp. 107–23.

people. Here we have a religious opiate of the Jewish people after the Nazi Holocaust.

In search of a stern realism one does well to ask how the ancient rabbis thought of the shofar at the End of Days. According to the Midrash, who will blow the final shofar? Elijah, the prophet who has seen all, knows all, and yet has retained the strength to wait for the End. At his first blow, the primal light which shone before the week of the Creation will reappear. (A great cosmic event!) At his second blow, the dead will rise and assemble around the Messiah from all corners of the earth. (After this, what more?) At his third blow, the *Shechinah*, the Presence of God, will become visible to all. (For the pious of many faiths the ultimate, unsurpassable consummation!) What, one may ask by way of a lapse into eschatological humor, can Elijah do for an encore? He can perform one climactic task. Indeed, only after all the preceding works are accomplished is it possible for him to perform it: he will slay Samael, the evil angel.[17] So utterly serious is the Midrashic eschatological expectation about the necessity to confront evil. So far removed is it from all escapism.

What of the other shofar, blown at Sinai and ushering in Jewish history? We read in Exodus:

> And it came to pass on the third day, when it was morning, that there were thunder and lightenings and a thick cloud upon the mount, and the voice of a horn exceeding loud. . . . Now Mount Sinai was altogether on smoke, because the Lord had descended in fire, and the smoke thereof ascended as the smoke of a furnace, and the whole mountain quaked greatly. . . . And the voice of the horn waxed louder and louder. [Exod. 19:16, 18–19]

Two questions arise. Who blew? We are not told. Was it God to arouse men? Or men to arouse God? Or, as one who does not believe in God might say, was it one man who blew, to arouse both himself and all others? We are not told, and perhaps it does

---

17. L. Ginzberg, *The Legends of the Jews* (Philadelphia: Jewish Publication Society, 1954), vol. IV, pp. 234 ff.

not matter. Perhaps what matters is not who blows but whether the sound is heard. This is the first question.

The second question is raised by the Midrash, and answered as follows: "Ordinarily the more the sound of a voice is prolonged the weaker it becomes. But here the longer the voice lasted the stronger it became. And why was it weaker at first? That the ear might get it in accordance with its capacity of hearing."[18]

There is now in process a great, hidden spiritual conflict concerning the Holocaust. It is hidden, for it is rarely articulated, and more rarely still in the right terms. It is great because it is meant by all or most of the articulated conflicts and discussions—between believers and secularists, Israel and the Diaspora, the Jewish people and the world. It is the great unspoken subject. Is the shofar of Rabbi Yitzhak Finkler of Piotrkov *wholly unlike* the shofar of Sinai? Does its sound grow ever dimmer with the passage of time so that even now it has perhaps ceased to be audible? Or is it, on the contrary, *wholly like* the shofar of Sinai? Is its sound waxing louder and louder, so that its sound mingles with the sound of Sinai, and no effort to silence it can ultimately prevail? All kinds of men try to silence that shofar which sounded a generation ago. Some do so innocently. Others are far from innocent. Some simply cannot bear to remember the crime. Others are heirs of the criminals. Others still are bystanders now as they were bystanders then. But the truth will not be silenced.

Epilogue

One morning, at the outset of the Yom Kippur War, an Israeli tank driver in the Golan Heights perceived a scene which he subsequently compared to a scene from a bad Italian movie. Wave upon unending wave of Syrian tanks appeared on the horizon, and between these thousand or more vehicles and the

18. *Mechilta de-Rabbi Ishmael*, ed., J. Z. Lauterbach (Philadelphia: Jewish Publication Society, 1949), vol. II, p. 223.

Israeli heartland there were a mere seventy-odd Israeli tanks. So, as he told the story to our friend Professor Yehuda Bauer, there was nothing to do but shoot until the ammunition gave out, rush for more ammunition, and come back to shoot again. The possibility of *not* returning to that hell, Professor Bauer commented when he told us of the incident, never occurred to this tank driver. The specter of a violent and total end of Jewish history, begun at Sinai, must have appeared before his mind but was immediately rejected. This secularist Israeli heard the shofar of Rabbi Yitzhak Finkler—and, mingled with it, the shofar of Sinai.

Another friend, Professor Pinchas Peli, edits an Israeli magazine called *Panim El Panim*. One day, in a German paper, he saw a picture of two soldiers in the Sinai during the Yom Kippur War, gun in hand, and dressed in the traditional phylacteries and prayer shawl. The picture of the older man reminded him of another picture of a Jew dressed in the same traditional garments. Where had he seen that face before? Soon he remembered a well-known picture of a pious Jew praying for his dead lying at his feet whom the Nazis had murdered, and he was surrounded by the murderers, jeering, laughing, and enjoying the fun. (One of them had photographed the scene, and this is how we have the picture.) So Professor Peli decided to write an article, and with this he printed the two pictures side by side.

Next week he received a letter from a hospital, saying something like this:

I am the other man in the picture in the Sinai, and the day it was taken I was shot. I am not writing for sympathy; indeed, I wish to remain anonymous. I am writing to tell you something. All my life I have thought of the generation murdered in the Holocaust as being collectively my father and mother. However, being collective, my relation to them was vague. Now it is no longer vague. I have seen that picture of the old man, praying for his dead, mocked and jeered at by the murderers of his people. And as long as I live, I will think of *this* man as my father.

This Israeli soldier heard the shofar of Sinai and, mingled with it, the shofar of Rabbi Yitzhak Finkler of Piotrkov.

Some may consider my citing these two cases as reflecting a vicarious Israeli chauvinism and militarism. It would be in keeping with the spirit of the times. Yet those uttering such condemnations would in fact condemn themselves. After Arafat's speech, Israeli Ambassador Tekoah gave verbal expression to the horn of Sinai when at the U.N. he reminded the world of the prophetic promise that the nations would beat their swords into plowshares. Even as he spoke most of those present walked away. Yet with the shofar of Sinai was mingled the shofar of Rabbi Yitzhak Finkler of Piotrkov, calling ever louder, ever more inescapably, to Israel, to the Diaspora, to the nations of the world, and indeed to God himself: "I shall not die but live, and declare the works of God."

14. Post-Holocaust Anti-Jewishness, Jewish Identity, and the Centrality of Israel: An Essay in the Philosophy of History

I

THE PREFIX "post" in the title of this essay may have two meanings. One signifies a merely temporal relation, so that any event after 1945 is "post-Holocaust." The other is historical in a pregnant rather than a merely trivial sense. An event succeeds another historically if the first somehow enters into its substance; if it is different from what it would have been if the first had never happened. Thus, much history is merely temporal. More importantly, historical events in the deeper sense are always of unpredictable import while they happen and even long thereafter. Only when they are assimilated by the historical consciousness of succeeding generations are they capable of transforming the future, and thus become historical in the deeper sense.

At least some current anti-Jewish attitudes are post-Holocaust in the historical sense. This is shown by the very terminology that is forced upon us. Prior to the Holocaust, many antisemites would protest—rightly so—their friendship for some Jews, and thus were called—rightly so—"decent" an-

Reprinted from Moshe Davis, ed., *World Jewry and the State of Israel* (New York: Arno Press, 1977). In this essay I refer repeatedly to other essays in the same volume.

tisemites. After the Holocaust, virtually all antisemites go to any length to deny, always to others (and often to themselves as well) that they *are* antisemites. The word "antisemitism," itself a nineteenth-century code word for anti-Jewishness, has become unusable for anyone seriously concerned to identify and comprehend post-Holocaust anti-Jewish attitudes.[1]

Only a few anti-Jewish attitudes may seem post-Holocaust in the historical sense. Moreover, these seem bound to diminish still further as the dread event passes from "experience" into "history."[2] However, the possibility is worthy of consideration that on both scores the exact opposite is the case. Not all forms of anti-Jewishness that look unrelated to the Holocaust are in fact unrelated to it. And while the Holocaust doubtless is passing from experience into history, it is only beginning to be absorbed by the historical consciousness—the consciousness both of those living in history and those writing about it.[3]

No one presently alive can answer the question raised by the relation between the Holocaust and the historical consciousness. We must at least pause, however, to ponder its momentousness. Will the Holocaust ultimately be forgotten or—perhaps this is the more precise way of putting it—be consciously and unconsciously expunged from the mind? Or will it, on the contrary, increasingly permeate both the lives of civilizations and the consciousness of its writers, philosophers and historians? In that case, the event may well assume a world-historical significance.

The question just raised is one for the future. In contrast, whether or not all forms of anti-Jewishness that look unrelated to the Holocaust are in fact unrelated to it is a question for the present. It may even now be illustrated by examples such as these:

1.   Germans of the new generation protest rightly that they are not guilty. This does not alter the fact that *any* form of

---

1. We shall generally use "antisemitism" in this essay only for pre-Holocaust forms of anti-Jewishness.

2. See Shlomo Avineri's essay in *World Jewry and the State of Israel.*

3. Raul Hilberg's assertion to this effect, made in 1961, is still substantially correct.

anti-Jewishness displayed by present and future Germans is historically post-Holocaust, for the slate of *no* people's history—that of Germans included—can be wiped clean. Unless they opt out of German history, i.e., emigrate, young Germans are burdened with the past and responsible for the future.

2.   Soviet Russia and other iron curtain countries actually try to wipe the slate clean, sparing no effort to make the Holocaust either a nonevent or a non-Jewish event. (There either are no memorials, or they are to the "victims of fascism.") This crime against the truth is enough to make all anti-Jewishness in these countries historically post-Holocaust.

3.   The Arab world protests that the sins of Christian Europe have been visited on its Palestinian segment. This protest is in bad faith when—to mention no others—it excises two facts from the record. One is the active participation of Haj Amin al-Husseini, Grand Mufti of Jerusalem, in Hitler's murder of Jewish children. The other is the link between Auschwitz and the war on the newly born Jewish state waged by five Arab armies. This attempt at politicide was encouraged by Hitler's practice of genocide with almost total impunity. And, of course, the victim in both cases—in the one case, actual, in the other, intended—was the same people.

To be fair, one may wish to doubt whether the third case of anti-Jewishness given is historically post-Holocaust, or even a case of anti-Jewishness at all; and in this spirit one may wish to consider the two excised events—the activities of the Grand Mufti during World War II and the Arab invasions in the 1948 war—as rightly excised, i.e., not as facts which, themselves shaped by the Holocaust, continued to shape subsequent history, but rather as random facts of the dead past. One's doubts are removed, however, by the present Arab propaganda system (assiduously assisted by the Communist) when it declares Israelis the new Nazis, Palestinian Arabs the new Jews, Arab refugees victims of a "holocaust," Zionism a form of racism and, by some mathematical tour de force, the Arab "victims" of "Zionism," in American terms, equivalent to six million.[4] It is

4. See Yassir Arafat's address to the United Nations General Assembly in 1974. See also above, pp. 201–03.

impossible to view this system as innocent, i.e., as truly ignorant of what happened a generation ago. One can only view it as
an attempt to wipe out the holocaust as a Jewish event, indeed,
to appropriate it as an Arab one, rewriting Israeli history as
being a "Final Solution of the Arab Problem."

That none of these forms of historically post-Holocaust
anti-Jewishness can be equated with the unsurpassable Nazi
kind goes without saying. (It requires saying only because of
the widespread dismissal of *all* Jewish explorations of *any*
post-Holocaust manifestation of anti-Jewishness as products,
either of a complex about the dread event, or of attempts to
exploit it. This extraordinary dismissal is itself in need of a
scrutiny that cannot be attempted here.) However, they are all
unable to claim or recapture the "decency" of pre-Holocaust
antisemitism. Only two decent Gentile relationships toward the
Jewish people remain. The one is that of being truly and
genuinely innocent of the fact that one generation ago the Nazi
regime first persecuted and then murdered the Jewish people,
while at the same time the rest of the world first shut its gates to
Jews fleeing for their lives and then failed to bomb the railways
to Auschwitz. (This "antisemitism" is a fossil, a relic from earlier, more innocent times. Its own innocence may be barbaric,
but it is an innocence all the same.) The other Gentile relationship to the Jewish people either always was free of anti-Jewish
animus or else, in response to the catastrophe, is trying desperately to rid itself of it. In contrast, all historically post-Holocaust
forms of anti-Jewishness are posthumous victories for Hitler
and witting or unwitting continuations of his work.

II

These consequences follow from the fact of Nazism. No historical fact is ever decisive proof of anything. However, being
the unsurpassable form of anti-Jewishness, Nazism comes as
close as possible to proving that *no* form of anti-Jewishness is
ever caused by Jewish behavior. This is not to say that it does
not matter what Jews do. It matters greatly, both in and for itself
and in response to manifestations of anti-Jewishness. In causal

terms, however, *all* forms of anti-Jewishness are strains of a Gentile disease. This might have been recognized when in nineteenth-century Europe right-wing antisemites hated "the Jews" because they were revolutionaries, while left-wing antisemites criticized them because they were capitalists, and when universalist liberals and particularistic nationalists complained, respectively, that "the Jews" mixed too little and too much with Gentile society. Occasionally anti-Jewishness was in fact recognized as a Gentile disease. Lessing did so in the eighteenth century.[5] In the twentieth century, the late, great Reinhold Niebuhr wrote: "When a minority group is hated for its virtues as well as its vices, and when its vices are hated not so much because they are vices as because they bear the stamp of uniqueness, we are obviously dealing with a collective psychology that is not easily altered by a little more enlightenment."[6] These words were written in 1942, before the worst was known. Now that it *is* known anyone responding by word or deed with the proverb "where there is smoke there is fire" is not a diagnostician of anti-Jewishness and its causes but himself a victim of the disease. This fact is in no way altered by assurances to the effect that the smoke is out of all proportion to any possible fire.

Like all theses about history, the present one requires qualifications:

1. An exposed social situation, whether of their own choosing (such as religious separatism) or of the world's making (such as spatial or social ghettoization) makes "the Jews" convenient scapegoats on which knaves and fools can blame the current ills of society. This theory is fashionable among the enlightened of

5. In Lessing's *Nathan the Wise* a Templar approaches a Christian Patriarch with the hypothetical case of a Jew who had pity on a Christian orphan and raised her in his home. The judgment he receives is that the Jew must burn at the stake. The troubled Templar's questions—what if he brought her up as a Jewess? What if he did *not* bring her up as a Jewess but simply as a decent person? What if, though the Jew could not save her soul, God in his power can save it?—all receive the same reply: "No matter! The Jew must burn!"

6. Reinhold Niebuhr, *Love and Justice: Selections from the Shorter Writings of Reinhold Niebuhr*, ed., D. B. Robertson (New York: Meridian, 1967), p. 133.

all ages, Gentile and Jewish. It turns the mind to a rational cure—the healing of the true ills in question. More important still, it denies the disease itself the sort of uniqueness that is forever anathema to the enlightened. However, by itself the "scapegoat theory of antisemitism" explains neither the tenacity of anti-Jewishness nor the variety of its forms, to say nothing of why other groups, no less exposed, were made into scapegoats rarely, differently, or not at all.[7]

2. "The Jews" can in fact show behavior that may seem to cause anti-Jewish attitudes. Jewish usury in the Middle Ages is a case in point. However, the fact that even then (to paraphrase Niebuhr) Jews were hated for the virtues as well as their vices would in itself suffice to overthrow this theory. Add that Jews were driven into usury by state and church policies *already* anti-Jewish in inspiration and purpose, and the Jewish "vice" in question emerges, not as the cause of anti-Jewishness, but rather as an effect of self-fulfilling anti-Jewish prophecies.[8] Never was the principle behind such prophecies expressed with such cynical openness as when Goebbels announced a policy of robbing Jews of their livelihood, thus driving them into crime, and then punishing them as a criminal group.

3. The above are cases of victimization. These must be distinguished from authentic actions. The most clearly authentic case of a collective Jewish action in recent history is the founding of the state of Israel. Obviously there could be no anti-Zionism without Zionism, and no Israel without Zionism. Somewhat less obviously, anti-Zionism may "spill over" into

7. In his *Anti-Semite and Jew* (New York: Schocken, 1948) Jean Paul Sartre achieves some deep insights into antisemitism but loses them totally when at one point he lapses into the scapegoat theory. See p. 54.

In a celebrated joke an antisemitic speaker at a meeting shouts "the Jews are our misfortune!" Heckler: "The Jews and the cyclists!" Speaker (puzzled): "Why the cyclists?" Heckler: "Why the Jews?" This joke, a classic illustration of the scapegoat theory, never cured a single antisemite. However, its enlightened tellers have always fondly believed it could.

8. In 1784, Moses Mendelssohn wrote: "We continue to be barred from the arts, the sciences, the useful trades and occupations of mankind . . . while our alleged lack of refinement is used as a pretext for our further oppression. They tie our hands and then reproach us for not using them." *Jerusalem: And Other Jewish Writings*, trans. A. Jospe (New York: Schocken, 1969), p. 146.

anti-Jewishness. Hence, it may seem that here is at least one bona fide case in which Jewish behavior can actually *cause* anti-Jewish attitudes where none existed.

However, even so drastic a Jewish action can at most only reinforce existing anti-Jewish attitudes. It cannot create them. In the "first world," why are Jews criticized for their "passivity" in Nazi Europe and for their "aggressiveness" and "intransigence" in Israel—often in the same quarters? Why do those praising Algerians and Vietnamese when they fight for liberty blame Israelis when they fight for life itself? In the "second world," why is "acquisition of territory through conquest" legitimate for large and safe nations—the Baltic countries by Soviet Russia, Tibet by Red China—but illegitimate for a small and beleaguered nation, and of all small countries, only for that of the Jews? In the "third world," why was an exchange of populations possible between India and Pakistan but remains inconceivable to this day between Arabs and Israelis? That Palestinian Arabs should have become hostile to the "invaders" is understandable, and perhaps natural or even inevitable. But one wonders whether, had these "invaders" not been Jews, their hostility—to say nothing of that of the Arab world—would have remained implacable. Indeed, except in the context of Muslim and post-Muslim Arab anti-Jewish attitudes, Arab policies toward Israel would appear to be unintelligible.[9]

Moreover, while in some quarters aggravating the disease of anti-Jewishness, we may ask whether in other quarters the fact of Israel has not helped alleviate or even cure it. Since we cannot replay history, we cannot answer this question. However, we should be faint-hearted if we did not at least raise it. Anti-Jewish attitudes in North American and some other Western countries have, in our age, reached their lowest ebb since pre-Christian times. Doubtless this is because the Holocaust has generated thought and contrition among Gentiles, and thought and militancy among Jews. However, except for Israel would anyone truly remember? Except for this unique witness,

9. See below, sec. IV.

would either Jews or Gentiles understand the radical fact that Jews *need* not be tolerees when they are not victims; and, having understood, would they seek to cure the Gentile world of the disease, the Jewish people of its effects?

III

If anti-Jewishness is a Gentile disease we must ask, especially in view of the durability of the phenomenon, why it should forever be necessary to restate this truth. One answer, applying to a variety of "group prejudices," will be readily accepted. However, this answer must be supplemented by a second, applicable to anti-Jewishness alone.

We use the word "prejudice" in quotation marks, for a disorder far deeper than obtuseness to "the facts" is involved in such relations as between racist and his victim or between colonizer and colonized. Nor can "enlightenment" by itself cure it. The oppressor, first, believes it to be true that the oppressed is inferior. Second, he acts out his belief so as to make it true. Third, his success is complete only when the oppressed accepts his own inferiority and the truth of his oppressor's belief. In that case, there is a harmony of sorts in the relation—the ultimate reason why it can last. In the eyes of neither oppressor nor oppressed is the oppression "real" oppression. Each knows—and has—his place.

This insight, first stated by Hegel and developed, in ways sound or not so sound, by such thinkers as Marx, Kojève, Sartre, and Fanon, is today widely accepted wherever serious attempts are made to end (rather than merely to alleviate) such social ills as racism and colonialism. And the slogan "Zionism is the liberation movement of the Jewish people" illustrates the belief that the social disease of anti-Jewishness and its cure are wholly parallel to these others.

However, even the relation between "antisemite" and self-hating Jew is not wholly parallel, and not all Jews are self-hating. The self-hating Jew hates his Jewishness, while the antisemite considers his Jew-hatred to be both caused and justified by the other's Jewishness. On his part, the Jew who is not self-hating hates not his Jewishness but rather his condition of exile which distorts his Jewishness, and he seeks to liberate his Jewishness from exile, not himself from his Jewishness. As for the antisemite, he hates (as we have already stressed) Jewish virtues as well as Jewish vices. And if and when forced to justify his hatred of *these* he emerges as hating the Jew, not for being or doing this or that; the doing of this or that is hated precisely when and because it is done by a Jew. He hates the Jew for being at all.

As we have seen, there can be a relation of false harmony between colonizer and colonized, or between racist and his victim. As for the antisemite, he is (as Sartre has rightly said) a criminal who seeks the Jew's death.[10] The Jew's place in *such* a relation would have to be not to exist at all—or to commit suicide. In fairness to all "decent" oppressors, racist and colonizer as well as antisemite, one must add that there are both degrees of hostility and ways of disguising it from others and, above all, from oneself. And in fairness to the "decent" antisemites of pre-Holocaust times, one must further add that the group-death of the Jewish people could be achieved in two ways—genocide or radical assimilation. As decent a thinker as Kant could assert that the "euthanasia" of the Jewish people was desirable for Jews and Gentiles alike. That this particular expression sounds singularly unfortunate two centuries later is hardly his fault.

If racism, colonialism, and anti-Jewishness were wholly parallel phenomena, one would expect opponents of the first two to be firm supporters of the state of Israel, however critical of this or that policy of an Israeli government. This, of course, is not so. In one kind of quarter, the Jewish state is hated because its Jews are no one's victims or tolerees; in quarters of another kind, because it willfully considers itself Jewish. (In 1944, Sartre wrote that "the antisemite reproaches the Jew with being Jewish; the democrat reproaches him with willfully considering himself a Jew."[11]) That fascist and Communist United Nations

10. Sartre, *Anti-Semite and Jew*, p. 49.
11. Ibid., p. 58.

representatives should have joined hands to denounce Zionism as a form of racism will always remain incredible. It would have been impossible if there were not two ways of destroying Jewish existence—one, by destroying the existence, the other, by destroying the Jewishness.

What elements, then, in addition to racism and colonialism, enter into anti-Jewishness—its unique persistence, mutability and nature? The first two factors may seem to be accounted for in terms of Diaspora history, a history longer and more varied than those, say, of black slavery in America and European colonialism in Africa. But this answer only raises the further questions of why the Jewish Diaspora was accompanied by antagonism (which is not true of all diasporas), and why even radical changes (such as that from the premodern to the modern world) did not, as was in fact hoped, end the antagonism but merely changed its nature, rationalizations and self-definitions.

We are driven, then, to pursue further the insight articulated by Reinhold Niebuhr. Had Jews been hated only by the virtuous for their vices (such as "usury" in the Middle Ages or "lack of refinement" at the time of Mendelssohn), anti-Jewishness should have ended with the disappearance either of the "vices" or the standards which considered them so. Had they been hated only for their virtues by the vicious, anti-Jewishness should at no time have had the social and spiritual respectability that has made it so uniquely powerful, lasting, and deadly. *It is the anti-Jewishness of the saints (in secular terms: the idealists), far more than that of the sinners, which characterizes the uniqueness of the disease.*

This conclusion disposes of a theory of anti-Jewishness long fashionable among traditional Jews and now also existing in a secularist form. There is *Sin'ah* (Jew hatred) because of Sinai, a Jewish tradition affirms. Jews are hated, claims its secularist counterpart, because they brought respect for human life into the world. This theory fails to explain why Jews are hated for their vices by Gentile fellow sinners. Far more seriously, it fails to account for the startling fact of saintly hatred, the more so when its object includes Jewish virtues. We are here speaking of people of love, grace, and humility, who care for the poor, the widows, and the strangers within their gates, and who would lay down their lives to save another; people whose own lives declare the sacredness of human life, their oneness with all human suffering, their refusal to justify evil, violence, and even a single tear. Yet there is the one exception, the hatred of "the Jews." Why should religious saints hate rather than love Jews on account of Sinai? Why should secular idealists hate rather than love them for having brought respect for human life into the world? In failing to answer these questions the theory implies that anti-Jewishness is incurable so long as there are Jews, when in fact (as we shall see) we must view it as obdurate but not beyond a cure. And, in failing to ask these questions, it fails to confront anti-Jewishness in the aspect that lends it its unique power, and among those who, once confronted, might be best able to cure themselves. We are referring, of course, to the anti-Jewishness of the saints and idealists.

Anti-Jewishness has its effective origins in Christianity and reflects these origins to this day. This thesis, like our earlier one, must be qualified and in this case (lest it be misunderstood) before it is even expounded.

1.   Anti-Jewish attitudes predate Christianity in pagan antiquity. However, the "saints" of the Greco-Roman world could and did recognize Jewish virtues. Thus, the philosopher Theophrastus "recoiled" from Jewish animal sacrifices, yet admired Jews as "philosophers by race."[12] Christianity not only perpetuated but also transformed pre-Christian anti-Jewish attitudes, and the transformation was crucial.

2.   Anti-Jewish attitudes postdate Christianity in modern secularism, i.e., pseudo-Christian right-wing nationalism, anti-Christian left-wing liberalism and radicalism and, most important, the Nazi idolatry which aimed at the destruction of Christianity as a goal second in importance only to that of the Jewish people.

However, the modern nationalist pseudo-Christianity would have been impossible without actual Christianity. The modern liberal-leftist aim to make "the Jews"—and no one but

12. See M. Stern, ed., *Greek and Latin Authors on Jews and Judaism*, vol. 1, (Jerusalem: The Israel Academy of Sciences and Humanities, 1974), pp. 8 ff.

the Jews—into men-in-general is a transformation of the Christian opposition to Jews-in-particular. And the Nazi murder camps were the apocalyptic nemesis of an anti-Jewishness that has persisted, at times dormantly, at times violently, among Christian saints through the centuries. At its bravest and most authentic, organized German Christianity resisted the Nazi onslaught on the Jewish people only because it was in reality an attack on Jesus Christ.[13] One can imagine Theophrastus consenting to attacks on the Jewish sacrifice of animals. But one cannot imagine him defending the "philosophers by race" on grounds no more forceful than that what was really attacked was philosophy.

3. *Not all Christians are or ever have been afflicted by the disease of anti-Jewishness.* In view of the content of the thesis, this qualification is crucial. However, while its truth would seem obvious its significance is complex, obscure, and possibly even beyond the powers of anyone's present comprehension.

In the present context, it must suffice to reject a false view of its significance. The distinction between the anti-Jewishness of "mere Christendom" and a "true Christianity" free of all hatred (and hence necessarily free of Jew-hatred) is obviously apologetic. That it is false as well is shown sufficiently by the fact of anti-Jewish saints, among them St. Chrysostom, St. Augustine, and Luther. That this fact of saintly Christian anti-Jewishness is significant beyond its Christian limits is indicated by the presence, in all post-Christian forms of the phenomenon, of anti-

13. Theodore A. Gill writes as follows: "And even after it got rolling, the Confessing Church was late in its perceptions. I simply cannot get gooseflesh over the systematic refinement in Barmen's discovery that the attacks on the Jews must be resisted because they were in reality attacks on Jesus Christ. That is not high theology. That is blasphemy, the unwitting blasphemy, I hope, of men playing a dandy hand at doctrine. It was played out to the end, too. In the letter sent around preparing for the Stuttgart confession after the war, was there much about the guilt against the Jews? Was there anything? [There was not. E.L.F.]

We have little to learn from any church or any prophet who cannot recognize murder until it is murder in the cathedral." "What Can American Learn from the Church Struggle?"in *The German Church Struggle and the Holocaust*, F. H. Littell and H. G. Locke, eds. (Detroit: Wayne State University Press, 1974), p. 286. See also above, pp. 76–77.

Jewish idealists. Thus, nineteenth-century secularist antisemitism—right-wing, left-wing, and liberal—all included secular saints, i.e., enemies and critics of "the Jews" inspired not by low passions but by high ideals. Had the target of these saints been only Jewish vices, real or imagined (as they often pretended, both to others and themselves), that target would not have been "the Jews." Yet while the Jewish defense organizations of those times kept stressing precisely that point, their labors were quite in vain.

Nazism escalated the logic of anti-Jewishness to its unsurpassable extreme. Jewish virtue and vice were irrelevant. Jewish birth was in itself a crime deserving torture and death. The most shocking fact about the most shocking Nazi crime, however, is that it was, in essence, an "idealistic" enterprise—the work not of petty scoundrels or vicious sadists but of men and women sacrificing all to the "Final Solution."[14]

Indeed, so shocking is this fact as to have rendered all historically post-Holocaust anti-Jewishness on the part of religious or secular saints seemingly impossible. It is all the more startling—and depressing evidence to the tenacity and mutability of the anti-Jewish virus—that the impossibility is only seeming; that saintly anti-Jewishness has not ended but rather developed a wholly new strain which, for the first time in history, goes to any length to deny that "the Jews" are its target. Pre-Nazi "decent" antisemites would salve their consciences by citing "exceptions" even while attacking "the Jews." Nazism

---

14. In a secret address to the S.S. given on October 4, 1943, Heinrich Himmler said the following: " 'The Jewish people is going to be annihilated,' says every party member. 'Sure, it's in our program, elimination of the Jews, annihilation—we'll take care of it.' And then they all come trudging, 80 million worthy Germans, and each has his one decent Jew. Sure, the others are swine, but this one is an A-1 Jew. Of all those who talk this way, not one has seen it happen, not one has been through it. Most of you must know what it means to see a hundred corpses lie side by side, or five hundred, or a thousand. To have stuck this out and—excepting the cases of human weakness—to have remained decent, that is what has made us hard. In our history, this is an unwritten and never-to-be-written page of glory" (Lucy Dawidowicz, ed., *A Holocaust Reader* [New York: Behrman, 1976], p. 133).

did away with the exceptions.[15] Post-Nazi saintly anti-Jewishness shrinks from this horror so radically as to attack only those Jews who are not "true" Jews.

From this stance there is only one step to the identification of "false" Jews with "Zionists," a step all the easier the more undefined the "Zionism." That this new distinction between "true" and "false" Jews is but the old disease in yet another form is obvious once one discovers who belongs in these two groups. The "false" Jewish Zionists include, first, *all* Israelis, right and left, religious and secularist, "hawks" and "doves", so long as they refuse to submit to politicide. They include, second, *all* Jews *anywhere* so long as they refuse to abandon the state of Israel to politicide. As for the "true" Jews, they reduce themselves to two kinds: those dissolving their Jewish identity for the sake of mankind; and those prepared—one generation after Hitler—to entrust their Jewish destiny to the mercies of the world. This new strain of the ancient anti-Jewishness finds its climax when the one calling the "false" Jews back to their "true" Jewishness claims himself to be—symbolically to be sure—the "true" Jew.[16]

The inquiry into the uniqueness of the disease of anti-Jewishness, its nature, tenacity, and mutability, thus refocuses itself into an inquiry into the hatred of Jewish virtues by Gentile religious saints and idealists. There are stirrings within the Christian community, few as yet to be sure, but compelling by

15. In the Himmler address quoted in the preceding note, the "decent" antisemites of earlier times have become insufficiently idealistic, and the new "decency" of Jew-hatred consists precisely of considering Jewish virtue and vice equally irrelevant to the crime of Jewish birth.

16. A. Roy Eckardt has analyzed this strain of anti-Jewishness as it erupted among certain liberal Christians following the Yom Kippur War, among them Professor Robert Cushman who asserted that decent respect for the opinions of mankind dictated that the price for Israel's existence was too high, and Father Daniel Berrigan who set himself up, before an Arab group, as the true—if symbolic—Jew. ("The Devil and Yom Kippur," *Midstream*, August to September 1974.) However, this strain has been evident at least since the Six Day War when voices from Geneva thought it their duty to remind Jews in Israel of their prophetic heritage. This was after the victory. Earlier, when Israel was threatened, Geneva had shown no signs of concern.

their courage and relentlessness, of an attempt to discover the primal roots of the dread plague within the Christian tradition itself. "The antisemitism in the New Testament" is no longer an uncommon phrase, although it still awaits a thorough exploration. For our purpose it suffices to indicate the profound ambiguity of the Books themselves which, on the one hand, affirm God's promise to keep his people Israel and yet, on the other, deny that very peoplehood: only "the faithful," but not all of Israel is Israel; and, read back into the "Old Testament," these faithful reduce themselves to but a few isolated individuals. The flesh-and-blood people is lost. Thus it is no wonder that for centuries the church considered herself as either the "true" Israel opposed to one always "false," or else as the "new" Israel opposed to one long dead.

Some Christians go even further. Is Jew-hatred built into the Christian Gospel itself? Is it part of the *kerygma* itself so that only the most radical attempt to identify the evil and transform the teaching can save the Good News?

Whatever the answer to these radical questions, the hatred of Jewish virtues by Gentile religious saints and secularist idealists may be said to have found its first systematic expression in the Patristic *anti-Judaeos* literature. Here the Jews are guilty *both* for obeying "the law" *and* disobeying it; of "legalistically" observing the Sabbath *and* giving to God only one day out of seven; and their wickedness is *both* imputable as though it were willed *and* incurable as though it were hereditary.[17] Add to this page from the "dark ages" the fact that Luther rewrote just that page even while writing a crucial page of modern history,[18] and it is no longer altogether obscure why nineteenth-century European nationalist idealists considered

17. To focus attention on the *anti-Judaeos* literature, for purposes of Roman Catholic self-criticism, is one of the great merits of Rosemary Ruether's *Faith and Fratricide* (New York: Seabury Press, 1974), chap. 3.

18. In our context it is worth recalling that the early Luther was decidedly pro-Jewish but matched or even exceeded his medieval predecessors in anti-Jewish venom in his old age, surely because Jews proved to be no less stubborn in insisting on surviving as Jews vis-à-vis the new form of Christianity as they had been vis-à-vis the old.

even patriotic Jews suspect because they *were* Jews; why their no less idealistic internationalist opponents considered even radical Jews suspect so long as they *considered themselves* Jews; why during the apocalypse German Nazis treated Jewish birth as a crime, not despite but because of their idealism; and why today high-minded post-Holocaust rightists and leftists unite to deny the legitimacy of the state of Israel—the one because this state is composed of and governed by Jews, the other because it is composed of and governed by people who wilfully consider themselves Jews.[19]

What remains still obscure in all these forms of saintly anti-Jewishness is its relentlessness and centrality in the respective schemes of things. What drove some Church Fathers into the radically un-Christian assertion that even baptism cannot redeem "the Jews"? What caused Eichmann's priorities when he redirected trains from the Russian front to Auschwitz?

In the nineteenth century, Bruno Bauer, ex-Protestant-theologian, left-wing atheist, and anti-Jewish archideologue, asserted the following. Not the Christian "daughter" is guilty for wishing to get rid of the Jewish "mother." The Jewish "mother" is guilty for wanting to live. The Jewish "mother" *had* to die if the Christian "daughter" and her secularist offspring were to live.[20] This piece of imagery diagnoses brilliantly, if unwittingly, the Gentile disease of anti-Jewishness,

---

19. Here is one reason why liberals and leftists are so easily taken in by the transparently fraudulent idea of a "Palestinian secular democratic state in which Jews, Muslims, and Christians can live together." That Arab propaganda does its best to exploit this liberal-leftist weakness was to be expected.

20. See Bruno Bauer, *The Jewish Problem*, trans. Helen Lederer (Cincinnati: Hebrew Union College, 1958). Bauer writes: "The hostility of the Christian world toward the Jews has been called inexplicable. Is not Judaism the mother of Christianity, the Jewish religion the predecessor of Christianity? Why this hatred of the Christians, this enormous ingratitude of the consequent for the cause, of the daughter for the mother?" (p. 7). He answers his own question as follows: "Not the daughter is ungrateful toward the mother, but the mother does not want to acknowledge her daughter. The daughter has really the higher right, because she represents the true nature of the mother. . . . If one wants to call both sides egotistical, then the daughter is selfish for wanting her own way and progress, and the mother because she wants her own way but no progress" (p. 18). On Bauer, see further my *Encounters between Judaism and Modern Philosophy* (New York: Basic Books, 1973), pp. 142 ff.

its nature, tenacity, and mutability. Why do some saints and
idealists, Christian and post-Christian, consider, in Jews and
Jews alone, those characteristics as vices that anywhere else
they would consider as virtues? Why is, to them, the viciousness of Jewish virtue both unredeemable and central in the
scheme of things? In Bauer's imagery, because the mere survival of the "mother" threatens the "daughter's" very life.
Otherwise put, because *for these saints and idealists their
self-affirmation is inseparable from the negation of "the Jew."*
On this point, the noblest saints afflicted by the disease are at
one with the most depraved sinners. Julius Streicher wrote:
"Who fights the Jew fights the devil. Who masters the devil
conquers Heaven."[21]

But Bauer's imagery also shows—this still more
unwittingly—that the disease of anti-Jewishness is neither inevitable nor incurable. The mother-daughter relationship need
not be antagonistic, to say nothing of taking the form of a life-
and-death struggle. Minimally, the two can part company when
the daughter has reached maturity. Maximally, each can find
strength and joy in the otherness of the other.

IV

Why do anti-Jewish attitudes exist outside the Christian
world? Almost no part of the globe is wholly outside Christian
or post-Christian influence. Moreover, the Streicher-inspired
cartoons prevalent in the pre-1967 Arab Press and the Arab
translations of European antisemitic tracts are evidence of the
ease with which even the most depraved strains of the anti-
Jewish virus can be exported. However, unless these exports
found a native response their effect would surely be marginal.

---

21. Quoted in *The Yellow Spot: The Extermination of the Jews in Germany*
(London: Gollancz, 1936), p. 47. This book, its title, and its date of publication
all refute the accepted view that "it wasn't known and couldn't have been
predicted." In fact, its anonymous compilers and the Bishop of Durham (who
wrote a moving preface) were voices in the wilderness. Why?

In the Arab world this is not so. A segment of Palestinian Arabs has opposed, to a self-destructive extreme, any form of Jewish state in their neighborhood. The most moderate of current Arab statesmen has described the small Jewish island in an Arab ocean as a "dagger" in the heart of his own far larger and more populous country. Indeed, Arab nationalism as a whole has a component so inextricably bound up with the negation of the "Zionist entity" as to cause wonder whether, were this negative end ever achieved, Arab nationalism—or at least its pan-Arab variety—would not disintegrate.

One need not go far afield in order to recognize that Islam, the second "daughter" of the Jewish "mother," too, has fallen prey to the disease of anti-Jewishness, and has done so on her own, quite apart from any influence of her "sister."[22] The ways are in some respects different, in others the same. The main difference: the Christian anti-Jewishness and its derivatives negate Jewish existence; the Muslim anti-Jewishness and its derivatives negate only Jewish equality, especially when it finds a political expression. The main resemblance: both forms of hostility include saints and idealists among their subjects and Jewish virtues among their objects.

The main cause of the difference is obvious enough: Christianity originated on Jewish soil, in the midst of a flesh-and-blood, still semi-autonomous, Jewish nation. When Islam originated, Jews had already been in exile for centuries and were, so far as the new religion was concerned, not a flesh-and-blood people but only a religious sect. In view of the vastness of this difference, the resemblance is all the more depressing: despite the "mother's" shadowy existence, the younger "daughter" found herself threatened by any sign of life shown by her, and is today shocked to the marrow by the "mother's" miraculous new youth. It is fortunate, however, that Muslim and post-Muslim-secular-Arab anti-Jewishness is neither universal nor inevitable. In this case, too, antagonism is not the only possible mother-daughter relation.

22. See Moshe Ma'oz's essay in *World Jewry and the State of Israel.*

V

The cure of the Gentile disease of anti-Jewishness can only be the task of the patients. The two "daughters" of the Jewish "mother" and their respective offspring can be healed by no one but themselves. However, the Jewish "mother" can assist in two interrelated ways. One is to remove herself, so far as she is able, from the reach of the other's power. (Of this more will be said below.) The other is to cure herself insofar as she has been infected by the daughters' disease, i.e., to break the circle in which the oppressor has made himself into a just accuser and the victim has confessed his guilt. The negative task of breaking this circle has as its positive counterpart the search for an authentic identity.

This search must obviously seek an end of all Jewish self-hatred, open or disguised. Less obvious is the need to end or transform a plethora of qualified Jewish self-affirmations, which are unauthentic to the extent to which they have yielded to and internalized a plethora of qualified anti-Jewish negations. The nineteenth-century German (or French or Hungarian) super-patriot of the Mosaic faith; his internationalist contemporary who expressed his Jewishness by dissolving it, thus leading all peoples in the march toward mankind; the open-minded Jew who kept his Jewishness from his son and daughter lest he deprive them of a free identity of their own when "they were old enough to choose": these and other Jewish identities were all unauthentic. Yet they all survive to this day. Others have been added by the events of this century. One is the Jew who forgets the Holocaust as if it were a guilty secret, or as if it were selfish for a Jew to remember it. Another is the "true" Jew who outdoes all other "anti-Zionists" in opposing all the "false" Jewish Zionists. An authentic Jewish identity is possible only if two questions are separated with absolute clarity: (1) How shall a Jew respond to anti-Jewish attitudes and, indeed, what Gentile attitudes can properly be viewed by him as being anti-Jewish? (2) What does, can, shall it mean to be a Jew, today and tomorrow?

This separation by no means marks the end of the contemporary Jewish identity crisis. It would be more correct to say that it only reveals it. For just as there are unauthentic Jewish identities, so there are also authentic identity crises. The emancipation of the search for a Jewish identity from the tyranny of all forms of internalized anti-Jewishness only brings into clear focus the fact that the authentic identity crisis of the contemporary Jew is without precedent. The premodern Jew knew his identity: he was covenanted to the God of Israel. His secularist modern descendant could seek a new Jewish identity by abolishing those "abnormalities" caused by a religious tradition to which he yet owed his very existence. However, the present-day religious Jew no longer can view the Jewish secularist as nothing but an apostate, and the present-day secularist Jew no longer can view the religious Jew as nothing but a dead relic. Each must include the other when defining his own Jewish identity, and while the problem is with us the solution has yet to come. This unprecedented crisis in post-modern Jewish identity is the result of two enormous facts. Of these one is the state of Israel. The other, however, has an enormity forcing us to view it quite by itself: *every Jew alive today would either be dead or be unborn but for a geographical accident.*

This is a *novum* in the human condition, without parallels inside Jewish history or outside it. Philosophers have not yet noticed this *novum*. Jewish thinkers have not done too much better. Its significance for Jewish identity is as yet obscure. Only one thing is clear and devoid of all obscurity: one cannot authentically cope with one's Jewish identity crisis without facing the *novum* in all its starkness and uniqueness. It is said that this is the first time in Jewish history when a Jew can cease to be a Jew without having to become something else, and that therefore the present Jewish identity crisis can authentically be solved by the dissolution of Jewish identity. It is not obvious that the conclusion follows from the premise. A generation ago Franz Rosenzweig knew that he could not authentically become a Christian without first knowing the Judaism he was about to leave. He never left, and subsequently helped write a new page in Jewish history. No Jew today can authentically abandon his Jewish identity without first asking whether in so doing he helps close the book of a history that should be closed, or abandons those who write a new page that cries out to be written; whether he leaves the ranks of pointless past victims or joins the ranks of possible future murderers and bystanders; whether he serves the cause of God and man or betrays it.

VI

It is doubtful whether the Jewish people could cure itself spiritually from its infection by the disease of anti-Jewishness were it not for the fact that one of its parts has removed itself physically from the reach of anti-Jewish power. It has done so by founding the Third Jewish Commonwealth. This event, momentous in Gentile as well as Jewish history (the former minimally to the extent that it has suffered from the disease of anti-Jewishness), has transformed the Jewish condition in two respects which concern our present purpose. Being a small yet independent state, Israel has given a new dimension to the unauthenticity of the Jew who lets his Jewishness be defined by others. And having built the Law of Return into its very substance, Israel has given a new dimension to the unauthenticity of the Jew who is voluntarily a toleree (to say nothing of being a victim) of the societies, theologies, philosophies, and ideologies of others. Thus it has come to pass, as a corresponding fact, that in the search for an authentic Jewish identity Israel is central.

These assertions may seem wayward or downright foolish at a time when the new, post-Holocaust "anti-Zionist" strain of anti-Jewishness has become so worldwide as to have given rise, among certain Jews, to complaints that the Jewish state, meant to solve the Jewish problem, has become the Jewish problem, and that, meant to be a spiritual center, it resembles more closely a beleaguered fortress.

Yet Herzl and Achad Ha-am, though each was wrong in one respect, were right in another. Herzl was wrong in his naive belief that a Jewish state would establish a natural Jewish existence and end the disease of anti-Jewishness; he was more right than he could have known in his belief that the Jewish people must stop tolerating what, since the Holocaust, has become intolerable: Jewish acceptance of the status of victim of those sick with anti-Jewishness, or the status of toleree of the semicured. Not long ago a Zionist leader proposed that Israel become the ward of the world community. Only a few years later it is clear that, so long as the world community is infected with the disease of anti-Jewishness, the guardian is unsuitable and that, if and when the disease vanishes, the guardian will not be necessary. Herzl was more right than many who came after him.

Achad Ha-am too was wrong and right. The Jewish state does not abound with synagogues filled with superior piety or universities of superior excellence. The life style of its citizens is too harried by the petty problems of daily existence and the deep worries about national existence to be of much help to Jewish visitors in search of a Jewish life style of their own. There is more leisure for matters spiritual at the periphery than at the center. The Jewish state is not, or not yet, a spiritual center of world Jewry in this sense. Yet, Achad Ha-am was right in a way he could not have known. Without Israel, the Diaspora's own spirituality would shrivel into mere fideism. Without the Jewish state, Diaspora Judaism, even after the Holocaust, would belittle "mere" Jewish survival unless it served ideals acceptable to others who would let Jews survive, provided they served just those ideals.[23] Without Israel's Law of Return Diaspora Judaism would make Jewish homelessness into a blessing, viewing the bitter fact of persecution as meaningful martyrdom, and the degrading condition of toleree as a chance to turn the other cheek. This would be true of the Judaism of the modern-minded. As for the Orthodox, they would try to rebuild ghetto walls which have crumbled beyond repair.

23. A decade ago Milton Himmelfarb exclaimed: "After the Holocaust, let no one call Jewish survival 'mere'!" Now Terrence Des Pres has written *The Survivor* (New York: Oxford University Press, 1976), a profound meditation which questions "a tradition that speaks of 'merely' surviving, as if in itself life were not worth much; as if we felt life is justified only by things which negate it" (p. 5). He finds "the grandeur of death . . . lost in a world of mass murder" (p. 6), and sees a significance both profound and universal in the defiant affirmation of life shown by inmates of the death camps.

VII

A modern view of great longevity has it that the Jewish people has survived through the ages only because of the pressures of its enemies. Friends holding this view have always wished an end of the enmity, foes holding it have always wished the end of the Jewish people. Still others, neither friend nor foe or a little of each, wanted an end of both. The pre-Holocaust version of this view extends to both the people and its faith. The post-Holocaust version professes to respect the intrinsic value and vitality of the faith, seeking an end only of the people, and of these only insofar as they insist on *being* a people. Only the "Zionists" and their "entity" are without intrinsic value and vitality, a pseudo-nation bound to dissolve once enemies cease to threaten it. "Zionism" and "antisemitism" belong together, and the first is the product of the second.

This is said to be the rationale of the current policies of Egypt, Israel's most peaceful Arab neighbor state. Peace with Israel is not considered incompatible with seeking her destruction but rather, on the contrary, the surest way to bring it about. An Israel at peace would be destroyed internally by factional strife—between secularists and Orthodox, Europeans and Orientals, rich and poor; she would be externally abandoned on the one hand, by Diaspora Jewry, on the other, by what is left of world conscience.

Jews cannot speak on behalf of world conscience. On their own behalf, however, they should accept this challenge, both the explicit challenge to Israel and the implicit challenge to the whole Jewish people. Let her enemies make peace with the state of Israel! And let the world cure itself of its anti-Jewishness! And let it then be shown by future history whether Jewish rebirth at Jerusalem after Jewish death at Auschwitz was, after all, a mere illusion—the birth a stillbirth—or whether, on the contrary, it was a live birth, with the prospect that the new Jerusalem might grow to be a blessing, matching or possibly even surpassing the old.

In the premodern world Yehudah Halevi wrote: "Jerusalem can be rebuilt only when Israel yearns after it to such an extent that we love even its stones and dust."[24] A post-Holocaust Jew might add: "In loving the stones and dust of Jerusalem, the Jewish people will rebuild itself after its greatest catastrophe; and only in rebuilding itself can it be a light unto the nations."

24. *Sefer Ha-Kuzari,* part V, sec. 27.

15. *On the Life, Death, and Transfiguration of Martyrdom: The Jewish Testimony to the Divine Image in Our Time*

I

THE COLLOQUY OF which this paper is part is doubly fashionable. Western religion, long self-enclosed, has now opened itself in all directions and to every influence. Western philosophy, having said little to a world wanting to hear much in its but recent tough-minded analytic extreme, is now swinging to an extreme so tender-minded as to define its critical function loosely when it defines it at all. The spirit of the age is thus well reflected in a meeting in which Christianity, Judaism, Islam, Hinduism, and Confucianism are all represented and in which, to judge by the titles, philosophy is as much an expression of religion as its critic.

But fashion is one thing, seriousness another. It is no accident that Western philosophy began with demythologizing the gods and that, even at a time when the man-made gods were replaced by the man-creating God, philosophy insisted on guarding its *lumen naturale* against incursions by an acknowl-

This paper was delivered at an International Philosophy Conference, held in New York City May 28–April 4, 1976, whose distinctive nature was an unprecedentedly large representation of non-Western philosophies. Reprinted from *Communio: International Catholic Review*, vol. IV, no. 1, Spring 1977.

edged *lumen supernaturale.* Nor is it an accident that the religions represented in this colloquy showed toward each other, for most of their history, an attitude of hostility, indifference, or at best of a tolerance not unmixed with condescension.

Can it be otherwise? Can philosophy let go of its critical function without self-betrayal? Can a religious witness believe himself to stand related to the Divine and yet let the truth of that relation be called into question by alternative or even conflicting religious testimonies? One thus wonders whether the current, superficially admirable looseness in philosophy does not hide a loss of direction, and whether the superficially no less admirable "dialogical" openness in religion is not an attempt to compensate for a lack of conviction. The last-named possibility was well expressed by a wit who defined ecumenism as the belief that anyone's religion is better than one's own.

Much of the current openness in religion and philosophy reflects a mere failure of nerve. At a deeper level, however, it responds to a historical necessity. The increasing, worldwide interdependence of civilizations, their religions included; a universal, steadily increasing secularization, accompanied by a rise of this-worldly expectations; and, perhaps above all, an accelerated pace accompanying all these manifestations of contemporary life, together with vast, mostly technologically induced promises and threats: these are just the most obvious facts necessitating looseness in philosophy and openness in religion. And the authentic question arising may be stated in the form of a dilemma. In response to the challenge of the age, religious and philosophical traditions may strive to dissolve their respective identities into a larger, possibly worldwide whole: but the universalism thus arrived at could only be a flattened-out syncretism. Alternatively, and in an attempt to preserve their identities, they may strive to withdraw from living contacts already actual into themselves: but the shell of such a particularism could only be frozen and sterile. The dilemma is between two forms of lifelessness, and the question is whether we can escape it.

II. Post-Hegelian Perspectives

This dilemma was anticipated and confronted with un-equaled profundity by the thought of Hegel. And, although it will appear that our own stance cannot be Hegel's own, we do well to begin with some relevant Hegelian theses:[1]

1. Philosophical thought is not divorced from but rather *rooted in* human existence. It *arises* from existential situations in order, partly or wholly, to rise above them.

2. Existence itself has an irreducible religious dimension. Marx, Freud, and others were to embrace a religious reductionism. This was repudiated and refuted by Hegel in advance. Religious truth must be understood as it understands itself before philosophy can rise to its conceptualization. Marxists and Freudians demythologize. Hegel transmythologizes. And unlike them he does not destroy religious truth but rather preserves it.

3. Committed to these principles, Hegel is faced with the very dilemma which we have already stated. Either the religious truth preserved by philosophical conceptualization is a "universal" religion of "mankind," whether culled from existing religious sources or wholly constructed by philosophy; but then it is a lifeless syncretism or construction, and philosophy does not preserve religious truth but rather helps destroy it. Or the religion conceptualized and preserved is one particular living religion: but then the philosophy which preserves its truth is guilty of parochialism and, moreover, finds its nemesis in other philosophies which conceptualize and preserve other, no less living, religions. Confronting the dilemma head-on, Hegel seeks to meet it with the crucial notion of *mediation*. Mediating philosophic thought must, first, do justice to every religion in *its own*, unique, self-understanding. It must, second, rise partly or wholly *above* this self-understanding. And it will, third,

---

1. The theses here merely asserted are developed in my *The Religious Dimension in Hegel's Thought* (Bloomington: Indiana University Press, 1968; Boston: Beacon Press, 1970). See also above, chap. 9.

prove the success of this rise if and when, partly or wholly, it mediates the conflict or divergence between one religion and some or all others.

4. Mediation is thus needed *among* religions. At least in the modern world, it is also needed *between* the religious sphere of life as a whole and an independent secular sphere of life. For it is the characteristic of the modern world that secular life, manifest in such forms as science and technology and, above all, in the social and political sphere, has emancipated itself from premodern religious authority. In the view of countless thinkers after Hegel, this fact has made all religion an anachronism. Hegel himself rejects and refutes this view in advance with his own mediation between religion and secularity, whose result is that modern religion stands in need of secular expression lest it lapse into a worldless pietism; and that modern secularity stands in need of religious inspiration lest it lapse into either spiritual chaos or spiritless fragmentation.

5. In theory, a religion may emerge from Hegel's mediating justice in one of three ways:

(a) Its truth may be preserved, encompassed, and hence superseded by a higher religion. In that case, the religion survives, if survive it does, only as an anachronism.

(b) Its truth may remain unencompassed by another. In that case, it depends for its authentic survival only on its own vitality and power of rejuvenation.

(c) Its truth may be a *novum* in history, relative to hitherto existing religious and/or secular forms of life, and responding to a *novum* in history itself. In that case, it necessitates a reappraisal of existing realities which may be worldwide in scope. And, if the *novum* is radical, the necessary reappraisal encompasses philosophy itself.

6. These three possibilities exist in theory. In practice they have reduced themselves to two in Hegel's own age. For Protestant Christianity is the "absolute" or all-encompassing religious truth, and between it and secular modernity there has come into being a mediation that is, in principle at least, all-encompassing and thus unsurpassable. Hence, first, no religious *novum* is either possible or necessary. Hence, second, all

existing religions that continue to exist side by side Protestant Christianity are, radically considered, anachronisms. Hence, finally, an absolute or all-encompassing mediation has become possible in the sphere of philosophical thought. The philosophy that has achieved this mediation is Hegel's own.

The above suffices not only as a summary of Hegel's thought but also as a proof why, on our part, we cannot be Hegelians but at most only post-Hegelians. For the sixth above thesis we non-Protestants are bound to reject as an expression of nineteenth-century Protestant-European imperialism. Moreover, most if not all contemporary Protestants would join us in rejecting it and indeed exceed us in vehemence. Finally, it is safe to say that Hegel himself would not be a Hegelian today.[2]

We say "post"- rather than "non"- or "anti-Hegelian" because Hegel's was not a thoughtless imperialism. Like Marx and others after him and on account of him, he foresaw that modern-secular European "freedom" would be of world-historical significance, and held that this secular emancipation *from* religion has been made possible by a religious emancipation *in* religion which had found in Protestantism its most effective if not sole expression. Unlike these heirs of his, he foresaw (as we have already stressed) that modern-secular freedom would degenerate into spiritual chaos or spiritless fragmentation unless it continued to be religiously nourished. Thus Hegel's European-Protestant imperialism is not a historically contingent aberration. It is a historically necessary experiment that failed.

It failed for three fundamental reasons:

1. While doing justice to non-Protestant religions to an astounding degree, Hegel does less than the full justice required by his own philosophy.

2. While anticipating the threat of fragmentation posed by "the Understanding," Hegel did not and could not anticipate that at least in one of its forms—technology—this threat would

2. See my "Would Hegel Today Be a Hegelian?" *Dialogue*, IX, pp. 222–26.

escalate into one to man's very humanity and, indeed, to his survival.

3. While allowing for relative evil, Hegel's philosophy cannot recognize absolute evil. In the religious realm, there is only relative idolatry which bears unwitting witness to a higher religious truth. In the political realm, even the worst state is better than no state at all, for it serves life and leads to a higher life. There is no room in Hegel's philosophy for an idolatry that revels in the defilement of everything human and blasphemes against everything divine; nor for an anti-society whose factories are geared to but one ultimate produce, and that is death. Leaving room for no absolute evil anywhere, his thought leaves room for it, least of all, in the Christian Europe of modern times. Yet precisely this was the space and time of Auschwitz and Buchenwald.[3]

The failure of Hegel's experiment transforms his remaining theses as follows:

1. Philosophic thought, having foundered in its attempt to achieve a transhistorical absoluteness, is cast back into history and becomes a historically situated reflection which (to use Kierkegaard's expression) points to a religious immediacy after reflection.

2. Religious immediacy, being *after* reflection, is forced to recognize *its own* historical situatedness. This imposes upon it a threefold obligation: the need to prove its own continued vitality and relevance; the need to meet the challenge of a *novum* if history produces a *novum;* and the need to be open to the challenge and testimony of other forms of religious immediacy. (This dialogical openness replaces Hegel's mediation.) However, especially in the age of Auschwitz, it is evident that this openness would degenerate if it were indiscriminate. It must be rendered discriminating by the power to oppose absolute evil.

---

3. The three reasons here merely stated are argued for in chap. 3 of my *Encounters between Judaism and Modern Philosophy* (New York: Basic Books, 1973). The chapter is entitled "Moses and the Hegelians."

III. The Jewish Testimony to the Divine Image

In the light of these criteria we shall now expound, first, a traditional Jewish religious testimony and then a contemporary *novum* concerning it. We shall confine ourselves to a single commitment, as made by one crucial witness at a crucial moment in Jewish history. The witness is Rabbi Akiba. His testimony is as follows:

> Beloved is man, for he was created in the image of God; but it was by a special love that it was made known to him that he was created in the image of God, as it is said, "For in the image of God made He man." [Gen. 9:6][4]

One is tempted to dismiss this affirmation as a high-sounding platitude so universalistic as to be discoverable anywhere and nowhere, committing an author to everything and nothing and thus costing him nothing. One is stopped short by the fact that this particular author died a martyr's death at the behest of Rome, the then citadel of universalism.

If taken seriously, Akiba's testimony raises an exegetical question. The rabbi cites a book. Like all books, it is a particular book. It is a—*the*—Jewish book. Could it be, then, that, its universalistic words notwithstanding, the scope of this testimony is confined to those who know the citation because they possess the book, that is, to Jews?

This "particularistic" exegesis is ruled out, however, not only by the context of the statement[5] but further by a well-known debate between Akiba and Rabbi Shim'on Ben Azzai. The task in this debate is to find a passage in the Jewish book which contains its greatest principle. Akiba cites "Thou shalt

---

4. *Pirke Abot* III, 18.
5. The particularistic exegesis would make a redundancy of the saying of Akiba which immediately follows. This reads: "Beloved are Israel, for they were called children of the All-Present; but it was by a special love that it was made known to them that they were called children of the All-Present, as it is said. 'Ye are children unto the Lord your God'" (Deut. 14:1).

love thy neighbor as thyself" (Lev. 19:18). Ben Azzai cites "This is the book of the generations of man" (Gen. 5:1). Ben Azzai does not wish to contradict Akiba, a close friend recognized by him as the greater man.[6] The debate is not an argument but rather a conjoining of two mutually inseparable principles. This exegesis is nicely confirmed by the fact that the debate exists in a second version in which the order of the two cited texts is reversed.[7]

The conjoining of the two principles has a twofold significance. First, the ethical commitment—love of neighbor—is mere sentimentality without the corresponding ontological commitment—the divine image in man—just as this particular ontological commitment remains empty if not fraudulent without an ethics, and just *this particular* ethics. Second, because of the content of this ethics and this ontology, there must be a conjunction of the metaphysically most radical universalism with the existentially most radical particularism. In *The Fathers according to Rabbi Nathan* we read:

He who sustains one soul is accounted by Scripture as though he had sustained a whole world . . . and he who destroys one soul is accounted by Scripture as though he had destroyed a whole world. . . . For thus we find of Cain who killed his brother Abel as it is said, *The voice of thy brother's blood crieth unto Me* (Gen. 4:10): though he shed the blood of one, it is said *damin* ("bloods") in the plural. Which teaches that the blood of Abel's children and the children's children and all his descendents to the end of all generations destined to come forth from him—all of them stood crying out before the Holy One, blessed be He.

Thus thou dost learn that one man's life is equal to all the work of Creation.[8]

6. On hearing a dispute concerning marital law in which Akiba espoused successfully the principle of a widow's human rights, Ben Azzai exclaimed, "Alas, that I did not have Akiba for a teacher!" (*Babyl. Talmud, Nedarim* 74b).

7. For the two versions, see *Sifra* 89b and *Genesis Rabba, Bereshit*, XXIV, 7.

8. *The Fathers according to Rabbi Nathan*, trans. J. Goldin (New Haven: Yale University Press, 1955; New York: Schocken, 1974), pp. 125–26.

The author of this statement is not Akiba but an unknown contemporary or near-contemporary. It is certain, however, that Akiba, like him, embraces a universalism so radical in metaphysical scope as to trace the divine image to Adam, and a particularism so radical in existential seriousness as to regard the life of even a single man as equivalent to the whole world.

Our exegetical question is thus answered. This answer, however, in turn gives rise to a question that is not merely exegetical but rather religious and philosophical. Does Akiba's ontology of the divine image in man refer to an unsullied human essence? Then why does this essence contrast so starkly with man's historical existence? Or is man's essence wholly manifest in and inseparable from his historical existence? Then what remains intact of the divine image—and of the God who created it? These questions are faced with unyielding sternness in a rabbinic debate reported in the Talmud as follows:

> The schools of Hillel and Shammai disputed two and a half years whether it would have been better if man had or had not been created. Finally they agreed that it would have been better had he not been created, but since he has been created, let him investigate his past doings, and let him examine what he is about to do.[9]

The debate reported in this text may have taken place before 70 C.E., when the Jerusalem Temple was destroyed by the Romans. Its conclusion makes its occurrence after the catastrophe more likely. Regardless of the scholarly question of dating the debate, however, much could have been said by the Hillelites, even after 70 C.E., in support of the view that it was better for man to be created, on the grounds of the divine image in man. And much could have been said by the Shammai'ites, even before the catastrophe, in support of the view that it would have been better for man not to have been created, on the basis of historical evidence. However, *nothing* could be and was said by *either* school, before or even after the event, to lend support

9. *Babylonian Talmud, Erubim* 13b.

to the view that this was not, after all, a divinely created world, and that hence man was not, after all, created in the divine image. Indeed, this view is explicitly defied with the demand that concludes the debate, to the effect that, even in a world giving every evidence against the goodness of being, man must *act* according to the divine image which he *is*. Such a demand, however, is possible only because the *knowledge* of man as the divine image remains accessible even at a time when the *reality* seems all but vanished. It remains accessible, if nowhere else, in the Jewish book.

In 70 C.E. Titus destroyed the Jewish state but permitted the study and teaching of the Jewish book. In 135 C.E. (after the collapse of the Bar Kokhba revolt) Hadrian went further. He forbade the study and teaching of the Jewish book on pain of death. The act of Titus had made inescapable, for the schools of Hillel and Shammai, the question whether for man, the divine image, it was better to be or not to be. The more radical act of Hadrian now raised for Rabbi Akiba the still more radical prospect of a time in which the very question could no longer be debated. After 70 C.E., the knowledge of the divine image remained even if the reality seemed all but vanished. After 135 C.E., Akiba had to reckon with the possibility of the destruction of the Jewish book, and hence the vanishing of the knowledge.

Akiba's response to this extreme situation—the most extreme in Jewish experience prior to the Nazi Holocaust—was astonishingly simple. The Jewish book teaches that man is created in the image of God. Reality shows that not every man *knows* that he is created in the image of God. It is therefore a Jewish duty to bear witness to this knowledge. This duty does not vanish at a time when the teaching of the Jewish book is forbidden. On the contrary, it then becomes most inescapable. If the penalty is death, then this risk must be taken. And if death comes as the result of defying the prohibition it assumes the form of martyrdom, the extreme act of testimony.

Akiba died pronouncing words from the forbidden book, "Hear, O Israel, the Lord our God, the Lord is One." It is significant that ever since Akiba's martyr's death, countless Jews have died many kinds of death with the same words on their lips. It is also significant that Rufus, the Roman officer in charge of Akiba's execution, made no attempt to silence him. On the contrary, he listened, and was astonished.[10]

IV. The Novum in Contemporary Jewish Existence

The Roman Empire was ignorant of the divine image. Heir to a bimillennial tradition, which included the Jewish book, the Nazi empire did not share this ignorance but rather repudiated the knowledge—consciously, deliberately, thoroughly. In its ignorance the Roman Empire violated the divine image, sometimes slightly, sometimes catastrophically, but always haphazardly. In its repudiation of the knowledge, the Nazi empire was neither haphazard nor content to violate the divine image. It sought to destroy the reality of the divine image so systematically as to make its rejection of the knowledge of it into a self-fulfilling prophecy. This empire was therefore a *novum* in human history; and the evidence around us—the cheapness of life, the banality of death, the ideological glorification of murder—shows that, for all its short duration, this *novum* was no mere episode.

Aiming at the destruction of the divine image of all peoples, the Nazi Empire focused its effort on one particular people. It asserted itself as "Aryan." Yet it could find no definition of

10. L. Finkelstein writes: "The popular story tells that the Romans killed him by tearing his flesh from his living body. As he lay in unspeakable agony, he suddenly noticed the first streaks of dawn breaking over the eastern hills. It was the hour when the Law requires each Jew to pronounce the *Shema*. Oblivious to his surroundings, Akiba intoned in a loud, steady voice, the forbidden words of his faith, 'Hear, O Israel, the Lord our God, the Lord is One. And thou shalt love the Lord thy God with all thine heart, and with all thy soul, and with all thy might.'

"Rufus, the Roman general, who superintended the horrible execution, cried out: 'Are you a wizard or are you utterly insensible to pain?' 'I am neither,' replied the martyr, 'but all my life I have been waiting for the moment when I might truly fulfil this commandment. I have always loved the Lord with all my might, and with all my heart; now I know that I love him with all my life.' And, repeating the verse again, he died as he reached the words, 'The Lord is one'" (*Akiba: Scholar, Saint, and Martyr* [New York: Atheneum, 1970], pp. 276–77).

"Aryan" other than "not-non-Aryan," and the "non-Aryan" was legally defined as a —full, half, quarter—Jew.[11] And the process which began with a definition making its victim rightless climaxed in an acted-out legal philosophy which defined the victim's very existence as a crime punishable by torture and death.[12]

If the Nazi empire was a *novum* in human history, this law was a *novum* in legal history. All periods of human history have had their share of lawless violence. All societies have had their share of unjust laws, not a few of them criminal. All law hitherto, however, defined crime as an *action*, something someone *did*. When, in the case of one group of persons, Nazi law defined *mere existence* as a capital crime, the society governed by it showed itself to be more than merely criminal vis-à-vis its victims, but rather an anti-society vis-à-vis the human race. In the view of Akiba and his friends, he who destroyed one soul had been as though he destroyed the whole world. In making *being* alive a *putative* crime for "non-Aryans," Nazi law

11. In commenting on the 1935 Nuremberg laws, Raul Hilberg writes: "It is to be noted that while heretofore the population had been divided only into 'Aryans' and 'non-Aryans,' there were now two kinds of non-Aryans: Jews and so-called *Mischlinge*. Half-Jews who did not belong to the Jewish religion or who were not married to a Jewish person on September 15, 1935, were to be called *Mischlinge* of the first degree. One-quarter Jews became *Mischlinge* of the second degree. The fate of the *Mischlinge* was never settled to the complete satisfaction of the Nazi party, and they were the subject of considerable discussion during the 'final solution' conferences of 1941 and 1942 (*Documents of Destruction*, ed. R. Hilberg [New York: Quadrangle, 1971], pp. 18–19.

12. In a book entitled *The Criminal Nature of the Jews*, published in 1944, Johannes von Leers asserted that since the Jews were not only a pseudo-people but also a race of born criminals, a nation had not only the right to kill the Jews living in its midst, but also the right, deriving from the juridical doctrine of hot pursuit, of seizing the Jews of its neighbors and exterminating them. Indeed, a nation harboring Jews was as criminally culpable as someone failing to take measures against cholera bacilli. (See the account by Erich Goldhagen, "Pragmatism, Function, and Belief in Nazi Anti-Semitism," *Midstream*, December 1972, p. 60.) Von Leers was Professor of History at the University of Jena.

Raul Hilberg's magisterial *The Destruction of the European Jews* (New York: Quadrangle, 1961) ends its concluding "Reflections" with this sentence: "When in the early days of 1933 the first civil servant wrote the first definition of an 'non-Aryan' into a civil service ordinance, the fate of European Jewry was sealed" (p. 669).

sought to implicate all "Aryans" in its domain in an *actual* crime, by the mere act—accomplished by the proof of one's "Aryan" ancestry—of *staying* alive.

In this manner the Nazi rejection of the knowledge of the divine image was translated into law. The law itself came closest to the self-fulfilling prophecy aimed at in the murder camp. The murder camp was not an accidental by-product of the Nazi empire. It was its pure essence.

The divine image in man *can* be destroyed. No more threatening proof to this effect can be found than the so-called *Muselmann* in the Nazi death camp. A survivor writes:

> On their entry into the camp, through basic incapacity, or by misfortune, or through some banal incident, they are overcome before they can adapt themselves; they are beaten by time, they do not begin to learn German, to disentangle the infernal knot of laws and prohibitions until their body is already in decay, and nothing can save them from selections or death by exhaustion. Their life is short, but their number is endless; they, the *Muselmaenner*, the drowned, form the backbone of the camp, an anonymous mass, continuously renewed and always identical, of non-men who march and labor in silence, the divine spark dead within them, already too empty to really suffer. One hesitates to call them living; one hesitates to call their death death.[13]

A recent writer comments:

> This is the empirical instance of death-in-life. No more awful thing can be said of the concentration camps than that countless men and women were murdered in spirit as the means of killing them in body.[14]

The *Muselmaenner* are a new way of human being in history, the living dead. What shall we say of those implicated in the

13. Primo Levi, *Survival in Auschwitz* (New York: Collier Books, 1961), p. 82. Cited by Terrence Des Pres, *The Survivor* (New York: Oxford University Press, 1976,), p. 89.
14. Des Pres, ibid., p. 88.

production of this way of being—propagandists, paragraph-experts, paper-pushers as well as those actually giving the orders and wielding the clubs—except that in murdering the "divine spark" in others they also killed it in themselves?

The murder camp did not succeed in destroying the divine image in all its victims. Akiba had died with words of the Jewish book on his lips. Countless nameless Akibas cited these same words at the time of death in the murder camps. Yet we cannot record this unprecedented spiritual triumph without at the same time recording an unprecedented spiritual tragedy. In making the teaching of the Jewish book a capital crime, Hadrian had created the possibility of martyrdom for Jewish believers. In making Jewish existence a capital crime, Hitler murdered Jewish martyrdom itself. When Akiba died with the words of the Jewish book on his lips, Rufus had listened in astonishment. When the nameless Akibas in the Nazi empire did likewise, the countless nameless Eichmanns reacted, either not at all, or with a new species of humor. Nor was this response without its logic. In the Roman Empire a martyr had *chosen* death. Since the Nazi empire destroyed this choice, a victim's retreat to the remaining choice—the manner of his death—was, in the eyes of all the murderers and most of the bystanders, either a triviality or an occasion for laughter. Humor has been defined as the experience that the small incongruities of life are not serious, and faith, as the commitment to the proposition that the large incongruities of life are not ultimate.[15] Since the Nazi empire spared no effort to make death itself banal, even the most sublime expression of faith—in this case, the manner of dying—reduced itself, in the context of that empire, to a small incongruity, that is, a case of the comical.

Yet believers will cry out that the testimony of the nameless Akibas, unheard on earth, is heard in heaven. Unbelievers will cry out that this proof of humanity will forever inspire humanity, even among persons without religious faith. Both will unite

15. By Reinhold Niebuhr, probably in part under the inspiration of Kierkegaard.

in the protest that the context of the Nazi empire is not *our* context, and must not be.

Both protests are powerful. Jointly they are irresistible. Yet they would lose all their power unless they face up to the question posed by the Nazi empire. This empire succeeded in destroying the divine image in some. It also succeeded in destroying an ancient way of testifying to the divine image in others. After this double success, carefully planned and executed, how can one witness to the divine image in man and hope to be believed? How can one believe one's own testimony? This question, in any case inescapable, is all the more so because the conditions that have given rise to it are not gone. The Nazi death camp is destroyed. The Soviet "Destructive Labor" camp[16] remains. Moreover, outside the Soviet empire the Nazi camp enjoys an afterlife of sorts. Death, forced into banality in the death camps, widely remains banal. And martyr and hero in behalf of a cause have given way to the terrorist whose glamor lies not in his ends but rather in his indiscriminate means.

The question is raised by the Nazi murder camp. An answer can come only *from* the murder camps—not from the philosopher reflecting on evil-in-general or the preacher inveighing against it but only from the testimony of the survivor. A recent book by that title[17] has three special credentials. The work of a non-Jewish author, the book disposes of the view that the Nazi empire is not in fact a *novum* in history but only viewed as such by traumatized Jewish writers. Encompassing the Soviet "Destructive Labor" camp as well as the Nazi death camp, it also disposes of the view that the *novum* was an episode, now dead and gone. Most important, the book does not psychoanalyze or otherwise explain the survivor. It exposes itself to his testimony.

This testimony—unprecedented in human history and a revolutionary challenge to religion and philosophy—may be summed up as follows. In an anti-society geared to torture and

16. Aptly so called by A. I. Solzhenitsyn.
17. See note 13. The following section is deeply indebted to this profound work.

death, mere living is not "mere." When law defines existence itself as a crime, illegality becomes sacred. When a system makes surrender to death the norm, survival becomes a heroic act of resistance. When every effort is made to reduce dying to a banality, life does not need to be sanctified. It already *is* holy.

This summary remains an empty shell without the actual testimony of the survivors: those who actually survived the Nazi empire to tell the tale; but also the far more numerous others who survived, not the camps, but only *in* the camps—a year, a month, or even a single day beyond imaginable human endurance—and whose story is told by others. And the story of most can never be told.

The weight of their collective testimony forces us to revolutionize our questions. One asks: why did many become *Muselmaenner*, the living dead? The true question is: why were there some who did *not* succumb to living death, and the answer is that they rallied a will-to-live no one knew existed. One asks: why were many reduced to what philosophers are wont to call the "state of nature," a war of each against all, with friend betraying friend, parent set against child and child against parent, all for a crust of bread? The true question is why not all succumbed to this state, and the answer is that, in a world that was no mere jungle but rather hell itself, some found an astounding need—indeed, an imperative and a law—to help others as much as to be helped by them. The contemplation of the murder camp as a system produces the most astonishing reversal of all. In an age in which men and women are programmed for all sorts of purposes, one takes for granted that the Nazi death camp, the supreme programming system of all, succeeded in programming its victims, and then wonders how men and women could be programmed into cooperating in their own destruction. The astounding fact is that the *recognition* of the system *as such* lent the intended victim his supreme power for resisting it. One survivor writes:

At the outset the living places, the ditches, the mud, the piles of excrement behind the blocks, had appalled me with their horrible filth. . . . And then I saw the light! I saw that it was not a question of disorder or lack of organization but that, on the contrary, a very thoroughly considered conscious idea was in the back of the camp's existence. They had condemned us to die in our own filth, to drown in mud, in our own excrement. They wished to abase us, to destroy our human dignity . . ., to fill us with horror and contempt toward ourselves and our fellows. . . . But from the instant when I grasped the motivating principle . . . it was as if I had been awakened from a dream. . . . *I felt under orders to live.* . . . And if I did die in Auschwitz, it would be as a human being, I would hold on to my dignity. I was not going to become the contemptible, disgusting brute my enemy wished me to be. . . . And a terrible struggle began which went on day and night.[18]

These answers, given not with words, but with lives lived beyond all limits of endurance hitherto known or imagined, are a testimony whose significance, to be contemplated by thinkers and poets present and yet unborn, is universal.

As for the Jewish people after the Holocaust, they are singled out by this testimony by dint of a simple, yet enormous and still all-but-unfathomable fact: but for an accident of geography, every Jew alive today would either have been murdered, or never been born, or be a survivor.

It is not possible for the post-Holocaust Jew to ignore or leap over this fact in an attempt to reenact or rejuvenate Rabbi Akiba's tradition, believing and behaving as though nothing had happened. More precisely, he can ignore or leap over the fact only by blaspheming against those who did or could not resist, and against those who could and did resist—a day, a year, or even by dint of good fortune until the enemy was destroyed. Prior to the Nazi empire, a Jew, in order to possess the Jewish book, had to view himself as though he had personally stood at Sinai. After the Nazi empire, a Jew is able to keep the Jewish book only if he views himself as though he had personally been present at Auschwitz or Buchenwald as well; and whether he then will still wish or be able to keep the book cannot be known in advance. Would he have been a *Muselmann?* Or have sum-

18. P. Lewinska, *Twenty Months in Auschwitz* (New York: Lyle Stuart, 1968), pp. 41 ff., 50. Cited by Des Preș, *The Survivor,* pp. 62 ff. (Italics added.)

moned the will to live? Would he have survived in a state of war against his fellow victims, or in alliance with them? By losing his human dignity or by finding it? He will never know. And he is required to re-enact *all* these possibilities and make them his own. Only then can he hope to emerge from reenactment without lapsing, either into a cheap faith in the divine image in man (a blasphemous honor to the Nazi criminals and a blasphemous insult to their victims, the living dead) or into a cheap despair (a disregard no less blasphemous of all resistance fighters everywhere, not least of those whose resistance took the form of survival in the murder camps). To new prisoners on their first night in Sachsenhausen, a survivor spoke these words: "I have not told you of our experiences to harrow you, but to strengthen you. . . . Now you may decide if you are justified in despairing."[19]

A Jew cannot take upon himself the age-old task of testifying to the divine image in man without believing his own testimony. In our time, however, he cannot authentically believe in this testimony without exposing himself *both* to the fact that the image of God was destroyed, *and* to the fact that the unsurpassable attempt to destroy it was successfully resisted, supremely so, by the survivor. *Hence the wish to bear witness turns into a commandment, the commandment to restore the diving image to the limits of his power.* And the prime witness to the knowledge that the destroyed image *can* be restored is not one who, like Akiba in his situation, is prepared to die for the knowledge. It is a new witness: the survivor, determined to *live and be human* in a world where murder was law and degradation holy; whose testimony consisted, with every breath, of restoring the divine image in himself even as it was ceaselessly being destroyed. A Bergen-Belsen survivor has said: "In my happier days I used to remark on the aptitude of the saying, 'When in life we are in the midst of death.' I have since learned that it is more apt to say, 'When in death we are in the midst of life.' "[20]

19. Cited by Des Pres, ibid., p. 209, as the concluding sentence of his book.
20. Quoted by Des Pres, ibid., p. 96. It is apt that this, as well as the preceding quotation—the conclusion of this article—should be anonymous.

16. *Midrashic Existence after the Holocaust: Reflections Occasioned by the Work of Elie Wiesel*

Absurdities

NEXT IN MAGNITUDE only to the crimes of the criminals and the suffering of the victims, the Holocaust presents us with unheard-of absurdities. Of these we here list the following:

1. The Jewish faith teaches that catastrophe is transient and salvation final. Yet the catastrophe suffered by this generation—the Holocaust itself—is unredeemable. And the daily news testifies that salvation—in our time, not, alas, in theirs, for the creation of Israel was then still impossible—cannot even now be taken for granted.

2. At Treblinka, the work of groundless hatred, Jews were singled out for death as inexorably as at Sinai they had once been singled out for life.[1] Can the mind grasp the juxtaposition of Sinai and Treblinka? It grasps at most only one of the other two shocks, the groundless hatred and the singling out of a people. Hence only the nasty people of this world tend to rec-

Based on a lecture given at a conference on the work of Elie Wiesel and the Holocaust Universe in September 1976 under the auspices of the National Jewish Conference Center and the Department of Jewish Studies, City College, City University of New York.

1. In a sense more so: Sinai gave the singled-out Jews the choice between life and death. Treblinka gave the choice only—and this only in the best of cases—between ways of meeting death.

ognize the Jewishness of the victims, prepared as they are to imply that the hatred was, after all, not groundless, that "the Jews" deserved some of what they got. On their part—a much harder blow—the good people, horrified as they must be by the great hatred, tend to flee into the view that the victims were essentially men-in-general, and only accidentally Jews. (In 1944, Jean Paul Sartre observed that antisemites reproach Jews for being Jews, while "democratic friends" reproach them for willfully considering themselves as Jews. This observation is still largely correct.)

3. A catastrophe surpassing all others, the Holocaust demands a moral and religious response far more insistently than did, say, the expulsion from Spain. Yet its very radicalism diminishes the likelihood of a response. The Jews expelled from Spain could at length give a new dimension to the Kabbala, for they lived; but the Jews of the Holocaust, except for a small remnant, are dead.

The Task

To see these absurdities clearly is to understand at once that the battle still rages, that the defeat of the great hatred requires the hearts and minds and strength of us all. Is Jewish catastrophe in our time unredeemable and deliverance still precarious? Precisely this unholy combination renders sacred the existence of the state of Israel. Do the nasty and good people of this world, otherwise poles apart, act as if united in this one specific area, that of blotting out the Jewishness of the victims, whether by transforming it into a guilty secret or into an irrelevance? All the more must the Jewishness of the victims as well as that of all post-Holocaust Jews be affirmed and testified to, not only against enemies but also, and indeed above all, against friends. Finally, if the survivors are few, what of us who are not survivors but are doomed to respond to the event without the voice of those it robbed us of forever—the songs of the Hasidim, the oratory of the Yiddishists, the prayers of the scholars, the battle cries of Bundists and Zionists? Surely we must cherish their memory, study as we would Holy Writ the diaries, books, records written in blood for our sake, relive their lives in songs of sorrow and joy. Surely we must do all this so that we may become heirs of their witness in this world and beyond.

The "Crime" of Jewish Existence

To confront the Holocaust is to be overwhelmed by inevitable failure. And to persist in the effort is to face a dilemma: if one seeks to grasp the whole, its horror dissipates itself into such meaningless abstractions as "the six million" or "the symbol Auschwitz"; and if one seeks the truth of the horror in some one particular, one encourages reactions such as the paradigmatic one of a German woman who, having seen the Anne Frank movie, exclaimed: "At least this one should have been spared!"[2] One can avoid this dilemma only by taking hold of individual examples which, at the same time, cannot be rejected by the mind as exceptions, aberrations, mistakes or excesses because they manifest altogether unmistakably the horror of the whole.

So totally integrated was the whole in question (rightly called by names such as "Holocaust Kingdom" or "Planet Auschwitz") that to find the required examples is not, after all, very difficult. Raul Hilberg cites two secret German army lists reporting capital punishment meted out in occupied Russia:

Punishable Offences by Members of the Population

Report I

Espionage	1
Theft of Ammunition	1
Suspected Jews *(Judenverdacht)*	3

Report II

Moving about with Arms *(Freischärlerei)*	11
Theft	2
Jews	2[3]

2. Reinhard Baumgard, "Unmenschlichkeit beschrieben: Weltkrieg und Faschismus in der Literatur," in *Merkur* XIX (January 1965), no. 1, p. 46.

3. Raul Hilberg, *The Destruction of the European Jews* (New York: Quadrangle, 1961), p. 657.

The meaning of these lists is shocking but simple. All others had to *do* something in order to be subject to punishment; in contrast, to *be* a Jew—indeed, to be under *Judenverdacht*—was *in itself* and without further ado a punishable offense *(strafbare Handlung)*.

One may object that the German war on Europe was one thing, the Nazi persecution of the Jews another; that while both reached a climax in Russia, they were only accidentally intermingled; and that to the end enemies of the *Reich* were punished for their deeds, whereas Jews, even when they were murdered, were not "punished." In short, the Holocaust, while quite possibly a whole-in-itself, was an accident—for historians a footnote—in the larger whole: the Nazi-German empire and its goals. Auschwitz, as it were, was a "mistake": not only Anne Frank, but all should have been spared.

Let those taking this view consider the following *Häftlings Personal Karte* (prisoner's identity card) which at this time of writing is on display at the Yad Vashem Museum in Jerusalem:

> *Name:* Kreisler, Andor
> *Place:* some town in Hungary
> *Religion:* Mosaic
> *Date of imprisonment:* 25.4.1944
> *Authority:* Gestapo Vienna
> *Concentration Camp:* Mauthausen
> *Reason:* Hungarian Jew
> *Previous criminal record:* none

Note, first, the archaic term "Mosaic" under the rubric "religion," a clear proof that (except in cases of Gentile converts to Judaism) religion, *as something one could freely accept or reject*, was of no interest to the authors of the form. Note, second, the utterly illogical but supremely revelatory sequence of these categories: "'reason' for imprisonment" and "previous criminal record." The illogic is obvious. "Previous criminal record" is senseless unless preceded by the category "crime"; and any "reason" for imprisonment other than "crime"—analogous, say, to wartime internment of Germans in Britain or Japanese in the

United States and Canada—is senselessly (and insultingly) followed by the category "previous criminal record." Yet precisely this illogic is revealing: the category "reason" *had* to be wide enough to include *for "punishment"* those who had *done* something as well as those for whom it was sufficient to *be* something. With the possible exception of the Gypsies, this latter group was Jews.

Yet a third point must be noted about the *Häftlings Personal Karte:* that it *was* a *Karte,* a form, carefully conceived, printed in countless copies, and used in who knows how many cases. This decisive fact demolishes any remnant of the idea that in the Nazi system the identification of Jewish existence with criminality was an accident.

However, we may still try to understand this identification as essential only to the murder-camp system, and not to the larger Nazi system of which it was a part. What gives us pause in this attempt is the fact that, though concealing the camps themselves, the Nazis made no attempt to hide the *beliefs* enacted in the camps. Indeed, years of propaganda concerning the "hereditary criminality" of the Jews had preceded a progression of actions which escalated until finally, so far as this crucial point is concerned, S.S. murder-camp forms and army lists of executed "criminals" can no longer be distinguished.

Disdaining to hide their beliefs from the populace outside the camps, the Nazis disdained even less concealment from the victims inside. At least as far back as 1938, concentration camp prisoners had their respective categories emblazoned on their uniforms in the form of triangles: red for "political," green for "professional criminal," brown for "unemployable," pink for "homosexual," and yellow for "Jew." Once again with the possible exception of the Gypsies (who were sometimes considered as *inherently* unemployable), everybody had to have *done* something in order to land in a concentration camp. Only Jews had simply to *be.* And, as if to underscore this distinction, when finally all Jews had conspired to do something—for such was the official theory about the assassination of Freiherr vom Rath by Herschel Grynszpan in November 1938—those Jewish members of the conspiracy who were incarcerated in concentration camps had *two* triangles on their uniform, neatly arranged into a Star of David: a red one for the political crime in which they had conspired, and a yellow one for "Jew." Significantly, Jews in the camps at the time seem to have had no adequate understanding of the explosive distinction of which they themselves were victims. The present writer, at any rate, did not have it. Indeed, on a visit to Yad Vashem just half a year ago he understood Andor Kreisler's *Häftlings Karte* sufficiently to copy it, but still not sufficiently to copy it in its entirety. This is why he cannot report the name of the town in Hungary which had once been Andor's home.

The distinction, then, between criminals-by-dint-of-actions and criminals-by-dint-of-birth was not only uniquely explosive but also applied with an insidiousness which even in hindsight staggers the mind. We must now face this insidiousness in its full scope. The late Leo Strauss has rightly observed that the Nazi regime was "the only German regime—the only regime ever anywhere—which had no other clear principle than murderous hatred of Jews, for 'Aryan' had no clear meaning other than 'non-Jewish.'"[4] If the "non-Aryan" was a criminal-by-dint-of-birth, then "man" no longer was, as once he had been, innocent-by-dint-of-birth. Each and every person was presumed to be guilty-by-dint-of-birth until he had proved his innocence, and this he could do only by proving his "Aryan" ancestry. So openly, yet insidiously, did the Nazi *Reich* implicate in its crime against the Jewish people, not only its direct agents and their accomplices, but each and every person proving, or even prepared to prove, his "Aryan" innocence. Indeed, even those surviving on the presumption of innocence of *Judenverdacht* are implicated. Only those rejecting outright the whole system of "non-Aryan" guilt and "Aryan" innocence are wholly pure, and those were sure to become honorary Jews, i.e., victims themselves.

We are thus forced to give up the comfortable conventional

4. "Preface to the English Edition of *Spinoza's Critique of Religion*," in *The Jewish Expression*, ed., Judah Goldin (New York: Bantam, 1970; New Haven: Yale University Press, 1976), p. 345.

wisdom that the Nazi tyranny was much like all other tyrannies, except of course for the shocking murder camps; and that the Nazi murder camps were much like other murder camps, except of course for treating a whole people as a "race" of hereditary criminals. The uncomfortable truth is rather the reverse. The murder camp was no accident of the Nazi system but its inmost essence. And what made the murder camp into a kingdom not of this world—the Holocaust kingdom—was an unheard-of principle: that a whole people—Jews, half-Jews, quarter-Jews, honorary Jews—are guilty by dint not of actions but of existence itself. The process governed by this principle climaxed in an apocalypse. It began before the first Jew was ever "punished" for his "crime." Hilberg writes: "When in the early days of 1933 the first civil servant wrote the first definition of "non-Aryan" into a civil service ordinance, the fate of European Jewry was sealed."[5] So, one must add, was the moral fate of the twelve-year *Reich*—the twelve years equal to a thousand—which has no analogue in history but at most only in the imagination when it pictures hell.

Hell Surpassed

History provides many examples of the strong vanquishing the weak without scruple, and of ideologies, recently taking the form of "social Darwinism," that endorse such unscrupulousness. But neither in such struggles nor in the ideologies endorsing them is weakness ever considered a *crime,* or the conquest or even "extermination" of the weak a *punishment.*

Again, history shows no dearth of societies governed by unjust laws. Yet the "criminals" of such societies are always punished for something they have *done,* namely, the breaking of the unjust laws. Hence, even the most unjust society cannot but recognize the free will, responsibility, rationality and thus humanity of its purported criminals. It is this circumstance that çaused Hegel to remark—controversially but intelligibly and even defensibly—that a bad state is better than no state at all.

5. Hilberg, *Destruction,* p. 669.

The Nazi state was no mere quasi-Darwinian, quasi-natural state, recognizing no right other than might.[6] It was not merely an unjust state, forced to recognize, if nothing else, the responsibility and hence humanity of its victims.[7] The identification of existence itself with criminality, involving as it did *all* human existence, "Aryan" and "non-Aryan" alike, caused *this* state to be neither a subhuman quasi-state nor an imperfect human state but rather an *anti-state*, that is, a system *absolutely* perverting *all* things human. Indeed, since the perversion is surpassable not in quality but only in quantity, the Nazi state was *the* anti-state *par excellence*. Hegel would condemn it as worse than chaos. As we have said, it has an analogue, if anywhere, only in hell.

Yet as one ponders this possibility, one wonders whether even hell is adequate. The devil is insidious in the ways he tempts us but does not place us into a kingdom, onto a planet, of which insidiousness is a built-in feature. He punishes sinners beyond desert but cannot so much as touch the innocent. He may have an infinity of time. But he has only finite power. Perhaps this is why Roy Eckardt has said that sooner or later the devil becomes a bore.[8]

We ask: what will limit the power of the devil if existence itself is a crime? If he can and does touch the innocent—

6. The presence of a social Darwinist element in Nazism and its antecedents is evident. (See e.g., H. G. Zmarzlik, "Social Darwinism in Germany," in *Republic to Reich*, ed., H. Holborn [New York: Vintage, 1973], pp. 436 ff.) However, a quantum leap is necessary if the "right" or even "duty" of the strong to "exterminate" the weak is to become a criminal prosecution in which the weak suffer "extermination" as a just punishment. This difference was fully revealed in the *Götterdämmerung*, when Hitler declared that the mighty Russians had, after all, historical right on their side, even as he wrote a last will and testament obligating future generations to complete the "Final Solution"—the "extermination" of a people which, in his view, fully matched the Russians in might.

7. The present writer was able to observe in 1938 that S.S. men, too, could land in a concentration camp and that, if they did, they were punished as brutally as the other inmates. But their punishment was, of course, for acts of disobedience.

8. In his classic "The Devil and Yom Kippur" (*Midstream*, August–September 1974) Eckardt deals with the monotonous repetition by antisemites in ever new code words, of the same false accusations and mendacious arguments. However, he does not deal with Nazism in this article.

indeed, them above all? What of a hell in which the question of punishment according to, or beyond, desert no longer arises? What will *then* limit the innocent suffering of the purported criminals, or the criminal actions of the purported judges and law-enforcers?

There can be no limit, or would have been none, if, by good fortune, Planet Auschwitz had not been destroyed. Hence, a whole generation after, we still accept its possibility only because of its brute facticity. We do not accept it because we understand it. Though the misbegotten creature of our civilization, Planet Auschwitz transcends the resources of our imagination, those pagan, on the one hand, those Jewish and Christian, on the other.

Wisest of the pagans, the Greek philosophers confronted the brute facticity of filth but could not conceive of an enthusiasm fired not by good but evil.[9] In contrast, biblically-inspired poets and theologians did indeed imagine such an evil, a fallen angel saying to evil, "be thou my Good!" But on their part, believing as they did in a divinely created world, they could not confront the facticity of filth.[10] One must therefore summon the resources of both our Western traditions to begin to grasp a kingdom which was *anus mundi* and hell in one; ruled in an eerie compact by "disgusting" pornographic Streichers and "fanatical National Socialist" idealists whose "cause" was "serious antisemitism";[11] and run by a wholly new species of human

9. In Plato's *Republic*, *thymos* or the emotional part of the soul which is capable of enthusiasm, is merely chaotic, not a possibility of the demonic; and the worst state is not hell but merely a tyranny governed by cynicism.

10. Hell is related to purgatory. But filth does not purge. See Terrence Des Pres, *The Survivor*, chap. 3, "Excremental Assault" (New York: Oxford University Press, 1976).

11. See Rudolf Hoess, *Commandant of Auschwitz* (London: Pan, 1974), p. 145. In this autobiography, written in prison, the Auschwitz *Kommandant* writes: "I was opposed to *Der Stürmer*, Streicher's anti-Semitic weekly, because of the disgusting sensationalism with which it played on people's basest instincts. Then, too, there was its perpetual and often savagely pornographic emphasis on sex. This paper caused a lot of mischief and, far from serving serious anti-Semitism, it did a great deal of harm. It is small wonder that after the collapse it was learnt that a Jew edited the paper and that he also wrote the worst of the inflammatory articles it contained."

beings: men and women who performed by day their quite new "jobs," and yet by night continued to relax as men and women have always relaxed—playing with their dogs, listening to fine music, and celebrating Christmas.

Commemorating the twenty-fifth anniversary of the liberation of Bergen-Belsen in nearby Hannover, Norbert Wollheim, a leading spokesman of the survivors, referred in his memorial address to Hitler as Goethe had referred to the devil: "misbegotten creature of filth and fire." Perhaps only the wisest of Germans—close to Christianity and classical antiquity and yet identified with neither—was able, if not to predict, prophesy or imagine, so at least to find words adequate to describe, of all the Germans, the most depraved. It is not certain how long the world will be inspired and instructed by the wisest German. But we must live with the grim certainty that the shadow of the most depraved German will never cease to haunt it.[12]

Midrashic Existence

How does one religious Jew respond to Planet Auschwitz, a place of limitless crimes and limitless suffering, surpassing hell?

Never shall I forget that night, the first night in camp, which has turned my life into one long night, seven times cursed and seven

---

The last sentence is, of course, quite untrue, but all the more significant when it is remembered that Hoess was in *total* command of *all* the actions at Auschwitz, the Streicher-type included. In his introduction to the German edition of the Hoess memoirs, Martin Broszat rightly notes how, even after, Hoess fancied himself as a decent person deeply moved by the murder of children—as if he had not himself ordered the murders! Broszat can find no better adjective than the obviously inadequate "schizophrenic" to describe this consciousness. M. Broszat, ed., *Kommandant in Auschwitz* (Stuttgart: Deutsche Verlags-Anstalt, 1958), pp. 17–18.

12. The preceding account is in no way opposed to the numerous investigations to the effect that not all Germans were Nazis, not all Nazis S.S. men, not all S.S. men murderers, and that the whole *Reich* contained within itself different and even conflicting fiefdoms. However, the *Reich*—if anything ever—was a whole which was more than the sum of the parts. If historical investigators lose sight of this truth they lose the whole.

times sealed. Never shall I forget that smoke. Never shall I forget the little faces of the children, whose bodies I saw turned into wreaths of smoke beneath the silent blue sky.

Pious Jews always dreamed of a time when "wickedness" would "vanish like smoke."[13] Now a wickedness never dreamed of snatched their symbol, turned it into a weapon of terrifying literalness and used it to murder their little ones and their prayers. Hence Elie Wiesel continues the above passage—there is none greater or more relentless in his writings—with these words:

Never shall I forget those flames which consumed my faith forever.[14]

How can a Jew say anything religious thereafter? [15]

The religious Word may be in flight from the world into the soul within or to heaven above, or even from this world altogether into a world-to-come; a Jew, however, even when he is sorely tempted, cannot flee from the world, for he belongs to a flesh-and-blood people—*a people with children*. Again, the Word may despair of the world and yet stay with it; but then surely the despair is of God as well, and the Word is no longer religious. The religious Word, then, seems no longer possible within Jewish existence. Yet, prior to Buchenwald, some Jews have always found it possible to hold fast to God, hold fast to the world, and affirm a bond between them with their lips and, indeed, with their very lives. The most authentic Word express-

13. Consider the following prayer in the traditional High Holiday service: "May the righteous see and rejoice, the upright exult, and the godly thrill with delight. Iniquity shall shut its mouth, wickedness shall vanish like smoke, when Thou wilt abolish the rule of tyranny on earth."

14. Elie Wiesel, *Night* (New York: Avon, 1972), p. 44.

15. This question will dominate the remainder of this essay. Except for the Epilogue, the essay does not consider possibilities which may exist outside Jewish existence or, within Jewish existence, for religious Jews who never committed themselves to words such as those just quoted, or for those who, having done so, remained silent thereafter, or for those who exist outside the sphere of Jewish religiosity.

ing this bond is Midrash, and a life witnessing to it may be called midrashic existence.

To affirm a bond between God and the world is always problematical. Midrash, however, is aware of this fact. Radically considered, a bond between a God who is truly God and a world which is truly world may well be considered as not merely problematical but nothing short of paradoxical. On its part, however, Midrash does not shrink from paradox, but confronts it and yet in the very act of confrontation reaffirms the bond.

This stance requires closer inspection. Philosophical reflection may find it necessary to choose between a God who is divine only if he is omnibenevolent and omnipotent, and a world which is truly world only because it contains elements contradicting these divine attributes, namely, evil and human freedom. Midrash recognizes the tension yet refuses to choose. Thus when the Israelites do God's will they, as it were, strengthen his power, and when they fail to do his will they, as it were, weaken it. Thus, too, redemption will come when men have become good enough to make the Messiah's coming possible, or wicked enough to make it necessary. It would be wayward to regard such Midrashim as insufficiently demythologized fragments of "philosophizing," the first groping for a "finite God-concept" which would at one blow "solve" the "problems" of evil and freedom, the second struggling with two conflicting "views of history," the one "progressive," the other "catastrophic." Midrash cannot embrace a "progressive view" of history, for this would dispense with the need for the acting of God; nor a "catastrophic view," for this would destroy the significance of the acting of man. Nor can Midrash accept a "finite God-concept" but must rather sweep aside all God-concepts so as to confront God himself—a God absolute yet "as it were" *(k'b'yachol)* finite in the mutual confrontation. The term *k'b'yachol* alone—a full-blown technical term in midrashic thought—suffices to show that Midrash does not "grope" for "concepts" in order to "solve problems" and dissolve paradox. The midrashic Word is story. It *remains* story because it both points to and articulates a life *lived with* problems and paradox—the problems and paradox of a divine-human relation. This life is midrashic existence.

Midrashic existence acts as though all depended on man and prays as though all depended on God. It considers itself worth nothing so that it can only wait for redemption; and worth everything so that a single pure deed or prayer may have redemptive power. It holds all these aspects together because it knows itself to stand in a mutual, covenantal relation—mutual even though the partners are radically unequal, for the one is man and the other is God. Climactically, midrashic existence endures the strain between these extremes without palliatives or relief. It cannot seek refuge from the real in a "spiritual" world, for it is the existence, not of souls, monks, sectarian individuals, but rather of a flesh-and-blood people—*a people with children.* Thus it is not surprising that during the trimillennial history of the Jewish people individuals and whole groups should always have failed to endure this tension. The truly astounding fact is much rather that endurance of the tension has been continuous; that prior to the Holocaust it has never been broken.[16]

Does this endurance extend over Planet Auschwitz? One cannot answer this question lightly. For one dare not ignore or belittle the fact that countless and nameless Jews persisted even then in acting as though all depended on them, and in praying as though all depended on God—all this as if nothing had changed. Nor dare we ignore the fact that everything *had* changed. The Midrash sees Israel, as it were, augment or diminish God's power. Elie Wiesel's most famous Midrash sees God hang on the gallows of a dying child,[17] despite prayers of saints meant to augment his power and because of acts of criminals meant to destroy it. The Midrash sees the Messiah come when men are either wholly righteous or wholly wicked. On

---

16. The above view of Midrash is summarized in a rather doctrinaire fashion because I have stated and defended it in many places over the years; see my *Quest for Past and Future* (Bloomington: Indiana University Press, 1968; Boston: Beacon, 1970), *passim*, and especially *God's Presence in History* (New York: New York University Press, 1970; New York: Harper Torchbook, 1973), chap. 1.

17. Wiesel, *Night*, pp. 75 ff.

Planet Auschwitz the Messiah failed to come even though both conditions were fulfilled. The "judges," "law-enforcers," and "ordinary employees" were wholly wicked, for the anti-world which they ruled, administered, and ran was wholly wicked. The "punished criminals" were wholly righteous for, as a statement wrongly attributed to Maimonides rightly says, a Jew murdered for no reason other than his Jewishness must be viewed as if he were a saint.[18] Hence the protagonist of *The Gates of the Forest* asserts that it is too late for the coming of the Messiah—that a Messiah who can come, but at Auschwitz did not come, has lost his meaning.[19]

Midrash is meant for every kind of imperfect world. It was not meant for Planet Auschwitz, the anti-world.

Mad Midrash

What then makes Elie Wiesel's work possible? No matter what its content—Israel, Russian Jews, Hasidism, the Bible— the Holocaust is always part of the hidden agenda. And no matter what its form—eyewitness reports, essays, a cantata, a play, to say nothing of the novels—it always has recognizable midrashic elements. The first is not accidental, for Wiesel cannot relate himself to *any* Jewish reality before and indeed after the Holocaust as though the dread event had not happened. The second is not accidental, for Wiesel cannot respond to the event by rejecting or fleeing from Jewish past and future—both informed by the hallowed tradition—but only by affirming both, and the most authentic and unmistakable verbal expression of this affirmation is Midrash. Indeed, precisely this togetherness of a relentless self-exposure to the Holocaust and a Jewishness steeped in tradition has given Wiesel the stature of a teacher.

18. The above two judgments are made with a view to guilt and innocence in the context of social structures. The issue "individual vs. collective guilt (or innocence)" becomes spurious and indeed evasive when it is abused to ignore these structures and their moral implications.

19. Elie Wiesel, *The Gates of the Forest* (New York: Holt, Rinehart & Winston, 1966), p. 225.

Yet the question "what makes his work possible?" is necessary, for it is just this togetherness that seems impossible.

This impossible togetherness produces the unprecedented phenomenon of mad Midrash. Moshe the mad *Shammash* appears on the very first page of *Night*, and no matter what guises he assumes in subsequent works he never disappears. At times he is only behind the scene. At other times his presence is manifest even though he is not the speaker. (Thus, the God who hangs on the gallows of the dying boy may seem close and assimilable to the Christ. But there is no suggestion of the death of God let alone of his resurrection: this God is part not of the Christian message but of a mad Jewish Midrash. Again, the outburst, "It is too late for the coming of the Messiah!" may seem close and assimilable to a tragic humanism. It becomes a mad Midrash through the sequel "precisely for this reason we are commanded to hope.")[20] The madness of mad Moshe is most unmistakable when he speaks with his own voice. This he does when he enters a small synagogue in Nazi-occupied Europe, listens for a while to the worshipers, and warns them not to pray so loud lest God hear them; lest He notice that some Jews are still alive in Nazi Europe.[21]

What is this madness?

Not insanity, if "insanity" is "flight from reality." It is just because it dare not flee from *its* reality that this Midrash is mad. This madness is obliged—condemned?—to be sane.

Not "irrationality," if this is ignorance or lack of discernment. There is, to be sure, a rationality of a lesser sort which one displays by discerning the ways of one's world, by going about in it, going along with it. But just a rationality of this sort shows its own ultimate irrationality when it goes along a road descending into hell and beyond. After all is over, such a rationality can only plead that it "did not know." Midrashic madness, in contrast, *knows*, in some cases has known all along. Its discernment is informed by a Truth transcending the world of

20. Ibid.
21. See my *God's Presence in History*, chap. 3.

which it is a victim. Irrational by the standards of lesser rationalities, its rationality is ultimate.

Midrashic madness, third, is not mysticism, if "mysticism" is a rise to a divine ecstasy in which innocence and guilt, joy and anguish, good and evil are all indiscriminately transcended. Midrash must hold fast to the world; mad Midrash cannot but hold fast to *its* world, the anti-world.

How then can it retain this stance and *remain* Midrash, that is, hold fast to God as well as its world? Only by dint of an absolute protest against the anti-world and its God—as it were, an anti-God over against mad Moshe, a God mad with him, or a God torn between these extremes. This protest is serious only if it turns into a determination to *restore* the world. To be sure, the world-to-be-restored will be, as it always has been, an imperfect world. But although tarnished by a thousand blemishes it is neither part of nor heir to the anti-world. On the contrary, the attempt to restore it strikes at the very core of the anti-world, thus aiming at its absolute overthrow. Thus, the mad midrashic Word turns into a *Kaddish* for all the victims of the anti-world, "that solemn affirmation full of grandeur and serenity, by which man returns to God His crown and sceptre."[22]

Mad Midrash and Post-Holocaust Jewish Praxis

Midrashic madness is not insanity, not irrationality, not a flight from the world into mysticism. These negations must forever be reenacted if midrashic madness is to preserve its integrity. Still a fourth negation is necessary, however, but this is in a class by itself. The negations made hitherto oppose threats and temptations from without. The negation to be made now opposes a threat arising from within the sphere of midrashic madness itself. This threat is its last temptation.

The midrashic Word was seen to point to, and be the linguistic expression of, midrashic existence. For this relation between

---

22. Wiesel, *The Gates of the Forest*, p. 225.

Word and existence, however, midrashic madness can have no counterpart. Midrashic existence is lived in and with an imperfect (albeit ever perfectible) world. The existence to which mad Midrash points, the anti-world, cannot be lived in and with but only opposed. To be sure, as we have seen, this opposition is already built into midrashic madness itself. Yet, no longer having an existential counterpart, the Word is tempted to withdraw into inwardness, expand this inwardness into a self-contained quasi-existence, and thus descend from literature into aestheticizing.[23] Already theo-political in its own right, mad Midrash must overcome this last temptation by pointing beyond the theological Word to a praxis whose politics forever questions all theology even as it remains itself theologically questioned. Thus, a clear road leads from *Night* to the *Jews of Silence*—a road understood only if its ultimate goal is not characters divorced from all else in a book but also a people outside and beyond the book: a people which (in no small measure thanks to *this* book) has ceased to be silent. A road too—though this one not so clear—leads from the final *Kaddish* for Leib the Lion in *The Gates of the Forest* to the final argument with Gad the Israeli officer in *A Beggar in Jerusalem*. Leib has fought against, but been killed by, the Holocaust Kingdom when it murdered his people. Gad is killed only after having helped save the state which is the heir of the murdered people. The *Kaddish* for Leib can do no more than restore to God a crown and scepter which have little power and majesty so long as the world remains unrestored. Gad helps restore the world—or at any rate, what after the anti-world has become its indispensable center—when he helps save the Jewish state, the heir of the annihilated Jews, from being itself annihilated.

This act on Gad's part is preceded by an argument with the protagonist. This latter knows (to paraphrase his words) that the

---

23. Perhaps the foremost aim of Kierkegaard's literary production is to wrestle with this last temptation. Still more instructive is Hegel's critique (in his *Phenomenology*), of the "beautiful soul's" withdrawal into inwardness, for in Hegel's account it is unambiguous that the withdrawal is from political action, and that its unadmitted purpose is to avoid the necessity of dirtying its hands.

world has not changed, that they would let it happen again, that Jews are still expendable and that, what with superiority of arms and men on the side of an implacable enemy, to expect victory—or, which is the same thing, survival—is irrational. (Although, as we have said at the very outset, the existence of the Jewish state, after what has happened, is sacred, it is not, to put it mildly, secure.) Gad in no way challenges these facts. Yet he affirms that "the national funeral" of the Jewish state "will not take place. Not now, not ever." He admits the protagonist's murmured protest that a faith such as this borders on madness yet insists that not madness but only death is to be feared and, indeed, that death can be driven away, some wars be won, by invoking madness.[24]

Gad wins this argument even though, as an individual, he is killed in the war "shortly thereafter." For midrashic madness points to *an existence in which the madness is transfigured.* Midrashic madness is the Word spoken in the anti-world which ought not to be but is. The existence it points to acts to restore a world which ought to be but is not, committed to the faith that what ought to be must and will be, and this is *its* madness. After Planet Auschwitz, there can be no health without *this* madness, no joy, no life. Without this madness a Jew cannot do—with God or without him—what a Voice from Sinai bids him do: choose life.

Epilogue

Almost a century ago Friedrich Nietzsche—not the wisest of Germans, but the one best equipped to understand madness—let a madman appear on the scene, crying that God is dead, that God stays dead, that men are his murderers, but that despite this fact the deed has not yet come to their ears.[25] Somewhat later he let Zarathustra—a sage beyond madness—prog-

24. Elie Wiesel, *A Beggar in Jerusalem* (New York: Random House, 1970), pp. 61 ff.
25. *The Gay Science,* #125.

nosticate two possibilities. The one hoped for—his "last will"—was:

Dead are all gods . . ., now let the superman live.[26] The dreaded possibility was the "last man":

> Alas, the time is coming when man will no longer give birth to a star. Alas, the time of the most despicable man is coming who can no longer despise himself. . . . A little poison now and then: it makes for pleasant dreams. And much poison in the end, for it makes for a pleasant death. . . . One still works, for work entertains. But one takes care lest the pastime cause fatigue . . .

> No shepherd and one flock. Each wants the same, is the same. He who feels differently enters the madhouse of his own accord.[27]

But Nietzsche's wisdom was not wise enough. A century after, the Nietzschean madness—mad because God is dead—is joined by a madness that is mad because he is alive.[28] And both are joined (surpassed?) by a new maturity which, amusedly or wearily but in either case condescendingly, dismisses the whole question.

This new maturity fancies itself as representing Nietzsche's prophesied superman. Yet in fact the notion of a superman fit to take the place vacated by God has become a sad joke. For

26. *Zarathustra*, end of pt. I. While significantly the earlier passage speaks of the death of God, the present one asserts the death of "all gods." Hegel— who preceded Nietzsche in both assertions—let the death of all gods happen in the Roman pantheon, with the consequence that the event did not encompass God, while asserting the death of God within the Christian realm, where it was followed by a resurrection. Hegel was unable to place Jewish existence within either of these contexts.

27. *Zarathustra*, pt. I, sec. 5.

28. See my *God's Presence in History*, chap. 3. The reader who wonders why this writer's second set of reflections on the work of Elie Wiesel, like his first, implicates thoughts by Nietzsche may be assured that this is not acciden- tal. In both cases there is a shared anguish—in the first, concerning the fate of God, in the second, concerning the fate of man. And in both cases there is a need to confront Nietzsche's post-Protestant view of the anguish with a Jewish view—a need which after the Holocaust brooks no compromise.

Planet Auschwitz murdered, along with men, women, and children, the idea of Man itself. And from Gulag and all the other heirs of Auschwitz resounds the daily cry: "Man is dead. Man stays dead!"

Thus of Nietzsche's three prognostications only the third has been borne out, and even this fails us in the end. It is not hard to recognize Nietzsche's "last man" in features of contemporary life, among them gray uniformity, computerized pleasure, an inability to create and an unwillingness to sacrifice. But behind such characteristics of decadence lurk far more ominous dangers. There is callous indifference to murder abroad and on the streets at home. There is an infatuation with death and perversity. And pleasure seeks escape from boredom, not just (as Nietzsche naively imagined) in a poison making sweet dreams but in quite a different poison which produces an ever-accelerating search for ever-new depravities. The specter of the Holocaust is quite unmistakably behind these phenomena. And it was only to be expected that sooner or later someone would make Auschwitz into a joke.[29]

In the beginning was the universe, and with it came man, the animal capable of laughter. He laughed at small incongruities—a man slipping on a banana skin—but stopped laughing when the incongruity became large—if the man broke his neck. Then came the Holocaust universe, and with it the S.S. man. He laughed only at large incongruities—the smashing of a non-Aryan baby's skull. Now the post-Holocaust universe has arrived, and it has produced a species of post-Holocaust man, Aryan and non-Aryan alike, who laughs at all the incon-

---

29. See Konrad Kellen, "Seven Beauties: Auschwitz—The Ultimate Joke?" *Midstream*, October 1976, pp. 59–66. This brilliant essay is a review not only of Lina Wertmüller's movie, *Seven Beauties*, but also of the reception it has received by the critics. Kellen writes: "Wertmüler uses the agony of Auschwitz not just as backdrop for some depraved and ridiculous sexual fantasy, but as a joke. This is something new, surpassing in intellectual and moral depravity all that "entertainers" have done so far. Even the Nazis did not treat the extermination camps as a joke. On visiting Auschwitz, Heinrich Himmler, inhuman though he was, became ill; but not Wertmuller or her giggling, guffawing audiences throughout the Western civilized world." (p. 59).

gruities once considered large—the crimes of the murderers, the anguish of the victims, and above all his own previous "unliberated" inability to laugh at either.[30] Man becomes human through his capacity to laugh. With *this* laughter his self-destruction is complete.

Or so it would be if the new maturity had really heard what it laughs at. However, though it wearily fancies itself as having heard everything it has as yet understood nothing. The deed is done, but it has not yet come to men's ears. If a few feel differently, it is because their ears have heard, if indeed they are not survivors who have seen with their own eyes. These few will *not* enter the madhouse of their own accord. Never! They *must* not enter the madhouse. The post-Holocaust universe is in need of them. It needs them if man is to become, not a superman replacing God, or a "last man" replacing man. It needs them if he is to become, after what has happened, once again human.

Yes, it *is* necessary for us who are not survivors to become heirs of their witness in this world and beyond.

30. Kellen's article gives numerous examples of critics, Jewish as well as non-Jewish, who found (or pretended to have found) the Wertmüller Auschwitz-as-fun "liberating." Why liberating? Because, Kellen replies, the people in question never rejected Nazism viscerally, as a "blemish on the entire human race." One need hardly add that this answer only begins a much-needed enquiry into this kind of "liberation."

17. The Holocaust and the State of Israel: Their Relation

I. Hope

Our Father in Heaven, the Rock of Israel and her Redeemer, bless Thou the state of Israel, the beginning of the dawn of our redemption. . . .

This prayer by the Israeli Chief Rabbinate does not hesitate to describe the state of Israel as "the beginning of the dawn of the redemption" of the Jewish people. That the official rabbinate of Israel should formulate such a prayer is in itself surprising: what is positively astonishing, however, is its wide acceptance by Jews everywhere. Religious Jews inside and outside Israel recite it in the synagogue, and secularist Israelis, who neither frequent synagogues nor recite prayers, recite *this* prayer, as it were, not with their lips but with their lives.

Reprinted from the *Encyclopedia Judaica Yearbook 1974* (Jerusalem: Keter, 1974), pp. 152–57. I have deliberately divided the three parts of this article into two parts, of which the second has two subparts, in order to emphasize that the beginning of part II (IIa) deals with a radical break rather than a mere "antithesis," and in order to forestall any suggestion that the end of part II (IIb) is a "synthesis" in which the "antithesis" is transcended. I have also deliberately placed this article at the end of the book and, just prior to it, two essays in which, once again, the Holocaust is central.

Messianic expectations by religious Jews are not new or unusual: neither is the association of these with the ingathering of the exiles in a restored Jewish commonwealth. More than merely unusual, however, if not altogether without precedent, is the linking of these, even by fervent believers, with a historical event *already clearly and unequivocally present*. No matter how cautiously interpreted, the messianic future cannot be shorn of an element of absoluteness, whereas the historical present is inexorably ambiguous in essence and precarious in its very existence. The state of Israel is not exempt from the condition of historicity. Hence a prayer which links this present state with the messianic future reflects a boldness that the ancient sages of the Gentiles might well have considered tantamount to *hubris*, or tempting the gods.

The rabbis of ancient Israel would have doubts of their own. Unlike the gods, their God is Lord of history. Moreover, he has given promises, the reliance on which is not *hubris* but rather fidelity. But *when* will the time be ripe for "the End?" And *how*—if at all—can one detect the signs? These questions receive only reluctant and conflicting answers from the rabbis. To be sure, they *must* link history with its messianic fulfillment, but prudently shrink from extending this linking to *particular* events *already present*. Thus the rabbis too understand, no less well than the sages of the Gentiles, that—this side of its messianic transfiguration—all history is precarious.

For this reason rabbinic imagery picturing the messianic days as gradually unfolding is inevitably at odds with its opposite, which views "the End" as ushered in by catastrophe. At one extreme, it is imagined that all foreign domination over Israel will cease *before* the coming of the Son of David, and that the "mountains will grow branches and bear fruit" for its returning inhabitants (TB Sanh. 98a). At the other, the End is pictured as preceded by impoverishment in the land, and indeed by a terror in Jerusalem so extreme that her gates will all be equal—not one will furnish escape (TB Sanh. 98a). The one projection can be furnished with a proof-text (Ezek. 36:8) which makes it the "clearest sign" of the End. But so can the other (Zech. 8:10, also Ps. 119:165). These and similar conflicting projections cannot but produce in all (or most) rabbis the insight that they are mere speculations—that all attempts to link the precarious present with the absolute future are themselves precarious and cannot be otherwise.

This condition cannot be transcended even when a sober appraisal of actual history brings about a near-consensus among the rabbis. Under the influence of idealism, some modern Jewish thinkers were to conceive of messianism as a mere ideal which, on the one hand, could only be approached and not reached and, on the other, was *being* approached in a linear or dialectial progression *already present*. Such notions are foreign to rabbinic realism, to which the messianic days are more than a mere ideal and which, at the same time, can see no clear messianic direction in past or present. Recognizing catastrophe as a persisting possibility, this realism creates the imagery of a pre-messianic travail—the "birth-pangs of the Messiah"—as an all but normative check on all gradualist or sentimental utopianism. Yet even so normative an image can bring about no firm link between the absolute future and historical events already present. Thus, in the midst of catastrophe, the pessimistic Rabbi Hillel can despair of messianism altogether, holding that King Hezekiah has already been the promised Messiah, and that none other is to be expected (TB Sanh. 99a). On his part, Rabbi Johanan cannot go beyond the admonition that "when you see an age in which suffering pours like a stream, then hope for him" (TB Sanh. 98a). But hope is not a certainty, and suffering, however harrowing, is not a proof. Thus the link between the forever precarious historical present and the messianic future is itself forever precarious, a fact poignantly expressed in Midrashim in which the Israelites plead with God to make an end of the painful historical alternation between exile and redemption, and bring the final redemption.

Yet unless the messianic future is to become ever elusive and thus irrelevant, its linking with a *possible* present, however precarious, is indispensable and, with its risks paradigmatically shown by Rabbi Akiba's support of the Bar Kokhba rebellion, this too becomes normative for the Jewish religious consciousness—and remains so, through the ages. Thus at one

extreme the mystical Nahmanides (1194–1270) does not hesitate to rob empirical history of its intrinsic precariousness by
means of the suspect ancient device of "calculating the End,"
maintaining that the rabbinic strictures against the practice no
longer apply when the End is so near.[1] (This view is to be
reiterated by more than one rabbi during the Nazi Holocaust,
with increasing conviction by those surviving to see the birth of
the state of Israel.)[2] Yet he *stays with* empirical history when he
sees messianic (albeit negative) *evidence* in the fact that, while
many Gentile nations have succeeded in destroying the land,
not one has succeeded in rebuilding it (Ramban to Lev. 26.32).
At the other extreme the sober Maimonides (1135–1204) as-
similates the messianic future to the historical present, sufficiently so as to reaffirm a rabbinic view that "the sole difference
between the present and the messianic days is delivery from
servitude to foreign powers" (TB Sanh. 91b). At the same time,
he must ascribe an *absolute* perfection to future men (Jews and
Gentiles alike) to be able to assert that the kingdom of the Son
of David, unlike David's own, will be destroyed neither by sin
within nor by aggression from without. He does not resolve but
only expresses this tension by echoing the rabbinic saying that
those be "blasted who reckon out the end" (TB Sanh. 97b).[3]

In view of this inherent and inevitable tension between contingent historical present and absolute messianic future in the
Jewish religious consciousness, it is not surprising that the
modern world should have produced a deep and widespread
desire or need to get rid of that tension. This is done covertly
when the absolute future is projected into an irrelevant infinity,
and overtly when it is abandoned altogether. The result is a
"normalization" which occurs when Jewish existence is classified without remainder in available categories, such as "religious denomination" or "ethnic subculture" and, above all, of
course, when there is total assimilation.

1. J. Lipschitz, ed., *Sefer Ha-Geulah* (London, 1909), especially pp. 3–16,
29.
2. See e.g., M. M. Kasher, ed., *Haggadat Pesah Arzi-Yisraelit* (New York:
American Biblical Encyclopedia Society, 1950), pp. 132 ff.
3. Maimonides, Yad, *Hilkhot Melakhim*, 5:11–12.

The modern Zionist movement originally appears on the scene as another normalization effort, and, indeed, at one extreme one so radical as total assimilation is at the other. No Jewish self-classification as "religious denomination" or "ethnic subculture" can ever be quite successful, not the one because one is born a Jew, not the other because one is somehow obliged to remain one, and various identity-crises reflect these difficulties. In contrast, Zionism characteristically seems to come on the scene with the aim of making Jews "a nation like any other nation," just as, at the opposite extreme, assimilationism aims at dissolving Jews *into* other nations. Thus Jewish "normalization" seems complete only at the extremes.

However, as Zionism unfolds in thought and action, it gradually emerges that the messianic future, ignored or even repudiated, lives on within it, changed or unchanged, as the hidden inspiration without which the movement cannot survive. To be sure, Herzl's "If you will it, it is no dream" is a strikingly secularist appeal, exalting as it does the will above all else: it may even be understood as an anti-religious protest. Yet the goal aimed at by this will is so radically at odds with all the "natural" trends of modern history as to require a mainspring far deeper and more original than the imitation of the varieties of nineteenth-century European nationalism, and one more positive and radical than escape into "normalcy" from what was then known as antisemitism. To this day this deeper inspiration has found little articulation in Zionist *thought*. Yet had it not existed throughout Zionist *life*—from the days of the early settlers through the Yom Kippur War—Herzl's dream would either not have become real at all or else not have stayed real for long. No other twentieth-century "liberation movement" has had to contend with all (or any) of these problems: the reuniting of a people rent apart by vast culture gaps of centuries; the reviving of an ancient language; the recreation, virtually overnight, of self-government and self-defense in a people robbed of these arts for two millennia; to say nothing of defending a young state for a whole generation against overwhelming odds, and on a territory virtually indefensible. Only a will in touch with an absolute dimension could have come anywhere near solving these problems; and even those acting on this will may well be astonished by its accomplishments. Hence it has come to pass that the categories "religious" and "secularist" (whatever their undiminished validity in other contexts) have been radically shaken by the Zionist reality, a fact that has produced strange bedfellows. On one side, ultra-religious Jews waiting for God's Messiah and secularist Jews wanting neither God nor Messiah are united in hostility to the will that animates the Zionist reality, obtuse to its meaning. On the other side, religious Zionists do not count on miracles, while secularist Zionists have been known to be astonished. These two are united as well, if not when things appear normal, at any rate in those extreme moments when all appearances fall away and only truth remains.

IIa. Catastrophe

The Holocaust is unique in history, and therefore in Jewish history. Previously, genocide has been a means to such human (if evil) ends as power, greed, an extreme of nationalist or imperialist self-assertion, and at times this means may even have become, demonically, an end *beside* these others. In the Holocaust Kingdom genocide showed itself gradually to be *the sole ultimate end* to which all else—power, greed, and even "Aryan" self-assertion—were sacrificed, for "Aryan" had no other clear meaning than "not-non-Aryan." And since the Nazis were not antisemites because they were "racists" but rather racists because they were antisemites, the "non-Aryan" was, paradigmatically, the Jew. Thus the event belongs to Jewish and world history alike.

Nor is "genocide" adequate to describe the Holocaust Kingdom. Torquemada burned Jewish bodies to save Jewish souls. Eichmann created a system which, by torturing with terror and hope, by assailing all human dignity and self-respect, was designed to destroy the souls of all available Jewish men, women, and children before consigning their bodies to the gas chambers. The Holocaust Kingdom was a celebration of degra-

dation as much as of death, and of death as much as of degradation. The celebrants willingly or even enthusiastically de-
scended into hell themselves, even as they created hell for their
victims. As for the world—it tolerated the criminals and abandoned the innocents. Thus the Holocaust is not only a unique
event: it is epoch-making. The world, just as the Jewish world,
can never again be the same.

The event therefore resists explanation—the historical kind
that seeks causes, and the theological kind that seeks meaning
and purpose. More precisely, the better the mind succeeds with
the necessary task of explaining what can be explained, the
more it is shattered by its ultimate failure. What holds true of
the Holocaust holds true also of its connection with the state of
Israel. Here, too, the explaining mind suffers ultimate failure.
*Yet it is necessary, not only to perceive a bond between the two
events but also so to act as to make it unbreakable.*

Historians see a causal connection between the Holocaust
and the foundation of the state of Israel. The reasoning is as
follows. Had it not been for the European Jewish catastrophe,
all the centuries of religious longing for Zion, all the decades of
secularist Zionist activity, together with all such external en-
couragement as given by the Balfour Declaration, would have
produced no more than a Palestinian ghetto. This might have
been a community with impressive internal achievements but,
rather than a "national home" for homeless Jews, it would have
been itself at the mercy of some alien government of dubious
benevolence. Only the Holocaust produced a desperate determination in the survivors and those identified with them, outside and especially within the *Yishuv,* ended vacillation in the
Zionist leadership as to the wisdom of seeking political self-
determination, and produced a moment of respite from political
cynicism in the international community, long enough to give
legal sanction to a Jewish state. Even so "the UN resolution of
1947 came at the last possible moment."[4]

This reasoning is plausible; no more so, however, than its

4. Walter Laqueur, *A History of Zionism* (London: Weidenfeld & Nicolson,
1972; New York: Schocken, 1976), p. 593.

exact opposite. Why were the survivors not desperate to stay away from Palestine rather than reach it—the one place on earth which would tie them inescapably to a Jewish destiny? (After what that destiny had been to them, the desire to hide or flee from their Jewishness would have been "natural.") Why did the Zionist leadership rise from vacillation to resoluteness rather than simply disintegrate? (Confronted by absolute enemies, it was at the mercy of its friends.) As for the world's respite from political cynicism, this was neither of long duration nor unambiguous while it lasted. Ernest Bevin and his Colonial Office were rendered more—not less—intransigent to Zionist pressures by the catastrophic loss of lives and power which the Jewish people had just suffered. And the five Arab armies that "surged in upon the nascent Israeli nation to exterminate it and make themselves its immediate heirs" were "encouraged by the way Hitler had practiced genocide without encountering resistance."[5] Thus while, as previously argued, the state of Israel after the Holocaust may be viewed as a near necessity, yet we now see that it may be viewed, with equal justice, as a near impossibility. Historical explanation falls short in this manner because all human responses to the Holocaust are ultimately incalculable.

If historical explanations (seeking merely causes) remain precarious, theological explanations (seeking nothing less than meaning and purpose) collapse altogether, not because they are theological but because they are explanations. They fail whether they *find* a purpose, such as punishment for sin, or merely *assert* a purpose without finding it, such as a divine will, purposive yet inscrutable. This theological failure is by no means overcome if the Holocaust is considered as a means, inscrutable but necessary, to no less an end than the "dawn of redemption," of which in turn the state of Israel is viewed as the necessary "beginning." No meaning or purpose will ever be found in the event, and one does not glorify God by associating his will with it. Indeed, the very attempt is a sacrilege. (I have

5. M. Sperber, . . . *Than a Tear in the Sea* (New York: Bergen-Belsen Memorial Press, 1967), p. XIV.

elsewhere argued that Jewish thought at its deepest level, especially vis-à-vis catastrophe, does not express itself in explanatory systems but rather in conflicting Midrashim, the goal of which is not how to explain God but how to live with him. Radicalizing the midrashic approach. I have also argued that to find a meaning in the Holocaust is impossible, but to seek a response is inescapable.)[6]

What then must be said of such as Rabbi Israel Shapiro of the city of Grodzisk who told his Jews at Treblinka that *these* were at last the *real* birth-pangs of the Messiah, that they all were blessed to have merited the honor of being the sacrifices, and that their ashes would serve to purify all Israel?[7]

First, this response must be revered *as a response;* however—in equal reverence for all the innocent millions, the children included, who had neither the ability, nor the opportunity, nor the desire, to be willing martyrs—it must be *rid totally of every appearance of being an explanation.* Did God *want* Auschwitz? Even the ancient rabbis sometimes seem to view the messianic birth-pangs not as a means used by a purposive (if inscrutable) divine will, but rather as, so to speak, a cosmic catastrophe which must occur before divine power and mercy can find their redemptive manifestation.

Second, Rabbi Shapiro's extreme of pious hope must be juxtaposed by opposites no less pious and no less to be revered. The pious men of a *shtibl* in the Lodz Ghetto spent a whole day fasting, praying, reciting psalms, and then, having opened the holy ark, convoked a solemn *din Torah,* and forbade God to punish his people any further. (Elsewhere God was put on trial—and found guilty.)[8] And in the Warsaw Ghetto a handful of Jews, ragged, alone, poorly armed, carried out the first uprising against the Holocaust Kingdom in all of Europe. The rabbis showed religious piety when, rather than excuse God or curse

6. Emil Fackenheim, *Quest for Past and Future* (Bloomington: Indiana University Press, 1968; Boston: Beacon, 1970), chap. 1; and *God's Presence in History* (New York: New York University Press, 1970; New York: Harper Torchbook, 1973), chaps. 1 and 3.

7. Cited in Kasher, *Haggadat,* p. 137.

8. *Ani Ma'amin* (Jerusalem: Mosad Ha-Rav Kook, 1965), p. 206.

him, they cited his own promises against him. The fighters showed secular piety when, rather than surrender to the Satanic Kingdom, they took up arms against it. The common element in these two responses was not hope but rather despair. To the rabbis who found him guilty, the God who had broken his promises in the Holocaust could no longer be trusted to keep *any* promise, the messianic included. And precisely when hope had come to an end the fighters took to arms—in a rebellion that had no hope of succeeding.

With this conclusion, every explanatory connection between the Holocaust and the state of Israel has broken down, the causal historical kind in part, the teleological religious kind entirely, and even the hope connecting the one event with the other competes with despair. Yet, as we have said, it is necessary not only to preceive a bond between the two events but also so to connect them as to make the bond unbreakable. Such a bond is *possible* because to seek a *cause* or a *meaning* is one thing, to give a *response* is another. And it is necessary because the heart of every *authentic* response to the Holocaust— religious and secularist, Jewish and non-Jewish—is a commitment to the autonomy and security of the state of Israel.

IIb. Response

The Chronicler Yosef Gottfarstein reports:

The Jews of Kelmé, Lithuania, were already standing beside the pits which they had been forced to dig for themselves—standing ready to be slain for the Sanctification of the Name. Their spiritual leader, Rabbi Daniel, asked the German officer in command of the operation to allow him to say some parting words to his flock, and the latter agreed, but ordered Rabbi Daniel to be brief. Speaking serenely, slowly, as though he were delivering one of his regular Sabbath sermons in the synagogue, Rabbi Daniel used his last minutes on earth to encourage his flock to perform Kiddush Hashem in the proper manner. Suddenly the German officer cut in and shouted at the rabbi to finish so that he could get on with the shooting. Still speaking calmly, the rabbi concluded as follows: "My dear Jews!

The moment has come for us to perform the precept of Kiddush Hashem of which we have spoken, to perform it in fact! I beg one thing of you: don't get excited and confused; accept this judgment calmly and in a worthy manner!"

Then he turned to the German officer and said: "I have finished. You may begin."

Gottfarstein continues:

. . .At Kedainiai the Jews were already inside the pit, waiting to be murdered by the Germans, when suddenly a butcher leaped out of the pit, pounced on the German officer in command, and sank his teeth into the officer's throat, holding on till the latter died.

When Rabbi Shapiro, the last Rabbi of Kovno, was asked which of these two acts he thought was more praiseworthy, he said: There is no doubt that Rabbi Daniel's final message to his flock concerning the importance of the precept of Kiddush Hashem was most fitting. But that Jew who sank his teeth into the German's throat also performed the precept in letter and in spirit, because the precept includes the aspect of action. "I am sure that if the opportunity had presented itself, Rabbi Daniel would also have been capable of doing what the butcher did," Rabbi Shapiro added.[9]

"I have finished. You may begin." We search all history for a more radical contrast between pure, holy goodness and a radical evil utterly and eternally beyond all redemption. The German officer saw what he saw. He heard what he heard. So did his men, How then could even one go on with the shooting? Yet they all did.

This unredeemable evil must have been in Rabbi Shapiro's mind when he did not hesitate to rank a simple, presumably ignorant, and perhaps not very pious butcher with a saintly rabbi learned in the ways of the Torah and earnestly obeying its commandments. For us who come after, the resistance as faith and dignity of Rabbi Daniel and his flock, the *kiddush ha-Shem*

9. "Kiddush Hashem over the Ages and Its Uniqueness in the Holocaust Period" in *Jewish Resistance during the Holocaust* (Jerusalem: Yad Vashem, 1971), p. 473.

of the butcher, and the judgment concerning these two forms of testimony made by Rabbi Shapiro of Kovno, itself a form of testimony, are nothing less than a dual revelation: a holy dignity-in-degradation, a heroic war against Satanic death— each a resistance to the climax of a millennial, unholy combination of hatred of Jews with Jewish powerlessness which we are bidden to end forever.

To listen to this relevation is inevitably to be turned from the rabbi who had only his faith and the butcher who had only his teeth to the Warsaw Ghetto fighters in their ragged dignity and with their wretched arms. Of the second day of the uprising one of the leaders, Itzhak Cukierman (Zukerman) reports:

> . . . By following guerrilla warfare theory, we saved lives, added to our supply of arms and, most important, proved to ourselves that the German was but flesh and blood, as any man.
>
> And prior to this we had not been aware of this amazing truth! If one lone German appeared in the Ghetto the Jews would flee *en masse*, as would Poles on the Aryan side. . . .
>
> The Germans were not psychologically prepared for the change that had come over the Jewish community and the Jewish fighters. They were seized with panic.[10]

Amazingly, the Holocaust Kingdom was breached. At least in principle, the millennial unholy combination was broken.

This fact recreated in Zuckerman hope in the midst of despair: "We knew that Israel would continue to live, and that for the sake of all Jews everywhere and for Jewish existence and dignity—even for future generations—only one thing would do: Revolt!"[11]

Another leader of the uprising, Mordecai Anielewicz, was to perish in the flames of the Ghetto. Yet in his last letter he wrote: "My life's aspiration is fulfilled. The Jewish self-defense has arisen. Blissful and chosen is my fate to be among the first

---

10. Meyer Barkai, tr. and ed., *The Fighting Ghettos* (New York: Tower, 1962), pp. 26 ff.
11. Ibid., p. 30.

Jewish fighters in the Ghetto." "Blissful" and "chosen" are almost exactly the words used by Rabbi Israel Shapiro of the city of Grodzisk as he led his flock to the crematoria of Treblinka, sure that their ashes would hasten the coming of the Messiah.

But *was* Jewish destiny so much as touched by the handfuls of desperate men and women in the ghettos and camps? And is it *true in any sense whatever* that the millennial, unholy combination of hatred of Jews and Jewish powerlessness has been so much as breached? Rabbi Shapiro was unable to sustain his faith in God without also clinging to the "aspect of action" in *kiddush ha-Shem*, as performed by the butcher. The fighters were unable to persist in their fight without staking their faith on future Jewish generations. Was not, in both cases, the faith groundless and hollow, overwhelmed by despair?

Mordecai Anielewicz died in May 1943. Named after him, kibbutz Yad Mordekhai was founded in the same year. Five years after Mordecai's death, almost to the day, a small band of members of the kibbutz bearing his name held off a well-equipped Egyptian army for five long days—days in which the defense of Tel Aviv could be prepared, days crucial for the survival of the Jewish state. The Warsaw Ghetto fighters had not, after all, been mistaken.

Their hope, however, had not been a rational one, much less a calculated prediction. It had been a blessed self-fulfilling prophecy, for the heroism and self-sacrifice of the prophets had been the indispensable element without which the prophecy could not have been fulfilled. The battle for Yad Mordekhai began in the streets of Warsaw. To this day the justly larger-than-life statue of Mordecai Anielewicz dominates the kibbutz named after him, reminding the forgetful and teaching the thoughtless that what links Rabbi Daniel, the butcher, the two Rabbis Shapiro, and the Ghetto fighters with Yad Mordekhai is neither a causal necessity nor a divine miracle, if these are thought of as divorced from human believing and acting. It is a fervent believing, turned by despair from patient waiting into heroic acting. It is an acting which through despair has recovered faith.

Behind the statue stands the shattered water tower of the kibbutz, a mute reminder that even after its climax the combination of hatred of Jews and Jewish powerlessness has not come to an end. However, the shattered tower is dwarfed by the statue, and is at its back. The statue faces what Mordecai longed for and never despaired of—green fields, crops, trees, birds, flowers, Israel.

Our Father in Heaven, the Rock of Israel and her Redeemer, bless Thou the state of Israel, the beginning of the dawn of our redemption. Shield her with the wings of Thy love, and spread over her the tabernacle of Thy peace. . . ."

Index